T0356919

God Shall Be One
Reenvisioning Judaism's Approach to Other Religions

Yakov Nagen
Sarel Rosenblatt
Assaf Malach

GOD
Shall Be
ONE

Reenvisioning Judaism's Approach to Other Religions

TRANSLATED BY
Daniel Tabak

PREFACE BY
Kenneth Brander

Ohr Torah Interfaith Center
Maggid Books

God Shall Be One

First English Edition, 2024

Maggid Books
An imprint of Koren Publishers Jerusalem Ltd.

POB 8531, New Milford, CT 06776-8531, USA
& POB 4044, Jerusalem 9104001, Israel
www.korenpub.com

© Ohr Torah Interfaith Center 2024

Cover design: Afaf Studio

The publication of this book was made possible
through the generous support of *The Jewish Book Trust.*

ISBN 978-1-59264-691-3, *hardcover*

Printed and bound in the United States

We greatly acknowledge
the support of
Dr. Giti and Jack Bendheim
for sponsoring the translation of this book
from its original Hebrew edition
Ushmo Echad (Maggid 2022)

Contents

Preface.. xi
    Rabbi Dr. Kenneth Brander

Introduction
The Relationship Between Jews and Non-Jews:
The Need for a New Source-Based Paradigm xv
    Yakov Nagen

Acknowledgments.. xxvii

PART I
FUNDAMENTAL ISSUES

Four Prophetic Models for the Future
of the Jewish People and the Nations........................... 3
    Sarel Rosenblatt

World Religions as Fulfilling Biblical Prophecies 17
    Yakov Nagen

The Seven Noahide Laws:
Prerequisites for Civilization or Religious Identity? 25
    Yakov Nagen

PART II
WORLD RELIGIONS IN MEDIEVAL JEWISH THOUGHT

Rabbi Nathaniel b. Rabbi Fayyumi:
Prophetic Revelation Outside of Judaism...................... 41
    Yakov Nagen

Rabbi Judah HaLevi and the *Kuzari*:
The Importance of World Religions 53
   Assaf Malach

Rabbi Moses Maimonides:
Noahide Law as the Exclusive Revelation to the Nations 71
   Yakov Nagen

Rabbi Menahem Meiri: Moral Behavior and
Theological Belief as the Basis for Fellowship with Non-Jews 91
   Sarel Rosenblatt

Rabbi Joseph Albo: A Noahide Law for Every Nation 111
   Yakov Nagen

PART III
WORLD RELIGIONS IN MODERN JEWISH THOUGHT

Rabbi Jacob Emden:
Christianity as a Positive Force of Noahide Religion 121
   Assaf Malach

Modern Halakhic Authorities on Christianity as
a Commendable Religion 141
   Assaf Malach

Rabbi Elijah Benamozegh: The Role of World Religions in
Realizing the Torah's Universalist Vision 169
   Assaf Malach

Rabbi Abraham Isaac HaKohen Kook: "Divine Religions" and
the Central Role of the Jewish People 187
   Sarel Rosenblatt

Rabbi Yehuda Léon Ashkenazi (Manitou): The "Equation of
Fraternity" and Interfaith Dialogue as Rectification
of the Primeval Murder 211
   Sarel Rosenblatt

Rabbi Jonathan Sacks's Approach to Other Religions 231
   Johnny Solomon

Religiosity as an Innate Quest for God 239
    Yakov Nagen

PART IV
DIVINE SERVICE OF GENTILES:
TORAH, TEMPLE, AND SABBATH

Sharing Torah with the World:
The Jewish People's Responsibility to Non-Jews............... 255
    Yakov Nagen

"A House of Prayer for All Peoples":
Non-Jews and the Temple 285
    Yakov Nagen

Shabbat for the Jews and Shabbat for the Nations 293
    Yakov Nagen

Afterword
Moving Forward: Interreligious Interaction Today 301
    Sarel Rosenblatt

About the Ohr Torah Interfaith Center....................... 309

Preface

*Rabbi Dr. Kenneth Brander**

For the first time in two millennia, the Jewish people are the sovereign power in a state of their own, whose inhabitants and citizens include Arab Christians and Muslims, Druze, Thai and Filipino migrant workers, Sudanese and Eritrean refugees, and other ethnic groups. How can we, and how ought we, make space for their religious identities and practices within our own state? What does the Torah demand of us in terms of our relations with them? Can religion serve as a basis for partnership? The same goes for the ongoing conflict in Israel, along with looming questions regarding Israel's alliances with other countries in the region and the world. Can religion, which has tragically contributed to so much strife in the world, be harnessed as a means toward advancing greater peace and cooperation? The vision of our patriarch Avraham as the ultimate mediator of the Abraham Accords is striking; how else can we use religious symbols to promote a vision of coexistence?

I am certain that some readers will approach this book, which addresses the subject of healing interfaith relations, with great excitement. Some will do so with curiosity, and yet others with hesitation and skepticism.

---

* President and Rosh HaYeshiva, Ohr Torah Stone

The skeptic will ask: What need is there to talk about the relations between the Jewish people and those of other faiths? When there are overlapping ethical and social concerns with other faith communities, we can simply form political alliances with like-minded partners. Why delve any deeper?

This skeptical approach may be theologically safe, but it misses a religious opportunity – indeed a religious mandate: despite theological differences, there is a greater vision for humanity that can only be realized, as we recite thrice daily in our prayers, when God's name will become one, *"ushemo eḥad."* We have a divine directive to work toward the global acknowledgment of God's dominion over the world. As Maimonides states, the purpose of other faiths is to pave the way for the Messianic era through the knowledge of the Divine they bring to the world (*Mishneh Torah, Hilkhot Melakhim* 11:4). Jewish theology therefore requires us to look at other religions and in turn evaluate our engagement with them.

With the Jewish people now inhabiting and governing an autonomous state, we have moved with centripetal force from an exiled people on the periphery, an ineffectual entity, to a nation that is a primary actor on the world stage, a history-making community. That reality should lead even the most hardened cynic to become a dreamer or, at least, to acknowledge that a new reality is possible. Our doctrinal disagreements with the Catholic Church, which caused generations of anti-Semitism and persecution, went through a significant transformation with the *Nostra Aetate* document of 1965. Many Catholics and Christians have become our most trustworthy and impassioned friends. Greater engagement with Muslims, Hindus, and Jains may yet enable us to achieve with other faith systems what emerged from the Second Vatican Council with the Catholic Church.

As the English edition of this groundbreaking volume is published, the need for deep, thorough, thoughtful consideration of how we ought to relate to other faiths and their adherents could not be more clear. At the most superficial level, the alliances and bridges we build with other religious groups require a firm account of what interfaith relations are all about. Religion is about both God and humanity. It is the way people connect with the Divine. *If we fail to acknowledge and appreciate others' faith, we also fail to recognize their humanity.* This, regrettably, has been the painful fate of the Jewish people for centuries; we must learn from our own history not to do the same to others. Respect for others requires respect for the *completeness* of the other, including their religion, as well as the recognition that the World to Come is not reserved for the Jewish people alone, but for all the righteous who walk the earth.

The Jewish people, particularly those in the State of Israel, are in dire need of traditional halakhic yet innovative paradigms for approaching these issues and the underlying theological questions upon which they rest. What does Judaism envision as the role of non-Jewish people and non-Jewish faiths here in this world and on the journey to redemption? What is God's vision for humanity? What is our own place, as God's "chosen people," in that vision?

Answers to these questions are remarkably hard to come by. Peruse the shelves of your average Jewish bookstore, or of a yeshiva or shul library, and you'll find a large number of volumes addressing not only traditional topics like Shabbat and *kashrut,* but even books that tackle contemporary issues such as waging war, technological advances and their impact on halakhic observance, how to follow the agricultural laws of the Land of Israel within a modern economy, and much more. Yet you will be hard pressed to find any works in the fields of halakha (Jewish law) or *hashkafa* (Jewish thought) that seriously engage with fundamental questions regarding Judaism and other faiths in our sovereign state of Israel and beyond.

UShemo Eḥad is an outgrowth of this vision, sharing ancient and contemporary religious sources that speak to the opportunities and challenges born of healing the relations between the Jewish people and those of other faiths. The fellows at Ohr Torah Stone's Beit Midrash for Judaism and Humanity and our Blickle Institute for Interfaith Dialogue are paving the way for a new Judaic legal and philosophical literature in this field. They consider seriously, and sensitively, the best approach to these halakhic issues; create points of reference for future learners and leaders; and offer tools for all those who wish to follow in the way of the Torah (or at least understand it) and engage appropriately with people of other faiths, in Israel and throughout the world.

I wish to thank the members of the Beit Midrash, particularly Rabbi Dr. Yakov Nagen, Rabbi Sarel Rosenblatt, and Dr. Asaf Malach, for the sacred work they invested into producing this volume, which deals with Judaism's approach to the religious world of the other. With God's will, we will merit to see many more holy books produced by them and the other fellows of the Beit Midrash, publications that enrich and uplift the discourse on the relations between the Jewish people and humanity. This book will yet be translated into other languages and will serve as the basis for further publications addressing even wider audiences in the future.

I also wish to thank Dr. Giti and Mr. Jack Bendheim for their support in helping bring this volume to publication. Giti and Jack bring a clarity of vision and a commitment to action in all their various and important philanthropic activities. Thank you for making this one of them.

This volume is dedicated to the memory of a cherished mentor of mine, Mr. Stuart Harris, Shimon Gedalya ben Pinchas Menachem v'Rachel *z"l*, by his loving family. Stuart was the kind of person who understood that ensuring a good and fulfilled life requires devoting energy to the great questions of the day. May his insights continue to be the blessing he was during his lifetime, and may his words continue to faithfully guide me, his wife Gloria, their three children – Jeffrey, David, and Rachel – their grandchildren, and their great-grandchildren, along with many, many others who were blessed by his wisdom, sharp mind, and deep sense of vision.

Introduction

The Relationship Between Jews and Non-Jews: The Need for a New Source-Based Paradigm

*Yakov Nagen**

JEWS AND THE NATIONS AT THE END OF DAYS

Over the past few decades, the Jewish people have been experiencing momentous reversals of fortune. Ancient prophecies about the ingathering of exiles and the return to Zion are being realized before our very eyes, and we are fortunate to bear witness to them. God has brought His people back to their homeland from the four corners of the Earth. As we observe and participate in events that are perhaps the most historic since the time of the Bible, we have to pinch ourselves to verify that we are not dreaming.

As history is in the making, what can we expect based on the eschatological prophecies of old? Interestingly, the prophets describe antithetical movements. In one direction, the return to Zion arcs inward;

---

* Rabbi Dr. Yakov Nagen is Executive Director of the Ohr Torah Interfaith Center and heads the Blickle Institute for Interfaith Dialogue and its Beit Midrash for Judaism and Humanity. Rabbi Nagen has published ten books that address Jewish spirituality, Talmud, and interfaith relations.

from a Diaspora where they have been mingled among the nations, the Jews separate themselves out and return to their homeland, the Land of Israel. In the other direction, the end of days sees the Jewish people fulfilling their mission to be "a light for the nations" (Is. 46:9), a light that radiates outwards from Zion – "from Zion shall the Torah go forth" (Is. 2:3). Why separate from the global community only to rejoin it?

The answer lies in a profound change of national mindset. In the period of redemption, Jews transform from reactive survivalists to proactive visionaries. In exile, Jews had to avoid at all costs losing their identities either to the domineering culture or to all others in the equalizing melting pot, which required distancing themselves from other peoples. Only when there is center, a national home, where Jewish identity can be safely preserved and reinforced, can Jews assuredly step out into the world and take their places on the world stage.

But as necessary as this metamorphosis is, the means and ends are indistinct. The time has come to reexamine the halakhic and theological issues regarding the relationship between Jews and the rest of humanity with a fresh pair of eyes. Historically, these questions have been tabled or too often decided in favor of cultural isolationism, to throw up what they hoped were insurmountable barriers that would keep foreign influences at bay. To generalize, Tractate Avoda Zara of the Talmud is an extensive guide of how *not* to act in matters involving non-Jews. Yet there is no complementary, positive treatise instructing Jews how to fulfill the mandate of being "a light for the nations" in the granular detail that is the hallmark of halakha. In the same way that we strive to make other eschatological predictions into realities, such as building up the Land and encouraging and making aliya, so should we be determining how to facilitate the ultimate realignment between Jews and non-Jews.

Another urgent reason for reconsidering this question is the accelerating pace of globalization. It is impossible today to ignore the existence of people who live in another hemisphere and speak languages that are alien to us. Everyone is inextricably linked to and affected by one another; the degrees of separation are steadily shrinking. Rabbi Abraham Isaac HaKohen Kook perceptively identified this process as precipitating one of the major transformations of the modern mind. Here is how he describes the premodern state of affairs:

Each and every community was circumscribed; an individual was visibly influenced only by their immediate environment. In their naïveté, every individual and community thought that the wide world was coextensive with their spiritual and physical environs.[1]

By the twentieth century, Rabbi Kook observed a massive change of consciousness:

> All individuals feel that they are not alone, that they are not hermetically circumscribed, that they act within and are acted upon by numerous expansive circles, various and even foreign milieux. As such, no one can dismiss any human being by saying, "I have no reason to pay them any mind at all" – even if they are in the farthest reaches.[2]

If a century ago one could not ignore the gravitational pull of cultures near and far on oneself and one's hometown, it is even more true today. Technological progress and the sense that we all live in the same global village has thickened and solidified the web of interconnection. In this new reality, we must reexamine how Jews should relate to non-Jews. The unavoidable contact can pose a challenge or threat to Jewish identity, but it simultaneously represents an opportunity for realizing the universalist mission of the Jewish people recorded in our prophecies, reinvigorating Jewish existence with a new sense of purpose.

The chapters of this book and their accompanying sources set out to lay the groundwork for a new perspective on one of the many crucial aspects of Jewish-gentile relations: the Torah's view on the beliefs and religious lives of non-Jews. The literature explicating and debating what God demands of the Jewish people is breathtakingly extensive, but this does not encompass the entirety of God's designs, which include the rest of humanity: "For from the rising of the sun to its setting My name is great among the nations, and in every place incense and pure grain offering are offered to My name – for My name is great among the nations,

---

1. *Orot HaKodesh* 2:539.
2. *Orot HaKodesh* 2:540.

said the Lord of Hosts" (Mal. 1:11). In a way, this neglect reflects the distorted view for which the book of Jonah is a corrective lens. The prophet shirks his God-given mission to the non-Jewish metropolis because of his ethnocentric view of the world, and God teaches him that he, like Jeremiah, is also "a prophet for the nations" (Jer. 1:5). The word of God extends beyond the chosen people to the entire human population.

The status of the religions practiced by non-Jews is not an incidental one raised by pressing historical circumstances, but an essential one that touches on the spiritual responsibility of the Jewish people to the nations of the world. This was first assumed by Abraham, about whom the Torah says: "Through you will all the clans of the earth be blessed" (Gen. 12:3). And it continues all the way to the end of history, when the Jewish people will become a "light for the nations" and spread Torah to them all:

> And many peoples shall go and say, "Come, let us go up to the mountain of the Lord, to the House of the God of Jacob, that He may instruct us in His ways, and that we may walk in His paths." For from Zion shall the Torah go forth, and the word of the Lord from Jerusalem. (Is. 2:3)

Jews are not meant to stand on the sidelines but to take to the global field and spread the word of God. How exactly are we to do this and what is the end goal?

THE SHARED ENTERPRISE OF DIVINE CORONATION

Many sources indicate that the revelation of God's sovereignty over the world is only possible in collaboration with our fellow human beings. The Jewish liturgy concludes with the *Aleinu* prayer, in which the supplicant yearns for a time when "all the world's inhabitants will recognize and know that to You must every knee bow, every tongue swear loyalty. [...] And they all will accept the yoke of Your kingdom." The prophet Zephaniah teaches us that the desire to call out to God and worship Him is universal: "For then I will transform peoples with a pure language, for them all to call in the name of Lord, to serve Him shoulder to shoulder" (Zeph. 3:9).

Spiritual fellowship does more than bring divergent forms of divine service into accord; it lays the foundation for peaceful relations and genuine cooperation between the separate oceans of humanity. As King David says in the book of Psalms: "I am a friend to all who fear You" (Ps. 119:63). On the surface, the psalmist is saying that there is a spiritual kinship between believers. On a deeper level, though, the verse expresses the idea that religiosity – too often the cause of antagonism – can be the very basis for solid friendship and broad partnership, provided that all worshippers respect one another's religious expression.

How this religious solidarity is to be achieved is an open question. Who has to change and how much to come closer together? One radical possibility is that spiritual fraternity requires the alteration of religious DNA. If so, one must ask what the new face of religion would look like. At the other extreme is a change in attitude alone. To partner with other nations in revealing God's kingdom, all that would be needed is acceptance and mutual respect for everyone driving humanity toward that goal.[3] An intermediate position would leave certain religions largely intact but require revising a number of basic tenets of faith. Again, one would need to iron out what precisely those are.

The sources collected and analyzed in this volume are intended to provide a launching point for thinking deeply about these and other issues that pertain to the relationship between Jews and the nations today, especially Judaism's perspective on non-Jewish religiosity. The medieval and modern authorities cited herein present a gamut of understandings

---

3. My dear friend and colleague Rabbi Professor Alan Brill has collected very important sources on the attitude of Judaism to other religions over the centuries in his *Judaism and Other Religions: Models of Understanding* (New York: Palgrave Macmillan, 2010). He categorizes Jewish thinkers according to the model of religious truth that they adopt: (1) Exclusivists admit only one truth and one means to redemption and salvation. (2) Inclusivists view the world through their particular religions but are able to acknowledge elements of truth in other faiths. (3) Pluralists posit the existence of multiple truths, so that no one religion can lay exclusive claim to the truth. (4) Universalists maintain that there is a single truth but it has many possible manifestations.

of the importance of non-Jews worshipping God. Some see the spread of monotheistic faiths influenced by Judaism as a giant leap for humankind toward the ultimate redemption of the world. From this historical fact, they even derive significant implications for Judaism's ideal relationship with the global community more generally, and with these monotheistic faiths in particular.

Additionally, Rabbi Kook saw in the return of the Jewish people to their land a basis for renewing our understanding of the Torah and mitzvot. This plumbing of the Torah's depths to bring to light the profound reasons for the mitzvot has a universalist orientation:

The recitation (*keriat*) of the *Shema* at night and in the morning gesture toward the two types of declaration (*keria*) of God's name that are incumbent upon the Jewish people. We must accept the yoke of Heaven on ourselves, and through our declaration of God's unity act so that ultimately all the world's inhabitants will recognize and know that the Lord, the God of Israel, is King, and His dominion extends over all.

> In exile, which is comparable to night, our primary activity concerns ourselves alone, so that we can withstand the waves that wash over us, in the name of God. Therefore, faith (*emuna*) pertains to the night: Whoever did not say *Emet VeEmuna* ("True and Faithful") at night did not fulfill their obligation. [...] But at the time of redemption, when the horn of Israel will be lifted, it will consequently be the time for the action of the recitation of the morning *Shema* – *Ahava Rabba* ("Great Love") – so that all peoples will say that the light of Israel shall be a light for the world. At that time, therefore, the reasons of the Torah will be revealed.... For in order to draw close those who are distant, words of truth (*emet*) must be perfectly clarified and the matter translated according to the superficial

conception of the non-Jews. That is why *Emet VeYatziv* ("True and Firm") of the morning is translated[4] into Aramaic.[5]

For Jews and non-Jews to coronate God as King at the time of redemption, not only will gentiles make adjustments to their belief systems, but Jews will have to reorient themselves as well to the universalist currents in the Torah. The generation of redemption will draw new light from the well of Torah and illuminate the world with it.

INTERFAITH DIALOGUE

The chapters and anthologized sources in this volume are also intended to serve as a springboard for reconsidering the role of interfaith dialogue and cooperation today, in a way that we think better suits the current political situation and spiritual state of the Jewish people, on the one hand, and the revised attitudes and beliefs of the major religions (especially Christianity, as discussed below), on the other. Every generation – and especially ours – ought to make an accounting of its success in fulfilling God's will in light of contemporary realities.

The motivations for and effects of interfaith dialogue can be various. At the most basic level, bloodletting can be stopped by religious leaders on all sides calling upon their faithful to lay down arms. Peace, or at the very least a truce, allows for additional, more meaningful levels of interaction. Practically, religious leaders can make common cause on social or spiritual matters. But sincere dialogue and deep connection has the potential to be positively transformational, to fundamentally reshape the represented religions and their interfaith postures. Whenever a religion, and this is particularly true of the flagship monotheistic ones, revises its attitude to and relationship with other religions, that change has a ripple effect on its core theology. Inclusive dialogue with other monotheistic

---

4. I.e., the word after *emet* in the morning blessing is *yatziv*, a Biblical Aramaic word from the book of Daniel, whereas the one in the nighttime blessing is *emuna*, which is Biblical Hebrew.

5. *Ein Aya*, Berakhot 1:1.

religions, which recognizes that we and they worship the very same God, is predicated on a more abstract conception of God that centers on His uniqueness and oneness. By the same token, when a religion conceives of itself as part of a panhuman fellowship serving God, the impediments to working together that flow from the delegitimizing of other religions, such as *jihad* and missionization, disappear. A legitimate partner is no enemy, and an attempt to convert a spiritual brother is an insult.

The starkest example of a before-and-after religious transformation is the mid-twentieth-century Catholic Church's reversal of its dim view of Judaism and the Jews. Change commenced in the 1960s when Pope John XXIII, who himself saved Jews in the Holocaust, began reforming the Church's position at Vatican II. *Nostra Aetate* (In Our Time), "the Declaration on the Relation of the Church with Non-Christian Religions," was promulgated in 1965, absolving the Jews of all blame in the death of Jesus and expressing the Church's reservations about labeling the Jews as rejected or cursed. This positive reappraisal continued to gradually develop until it culminated in a document produced by the Vatican in 2015 titled "The Gifts and the Calling of God are Irrevocable." This officially put an end to missionary activity among the Jews due to the recognition that God's covenant with them remains in force.[6]

With Islam, too, one can see that countries that maintain good relations between members of different faiths tend to interpret *jihad* as a spiritual struggle within the individual, not a violent war to be waged by one people against another. Simply engaging in dialogue and encountering one another, even without coming to any formal resolution or determination, steers world religions onto a more inclusive course toward the Other.

When lines must be drawn, however, Judaism has never been afraid to draw them. It has challenged polytheism and championed unadulterated monotheism. There is room for withering criticism of unacceptable or extremist elements of other religions. Just as Judaism is open to cooperation, it withdraws when necessary. Legitimization of

---

6. See Dina Porat, Karma Ben Johanan, and Ruth Braude, eds., *In Our Time: Documents and Articles on the Catholic Church and the Jewish People in the Wake of the Holocaust* [in Hebrew] (Tel Aviv: Tel Aviv University, 2015).

other faiths and respectful discourse do not translate into unconditional acceptance of every religious belief, behavior, or phenomenon.

INTERFAITH ENCOUNTER AS A STRENGTHENER OF JEWISH IDENTITY

To adopt a position of legitimization and respect for other religions – not to mention one of cooperation – can dilute one's own religious identity. When Rabbi Kook wrote about modern interconnectivity and the tidal pull of groups the world round on every individual, he did not neglect to spell out the danger: the more identity is stretched in every direction, the more likely it cannot hold onto its particularistic contents. This is especially true when identity is contrastive, emerging from a negation of and separation from the Other. Consequently, when one acknowledges the religious identity of the Other, the luminosity of one's own identity is liable to be dimmed.

However, strengthening connections and cooperation with members of other faiths need not weaken Jewish identity. To the contrary, it can work to solidify it. First, the greatest threat to all religiosity today is from the secular materialism of the West. Standing shoulder to shoulder with other religions against this danger strengthens everyone's religious identity vis-à-vis secularism. Second, identity erosion from the recognition of other faiths as legitimate is primarily a concern within the isolated communities of the Diaspora, which are enveloped by the more "successful" and "alluring" religion of the majority. In the Jewish State, belonging to the majority minimizes this risk.

Moreover, the post-modern world we live in is allergic to meta-narratives that claim to possess the exclusive truth and to dismiss all others as false. Over a century ago, Rabbi Kook foretold this danger of a relational, rather than substantive, religious identity:

> There are others who believe it impossible to genuinely believe in the truth of the Torah unless one also believes that all other faiths are worthless, and that those who adhere to them gain

nothing from them. But this is not true. [...] This ill-conceived line of thinking has many negative repercussions.[7]

Rabbi Kook utterly opposes the notion that to be a true believer entails rejecting all other faiths and dismissing them as valueless. For him, taking this position weakens Jewish belief. The proper approach is to find the value in other belief systems and thereby strengthen one's faith:

The scorn for other faiths deeply ingrained in the masses is also responsible for the wicked and godless treating the pure belief of the Jews in the same way. They claim that they are identical: this is religion and that is religion. Therefore, to save our youngsters from corrosive influences such as these, we must instill the value of other faiths according to the Torah.[8]

Finally, experience – the greatest teacher – indicates that the encounter with other Abrahamic religions, and the resulting understanding of just how central Judaism is to their story and tenets of faith, ought to reinforce Jewish identity and pride. When a Jew meets a Christian who thinks of the Jewish people as his "older brother," or when a Jew encounters a Muslim who views that person as a member of the "people of the book" (*ahl al-kitāb*) who merited receiving the Torah from Heaven, the eyes of the Other reflect the importance of Judaism back to the Jew and reinforce the sense of collective Jewish responsibility to other peoples and faiths. Large segments of humanity model their lives on that of Abraham and perpetuate his legacy, a fact that should imbue Jewish life with greater, more universal significance.

*   *   *

THE STRUCTURE OF THIS BOOK

To reopen the wide-ranging questions, both halakhic and philosophical, that bear on the relationship between Jews and the nations, the Ohr Torah Stone network founded a think tank called the Beit Midrash for Judaism and Humanity. The work before you is the fruit of its intellectual

---

7. *LiNevukhei HaDor* 14:1.
8. Ibid.

labors, the result of the joint study of four members: Rabbi Dr. Yakov Nagen, head of the Beit Midrash, Rabbi Sarel Rosenblatt, Dr. Assaf Malach, and Mrs. Gita Hazani-Melchior. Each chapter was authored by a different fellow, but it expresses the collective insights of the group. We are also grateful to Rabbi Johnny Solomon for contributing a chapter about the thought of Rabbi Jonathan Sacks.

The chapters of this volume all relate to the importance of religiosity and service of God among non-Jews. The book is divided into four parts. Part I addresses fundamental issues. First, it examines the nature of the eschatological relationship between the Jewish people and the nations of the world that emerges from studying the Prophets. Since the various seers describe this relationship differently, there is more than one way to understand the place of world religions in the future. The next chapter analyzes the character of Noahide law in rabbinic thought and concludes that it is a necessary condition for human civilization. Once that condition is met, each nation has a blank canvas on which to paint its own rich religious experience. Part II explores the attitude toward world religions in medieval Jewish thought, and each chapter thereof is dedicated to the thought of one celebrated thinker on the issue. Rabbi Judah HaLevi holds that these religions accord with human reason or morality but are essentially distinct from revealed religion, whereas Rabbi Nathaniel b. Fayyumi stakes the claim that there are revealed religions, having been revealed independently of the giving of the Torah to Moses. Rabbi Menahem Meiri argues that their legitimacy stems from their fundamental ethical decency and theological foundations, and he even allows for interreligious fraternity. Rabbi Joseph Albo spells out the necessary theological foundations for all true religions, while attributing their variability to national character. Against all these thinkers stands Rabbi Moses Maimonides, who grants no legitimacy to world religions and identifies the seven Noahide laws with the proper religion for non-Jews – and only precisely because these mitzvot were revealed at Sinai. Nevertheless, even Maimonides shows appreciation for the divine service of exceptional non-Jews. The third part of the volume moves to the modern period, ranging from the eighteenth to the twenty-first century. It covers dedicated treatments of the topic by Rabbi Elijah Benamozegh, Rabbi Abraham Isaac HaKohen Kook, Rabbi Yehuda Léon Ashkenazi

(Manitou), and Rabbi Lord Jonathan Sacks. These chapters highlight the modern call to focus on the universal role of the Jewish people and the Torah, and on the important place of world religions – especially Christianity and Islam – in the grand narrative of humanity.

The final section of the book discusses the participation of non-Jews in three core areas of Judaism: Torah study, the Temple service, and Shabbat observance.

Every chapter is an independent essay of variable length that contextualizes and interprets a selection of sources, and then concludes with key points or lessons for reflection. It is followed by a section titled "Sources," in which texts cited briefly in the chapter are expanded and other relevant sources appear.[9] This format affords readers unmediated access to the source materials so they can form their own impressions, grasp the sources' full meaning, and – it is our hope – come to a new understanding of Jewish-gentile relations. All sources that appear at the end of the chapter are numbered for ease of reference.

The book sets forth the findings of the Beit Midrash by presenting its interpretations of the sources and charting a cogent course through them. As the general thesis is elaborated chapter after chapter, the reader will come to see that this makes room for inclusive and respectful interfaith dialogue, and even deems other faiths partners in humankind's all-inclusive service of God – "for them all to call in the name of Lord, to serve Him shoulder to shoulder." Of course, this should not be taken to mean that Judaism grants legitimacy to any and every religious movement. In another volume, we will treat the relationship between Judaism and polytheism in all its ramifications.

It is our hope that the sources we have woven together in this volume to spur new avenues of thought will not remain theoretical but will find application in the great work of revealing God's glory in this world, a process that we aspire to advance through connection, cooperation, healing, and interfaith dialogue. As we pray thrice daily: "May all of humanity call out in God's name, and everyone accept the yoke of His kingdom."

---

9. In some chapters, the nature of the presentation and argument requires incorporating the relevant sources into the body of the chapter, so that there is no appended "Sources" section.

Acknowledgments

This book is the inaugural volume of the Beit Midrash for Judaism and Humanity. As part of the Ohr Torah Stone network, we owe its staff a tremendous debt of gratitude. First and foremost, we thank its President, Rabbi Dr. Kenneth Brander, whose vision, initiative, support, and practical guidance keep the Beit Midrash going. From the beginning, Rabbi Brander recognized the urgent need for a think tank dedicated to probing the relationship between Judaism and humanity. Additional thanks go to the Director General, Mr. Yinon Ahiman, for assuring the financial success of the Beit Midrash; Ohr Torah Interfaith Center's managing director Rabbi Dr. Aharon Ariel Lavi for promoting our projects; Deputy Director of Education, Rabbi Yehuda Shtauber, whose door is always open for the generous dispensation of insightful advice; Rabbi Nehemiah Krakover, for his professional guidance of the Beit Midrash; and Mr. David Katz, for everything he does behind the scenes.

I am grateful to the team of talented people at Maggid Books. At every stage they have given their input with dedication, professionalism and marvelous advice. I thank the publisher Matthew Miller, the chairman of the editorial board Rabbi Reuven Ziegler and the production manager Caryn Meltz.

Thank you to Daniel Tabak, for producing a superb translation and succeeding in the daunting task of making a work of rabbinical literature of multiple genres readable in English without sacrificing detail. And to Rabbi Dr. Tzvi Sinensky the copy editor, for your fine-tuning of the text. Thank you also Tsofia Harband for the beautiful cover, Estie Dishon for a layout that is pleasing to the eye, and Faigy Badian for your precise proofreading.

We conclude by thanking the Master of the Universe for allowing us to be part of the generation of the redemption, and to personally witness God's favor showered upon His people in the Land. In every generation, the Jewish people face challenges. It is our fortune that ours are bound up with the reconstitution of the Jewish nation in the Holy Land and in the founding of Israeli society on the Torah – on the principles of peace, justice, and righteousness. "Were our mouths as full of song as the sea, and our tongue's praise like the roar of its waves…we still would not be able to thank you enough, the Lord our God."

PART I:
FUNDAMENTAL ISSUES

Four Prophetic Models for the Future of the Jewish People and the Nations

*Sarel Rosenblatt**

A BIRD'S-EYE VIEW OF TANAKH

Many of the prophecies about the end of days look beyond the internal affairs of the Jewish people to issues that concern the nations of the world. What will be their relationship with the Jewish people? What will their belief system look like? How will they respond when the final redemption is at hand?

Upon closer examination, the prophetic focus on the fate of non-Jews is part of a thematic, historical envelope pattern in Tanakh. Genesis opens with the widest lens possible by following the life of Adam, progenitor of all humankind. When, only a few chapters later, God chooses to make a covenant with Abraham, the frame narrows to a single man and his progeny for the rest of the book. Exodus expands the narrative aperture just enough to capture the entire people descended from Abraham, who make a special covenant with the Creator. If we then fast-forward

* Rabbi Sarel Rosenblatt is the Rosh Yeshiva of the Ohr Torah Stone network's Robert M. Beren Machanaim Hesder Yeshiva, Co-founder and Senior Fellow at the Ohr Torah Interfaith Center, and the Dr. Monique and Mordecai (*z"l*) Katz Fellow at its Beit Midrash for Judaism and Humanity.

3

to prophecies about the end of history, the field of view snaps back to its original setting, taking in all of humanity.

In the biblical narrative, other peoples – typically local inhabitants or foreign invaders – pop in and out of the frame, but the focus remains steadily on the Jewish people. Contrast that with the eschatological prophecies, in which the nations of the world are not side players but have a starring role in the destiny of the Jewish people and the entire human race. Their precise political and religious relationships with the Jewish people and God may vary from prophet to prophet, but one cannot ignore the fact that they are in some way or another integral to the grand scheme of the ultimate redemption.

This very fact seems to gesture toward the revolutionary contribution of the Torah to the world. Where idolaters worship gods associated with a specific topographic feature or geographic region, deities that constantly strive with fellow gods and mere mortals, Jewish Scripture reaches over the horizon to embrace all humankind in its utopian vision of peace and harmony through knowledge of God. This conception of the end of days is the product of monotheistic belief and the view of the human being as fashioned in God's image.

Many scriptural passages relate to the non-Jewish world during the end of days, but the discussion below concentrates on those that deal specifically with the religious angle: the connection of non-Jews to God, the Torah, Jerusalem, and the Temple.

Each prophet envisions the end differently, and this includes the place of the nations. Will Jews and non-Jews enjoy identical stature, or will a hierarchy prevail? Will war precede a lasting peace, or will the nations come to their senses, having been touched by the word of God broadcast from Jerusalem? Will the Jewish Temple be the exclusive cultic site for all peoples, the sole *axis mundi* marked on the globe, or will there be other places of worship as well?

In the proceeding analysis, I plot the trends that emerge from the welter of prophetic statements onto multiple axes: hierarchy versus egalitarianism, centralization versus decentralization, and subjugation versus peaceful enlightenment. I then address the relationship between these prophecies, considering whether they complement or contradict one another.

HIERARCHY VERSUS EGALITARIANISM

In the prophecies that foretell of a future hierarchy, the Jewish people are set apart from everyone else. This is expressed in multiple ways. According to Ezekiel, the Temple precincts are off-limits to non-Jews: "No foreigner, uncircumcised of heart and uncircumcised of flesh, shall enter My sanctuary; no foreigner who is among the Israelites" [8]. In Isaiah's prophecy, though, the division of physical and spiritual labor creates a harmonious society: "And foreigners shall stand and tend your flocks, and strangers shall be your farmers and your vinedressers" [6]. Isaiah [1] and Zechariah [10] appoint the Jewish people as teachers and disseminators of Torah, as well as judges who rebuke the nations.

Note that none of these prophets severs contact or puts distance between Jews and everyone else. In fact, they unanimously attest to a close connection between them. In their prophecies, everything is oriented around the Land of Israel, so the Jews have a special calling. This disparity in roles is not due to some ingrained racial difference but due to the sanctity of the Jewish people or their intimate knowledge of the Torah. Redemption, in this account, flows from the success of the Jewish people in the global spiritual economy, and from the rest of the nations taking their respective places in this new spiritual-political world order.

The egalitarian prophecies could not be more different. The line separating Jew from non-Jew fades, partly or more fully, with respect to religious service and the relationship with God. This is not a byproduct of the redemption but its central feature. According to Isaiah, God invites the nations to Jerusalem for two reasons: (1) to dissolve this perception of difference – "Let not the foreigner who has attached himself to the Lord say, 'The Lord will surely separate me from His people'"; and (2) to include them within the holy community that serves Him – "And the foreigners who attach themselves to the Lord to serve Him and to love the Lord's name, to become His servants … I will bring them to My holy mountain …."[1] Why? "For My house shall be called a house of prayer for all peoples" [5].

---

1. Who are these "foreigners"? Ex. Rabba (19) and Rashi (ad loc.) imply that these are converts. Rabbi Moses Alsheikh, on the other hand, thinks they are non-Jews. I

It goes even further. In Isaiah, non-Jews are welcomed to the Jewish Temple; in Zephaniah, they participate in common worship: "For then I will transform peoples with a pure language, for them all to call in the name of Lord, to serve Him shoulder to shoulder" [9]. The talmudic interpretation of this verse understands that in the future non-Jews will spurn idolatry and associate themselves with the Jews so they can worship God together. Redemption here erases a near-essential differentiator imprinted already in the womb: one's mother tongue. The instatement of a lingua franca undoes the punishment for the Tower of Babel, the fragmentation of human language into mutually unintelligible families. Recall that that story precedes God's selection of Abraham from all humankind. In the eschatological era, these markers of difference will have outlived their usefulness, so that all humanity will be reunited through a single language and worship God "shoulder to shoulder."[2]

CENTRALIZATION VERSUS DECENTRALIZATION

The question of centralization does not turn on relations between peoples but on the geopolitical and spiritual centrality of Jerusalem, the Temple, and the Jewish God. The centralized worldview is given voice by Zechariah: "And many peoples and mighty nations shall come to seek the Lord of Hosts in Jerusalem, and to entreat the Lord" [10]. In another vision of the prophet, the nations are called to Jerusalem to celebrate Sukkot, by which their faith in "the King, the Lord of Hosts" will be tested [11].

---

think that his is the simplest reading of the verse, since the immediately preceding verse speaks of "the man" and "the son of man" (Is. 56:2), and the prophecy ends with a house of prayer for "all peoples."

2. Thus does the Maharsha explain the verse in Zephaniah. He adds: "The world was first settled due to the activity of the generation of dispersion, which had a single language in the Holy Tongue. They set out to rebel against God, so He confused that Holy Tongue. He says here that when the idolaters return to God's worship, He will transform a pure language for them, and this is the Holy Tongue, because all the languages that are not 'pure language' are called *laaz* (imperfect speech) with respect to the Holy Tongue" (*Hiddushei Aggadot*, Avoda Zara 24a).

With Jerusalem at the heart of everything, the world can be either hierarchical, as in Ezekiel's prophecy [8], or egalitarian, like in Isaiah's [5]. Common to both visions is the relinquishment of non-Jewish hegemony via recognition of the sacred supremacy of Jerusalem, the Holy of Holies. In other words, when Isaiah articulates his universalist and cooperative prophecy in which the Temple is the house of prayer for all nations, there is a flipside to it. If Jerusalem is the epicenter of all that is good and holy in the world, then no other religion can claim that another cultic site on Earth is the exclusive – or even the central – place of worship. A life that does not exclusively revolve around the Temple in Jerusalem is perhaps the most surprising vision of the future found in Tanakh. When Micah writes that people of the world will stream to God's mountain, he does not depict Zephaniah's monolingualism and mono-religiosity [9] but extreme religious diversity: "For all the peoples shall walk, each in the name of its god, but we shall walk in the name of the Lord our God, forever and ever" [2]. The simplest reading of Micah's prophecy is that ascending the Temple Mount is the pinnacle of religious experience, but the nations of the world are not expected to ring Jerusalem with permanent residences and live in its spiritually rarefied atmosphere. They go home and resume their previous religious practices, spiritually recharged and enlightened.[3] Another decentralized version of the future is presented by Isaiah:

---

3. According to Rashi, Radak, and other commentators, Micah refers here to the past. That is, throughout history the nations of the world have followed the path of their respective gods, but now, with the redemption at hand, they reject their idolatry and worship God alone. Rabbi Moses Alsheikh (on Ps. 102:23), however, claims that Micah is speaking of the future redemption entirely. The approach taken in the body of the text here connects these verses with a kabbalistic tradition present in Rabbi Moses Nahmanides's Bible commentary (on Lev. 18:24) and in the Zohar (see *Zohar Ḥadash, Tikkunim* 97b), that all the nations of the world have supernal figures appointed over them that are ultimately subject to God's will, whereas the Jewish people have a direct, unmediated connection with God. This conception of the existential order may find halakhic expression in the tradition that non-Jews are not cautioned against *shittuf*, associating the name of God with something else (see *Tosafot*, Bekhorot 2b, s.v. *shema*, and Rema, *Oraḥ Ḥayim* 156).

> On that day there shall be an altar of the Lord in the midst
> of the land of Egypt, and a pillar to the Lord at its border.
> [...]
> On that day, Israel shall be the third with Egypt and
> Assyria, a blessing in the midst of the earth, which the
> Lord of Hosts conferred saying, "Blessed be My people
> Egypt, My handiwork Assyria, and Israel My inheritance."
> (Is. 19:19, 24–25) [3]

At the end of days, according to Isaiah, the nations will worship the Jewish God exclusively, but Jerusalem is not the only acceptable place to do that. Even Egypt will have "an altar of the Lord." The biblical model of a single chosen nation is modified so that the two mighty empires of the biblical period – Egypt and Assyria – join spiritual forces with Israel. The language here is noteworthy: God calls Egypt "My people" and Assyria "My handiwork." Previously, God referred exclusively to the Israelites in such loving terms. Like Isaiah, Malachi also envisions a world with altars as far as the eye can see: "in every place incense and pure grain offering" are brought to God's name. This attests to the fact that God's name is "great among the nations" [12].[4]

SUBJUGATION VERSUS ENLIGHTENMENT AND PEACE

Another tension between the many eschatological prophecies surrounds the unfolding of events. One foretelling has it that cataclysmic wars and extraordinary natural disasters will make the nations of the world submit and recognize that the God of Israel reigns supreme and that Jerusalem is His chosen city. For example, Zechariah depicts a world war in which the two forces meet on the battlefield of Jerusalem, where victory is decided by earthquakes, the splitting of the Mount of Olives,

---

4. The verses in Malachi are also significant because Malachi is speaking of his own day and not of the future. We know that during his time nations were not coming to the Temple to offer sacrifices nor to Jerusalem to learn Torah, yet he still considers their religious worship as magnifying God's name in the world. This is also implied by Menaḥot 110a.

and a brilliant light at night. The ranks of the enemy are devastated, and survivors have no choice but to accept that God is King of kings. The threat of plague and drought looms over their continued faithfulness to God. The path to the end of days is therefore lined with bent knees.

Where Ezekiel foresees the illumination of a decimated landscape on a scale we associate with the end of days, Isaiah [1] (and in chapter 11) instead sees a spiritual beacon that illuminates the world with knowledge of God through the teaching of Torah and the pursuit of justice. The divine spirit – imparting wisdom, discernment, understanding, and fear of God – rests on a scion of King David, whose fight for what is good and right is heard round the world. As the Torah goes forth from Zion, the nations embrace it and decide to seek out God in Jerusalem, to study His Torah and be judged by His wisdom. It is not only that no force is applied to make the nations see the light, but that the ensuing enlightenment does more than lead them to coronate God as King. As the divine wisdom is disseminated throughout the world, a new world order arises, in which all weapons of war are irrevocably transformed into tools of peace.

THE CHOICE IS OURS

How the world will ultimately look and how it will get there is the subject of differing prophecies, and we must consider the possible relationship between them. Theoretically, the analysis can go in one of two directions. The first approach harmonizes the incongruities as much as possible to produce a synthetic account. This is theologically advantageous, because it takes a holistic view of God's will. The denouement of history is carefully plotted, and we can discover how all the loose ends will be tied up. What of the glaring incompatibilities? These can be attributed to the fact that every prophet sees what will come to pass through a unique pair of eyes. As R. Yitzḥak says in the Talmud, "A single matter may appear to several prophets, but no two prophets express it identically in prophecy."[5] The prophecy beheld is raw data that must be parsed and interpreted through the organs of the prophet's mind and

---

5. Sanhedrin 89a.

spirit. No two minds are alike, so no two prophecies are identical. This approach, however, faces nearly insurmountable interpretive hurdles, because some aspects of the visions are in direct conflict, or are even diametrically opposed.

It is possible to soften this position and argue that each prophet has a different vantage point from which he observes part of the future reality, and so offers us one slice of it. For example, one can describe a person independently, as an isolated being distinct from family, friends, and society, but one can also locate an individual within the great web of humanity. The relationship between the Jewish people and the rest of humanity similarly lends itself to being presented in terms of separation and cooperation, and both can be simultaneously true. One would have to be able to show exactly how each prophecy aligns with some facet of this multifaceted reality.

The second approach fits more smoothly with the language and content of the biblical passages, because the prophets do sound like they are bearing witness to fundamentally distinct worlds. This interpretation accepts the prophecies for what they are: alternative possible futures. Rabbi Moses Maimonides appears to take this approach when he writes:

> Regarding all of these and similar matters, nobody knows how they will occur until they do, for these matters are obscure in the Prophets, and the Sages possess no tradition about them. All we have is the most persuasive interpretation of the verses, which is why there is a dispute about them. Be that as it may, neither the order of events nor their details are religious dogma, and a person should never preoccupy oneself with aggadic statements. One should not dwell overmuch on the midrashic homilies about these and similar matters, nor should one treat them as essential, for they do not bring one to fear or love [God]. Similarly, one should not calculate the end; the Sages said, "May those who calculate the end be cursed."[6] *One should*

---

6. Sanhedrin 97b.

*instead wait and have general faith that it will happen, as we
have explained.[7]*

Clearly, Maimonides views the sources as contradictory, which is precisely why he discourages spending time to try to work out what will happen. There is no definitive answer to be reached.

According to the Torah, the future is not set in stone; otherwise, we would not have divergent prophecies. It is not pointless to weigh and act upon the possibilities, because the Torah expects us to be active participants in shaping the future, not passive spectators observing the unfolding of God's master plan. By giving us glimpses of how things could be, God has also given us the free will to make one of them a reality. The Sages similarly pin the timing of the ultimate redemption on Jewish activity. In trying to make sense of the prophetic promise that God will "hasten" the end "in its time" (Is. 60:22), the Sages remark: "If they merit it – 'I will hasten it'; if they do not merit it – 'in its time.'"[8] This is more limited because it refers only to the collective merit of the Jewish people accumulated by Torah study and mitzva observance. In the prophecies discussed here, the nations of the world have greater input through their choices and actions, but the Jewish nation still has an effect on whether redemption will be hierarchical or egalitarian, centralized or decentralized, militaristic or didactic.

In considering all these options, we should bear two things in mind: the nations of the world will always be part of the picture, and the utopian reality will only be achieved through a combination of human action and divine orchestration.

Sources

[1] Isaiah 2:2–4
It shall be at the end of days that the mountain of the Lord's house shall be established at the top of the mountains and tower above the hills, and all the nations shall flow to it. And many peoples shall go and say,

---

7. *Mishneh Torah, Hilkhot Melakhim* 12:2.
8. Sanhedrin 98a.

"Come, let us go up to the mountain of the Lord, to the house of the God of Jacob, that He may teach us of His ways and that we may walk in His paths." For from Zion shall the Torah go forth, and the word of God from Jerusalem. And He shall judge between the nations and arbitrate for many peoples. And they shall grind their swords into plowshares and their spears into pruning hooks. Nation shall not raise sword against nation, nor shall they learn war anymore.

[2] Micah 4:1–5

It shall be at the end of days that the mountain of the Lord's house shall be established at the top of the mountains and tower above the hills, and peoples shall flow to it. And many nations shall go and say, "Come, let us go up to the mountain of the Lord, to the house of the God of Jacob, that He may teach us of His ways and that we may walk in His paths." For from Zion shall the Torah go forth, and the word of God from Jerusalem. And He shall judge between many peoples and arbitrate for mighty nations from afar. And they shall grind their swords into plowshares and their spears into pruning hooks. Nation shall not raise sword against nation, nor shall they learn war anymore. But every man shall sit under his grapevine and under his fig tree, with none to make him afraid, for the Lord of Hosts has spoken. For all the peoples shall walk, each in the name of its god, but we shall walk in the name of the Lord our God, forever and ever.

[3] Isaiah 19:18–25

On that day, five cities in the land of Egypt shall speak the language of Canaan and swear to the Lord of Hosts. Of one of them it shall be said "the city of destruction." On that day there shall be an altar of the Lord in the midst of the land of Egypt, and a pillar to the Lord at its border. It shall be a sign and witness for the Lord of Hosts in the land of Egypt, so that when they cry out to the Lord because of oppressors, He will send them a savior and champion who will save them. And the Lord shall make Himself known to Egypt, and Egypt shall know the Lord on that day, and worship with sacrifice and grain offering and make a vow to the Lord and fulfill it. And the Lord shall afflict Egypt, afflicting and healing, and they shall return to the Lord, and He shall hear their entreaty and heal them. On that day, there shall be a highway from Egypt to Assyria: Assyria shall come into to Egypt and Egypt into Assyria, and Egypt shall worship with Assyria. On that day, Israel shall be the third with Egypt and Assyria, a blessing in the midst of the earth, which the Lord of Hosts conferred saying, "Blessed be My people Egypt, My handiwork Assyria, and Israel My inheritance."

[4] Isaiah 42:5–7

Thus said God, the Lord, who created the heavens and stretched them out, who spreads out the earth and its issue, who gives breath to the people upon it and spirit to those who walk on it: I, the Lord, have called you in righteousness and held your hand, and kept you and made you a covenant for peoples, a light of the nations, to open blind eyes, to bring out the confined from prisons, those sitting in darkness from dungeons.

[5] Isaiah 56:3–8

Let not the foreigner who has attached himself to the Lord say, "The Lord will surely separate me from His people," nor let the eunuch say, "See how I am a withered tree." For thus said the Lord, As for the eunuchs who keep My Sabbaths, choose what I desire, and hold fast to My covenant, I will give them in My house and within My walls a monument and a name better than sons and daughters; I will give them an everlasting name that shall not be cut off. And the foreigners who attach themselves to the Lord to serve Him and to love the Lord's name, to become His servants; all who keep the Sabbath from profaning it and hold fast to My covenant – I will bring them to My holy mountain and give them joy in My house of prayer. Their burnt offerings and sacrifices shall be welcome on My altar. For My house shall be called a house of prayer for all peoples. Thus said the Lord God who gathers the dispersed of Israel, I will gather still more to those already gathered.

[6] Isaiah 61:5–6, 9

And foreigners shall stand and tend your flocks, and strangers shall be your farmers and your vinedressers. As for you, you shall be called the Lord's priests; it shall be said that you are "servants of our God." You shall consume the wealth of nations and revel in their glory. […]

And their seed shall be known among the nations, and their off-spring among the peoples. All who see them shall recognize that they are the seed the Lord has blessed.

[7] Isaiah 66:18–23

As for Me, [I know] their acts and their thoughts. [A time] is coming to gather all nations and tongues, and they shall come and see My glory. And I will set a sign upon them and send from them survivors to the nations, to Tarshish, Pul, and Lud, who draw the bow; Tubal and Javan; the faraway isles that have not heard tell of Me and have not beheld My glory, and they shall relate My glory among the nations. And they shall bring all your brothers from all the nations as an offering to the Lord, on horses, in chariots and covered wagons, on mules and dromedaries, to My holy mountain in Jerusalem, said the Lord, as the Israelites bring a grain offering in a pure vessel to the house of the Lord. And from them, too, I shall take to be priests and Levites, said the Lord. For as the new heavens and the new earth that I make stand before Me, said the Lord, so shall your seed and your name stand. And it shall be, from one month to the next and from one Sabbath to the next, all flesh shall come to bow before Me, said the Lord.

[8] Ezekiel 44:6–10

And you shall say to the rebellious, the house of Israel, Thus said the Lord God, All your abominations are enough for you, house of Israel: when you bring foreigners, uncircumcised of heart and uncircumcised of flesh, to be in My sanctuary, to profane My house, when you offer My food, fat, and blood, and they violate My covenant with all their abominations. And you have not kept the charge of My sacred things, but you have set them for yourselves as keepers of My charge in My sanctuary. .Thus said the Lord God, No foreigner, uncircumcised of heart and uncircumcised of flesh, shall enter My sanctuary; no foreigner who is among the Israelites. Only the Levites, who distanced themselves from Me when Israel strayed, straying from Me after their foul things, and they shall bear their iniquity.

[9] **Zephaniah 3:8–9**
Therefore, wait for Me, said the Lord, for the day I rise as witness, for
My judgment is to gather in nations, to assemble kingdoms, to pour out
My wrath upon them – all my blazing anger. For the entire earth shall
be consumed by My zealous fire. For then I will transform peoples with
a pure language, for them all to call in the name of Lord, to serve Him
shoulder to shoulder.

[10] **Zechariah 8:20–23**
Thus said the Lord of Hosts, Peoples and the inhabitants of many cities
shall yet come, and the inhabitants of one shall go to another, saying,
"Let us go to entreat the Lord and to seek the Lord of Hosts; I will go,
too." And many peoples and mighty nations shall come to seek the Lord
of Hosts in Jerusalem, and to entreat the Lord.

Thus said the Lord of Hosts, In those days, ten men from nations
of every tongue shall grasp – they shall grasp the border of a Jew's gar-
ment, saying, "Let us go with you, for we have heard that God is with you."

[11] **Zechariah 14:2–3, 9, 12, 16–19**
And I will gather all the nations against Jerusalem for battle. And the
city shall be captured, the houses plundered, and the women ravished,
and half the city shall go out into exile, but the rest of the people shall
not be cut off from the city. Then the Lord will go forth and do battle
with those nations, as when He fights on the day of battle. […] And
the Lord shall be king over all the earth; on that day the Lord shall be
one and His name one. […]

This shall be the plague with which the Lord shall strike all the
people that warred against Jerusalem: their flesh shall rot while they
stand on their feet, their eyes shall rot in their sockets, and their tongues
shall rot in their mouths. […] It shall be that whoever remains from the
nations coming up against Jerusalem shall go up, year after year, to bow
to the King, the Lord of Hosts, and to celebrate the festival of Sukkot.
And it shall be that whoever of the clans of the earth does not go up
to Jerusalem to bow to the King, the Lord of Hosts, shall have no rain
upon them. And if the clan of Egypt does not go up and does not come,
and there is no overflow, there shall be the plague with which the Lord

strikes the nations that do not go up to celebrate the festival of Sukkot. This shall be the punishment of Egypt and the punishment of all the nations that do not go up to celebrate the festival of Sukkot.

[12] Malachi 1:11

For from the rising of the sun to its setting My name is great among the nations, and in every place incense and pure grain offering are offered to My name – for My name is great among the nations, said the Lord of Hosts.

World Religions as Fulfilling Biblical Prophecies

Yakov Nagen

We are privileged to live in an age in which much of what the prophets envisioned is being fulfilled: the return to the Land of Israel, the establishment of Jewish sovereignty within its borders, and the liberation of the Old City of Jerusalem, including the Temple Mount. Throughout the ages, religious Jews believed that the fulfillment of the biblical prophecies could be influenced only indirectly, in accordance with mitzva observance. Performance of the commandments would draw the final redemption closer, and their transgression would push it further away. By contrast, the fundamental insight of Zionism was to recognize the need to actively and directly change the course of history by partnering with God through human initiative. As the Talmud says, "In the future, a heavenly voice will call out in the tents of the righteous and say, 'Let whoever acted in concert with God come take their reward.'"[1] For example, the return to Zion was realized due to intensive and dedicated

---

1. Y. Shabbat 6:9.

human endeavor, not by passively waiting for God to fulfill His promise "to bring your children from afar" (Is. 60:9).

The establishment of the State, mass aliya, and other elements of the foretold return to Zion have already come to pass or are far along in their process of realization. But these constitute only the beginning of the future foreseen by the prophets. One very important domain of Jewish eschatology that has yet to be fulfilled is the topic of this volume: building and healing the relationship between the Jewish people and the rest of humanity.

The problem is that even for the close reader of Tanakh who is open to its universalism, the words of the prophets are obscure, making it difficult to translate vision into action. For instance, Zephaniah relates about religious fellowship: "For then I will transform peoples with a pure language, for them all to call in the name of the Lord, to serve Him shoulder to shoulder" (Zeph. 3:9). What does this mean in concrete terms? For non-Jews to "call in the name of the Lord," must they convert to Judaism, or can there be a pan-religious identity, similar to the Noahide category in halakha? Or perhaps each religion retains its distinctive identity, and fraternity entails serving God with mutual respect and agreement on certain core principles of faith?[2]

These questions go beyond theoretical interpretation; they have practical implications. If we want to "act with God" in fulfilling prophetic visions, we must address where and how to do so. In what ways can we best promote interfaith relations and cooperation? And how far away are we from achieving this goal? The answer depends on how we interpret the words of Zephaniah and other biblical prophets. If unity implies that the other nations will substitute a new religious identity for their own, such a circumstance is, to all appearances, a long way off. But if unity can encompass the idea that all peoples retain their own faiths, we can promote this goal – if we are willing to shift our attitude toward relations with other nations and religions in fundamental ways.

---

2. See the discussion in Avoda Zara 24b. Note that in the rabbinic period this final possibility did not exist, since the major world religions were still polytheistic.

PARTNERS IN SHAPING PROPHETIC MEANING

I wish to suggest that we must strive to answer such questions through active dialogue with God. Our task is not merely to observe, uncover, and execute a preordained divine plan. Rather, we are partners with the Almighty in shaping the meaning of the prophecies themselves. This is an essential element in the profound partnership between God and the Jewish people. This partnership touches on the essence of our humanity, the Torah, and prophecy.

(1) Humanity

Consider the first human being, Adam. Having been created "in God's image" (Gen. 1:27), he becomes an ongoing partner in Creation and in ruling the world. But his power is not restricted to the plane of physical activity. He also gives the world meaning. In Genesis 1, God names the light and the darkness, the firmament and dry land, but in Genesis 2, this divine capacity is vouchsafed to man:

> And the Lord God formed from the earth every beast of the field and every fowl of the sky, and He brought them to the man to see what he would call it; and whatever the man called each living creature, that was its name. (Gen. 2:19)

Astonishingly, the Torah describes God Himself waiting with bated breath, as it were, to hear Adam's choices. Had the Torah not said this, it would be theologically untenable to entertain such a scenario. God lets Adam mint the names and then gives them His stamp of approval.

What is the significance of naming? According to Jewish tradition, a name encapsulates and shapes its bearer's essence:

> Whence do we have it that a name is determinative? R. Eliezer said: Since the verse says, "Go see the acts of the Lord, who has made desolations (*shammot*) on earth" (Ps. 46:9) – don't read "desolations" (*shammot*) but "names" (*shemot*).[3]

---

3. Berakhot 7b.

The insights that post-modernism has afforded us enable us to better grasp how the way we think and talk about things can, in addition to being descriptive, be prescriptive as well. The Jewish position is thrown into sharper relief when it is contrasted with the parallel story in the Quran. There, God names everything; man is special in that he is privy to this list of names. In the Torah, however, Adam assigns all living things their uniquely suited names, because it is he who determines their essential quality and endows them with meaning.

(2) The Torah

In Torah study, too, humanity partners with God in Creation. This is the very essence of the Oral Torah, which develops through active interpretation and passionate debate. Contemporary hermeneutics dispenses generally with the idea of interpretation as revealing a preexisting meaning in a text, and argues that meaning arises from the encounter between reader and text. Rabbi Abraham Isaac HaKohen Kook underscores the human component that differentiates the Oral Torah from the wholly divine Written Torah:

> With the Oral Torah, we have moved downward to Life.
> [...] We feel that the unique character of the national spirit,
> bound like a flame to a coal in the light of the true Torah,
> is what lends the Oral Torah its unique form.[4]

This is just as true of Jewish thought and Kabbala as it is of halakha. The introduction to the Zohar says that humanity's innovative perception into the Torah and the divine realm has the creative effect of partnering with God: "'And saying to Zion, You are My people' (Is. 51:16) – don't read 'you are My people (*ammi*)' but 'you are with Me (*immi*),' to be My partner."[5]

---

4. *Shemona Kevatzim, Kovetz* 2:57.
5. Zohar, I:5a.

(3) Prophecy

One might think that the actualized meaning of prophecy – the word of God placed in the mouth of human beings – would come entirely from God, but that is not necessarily the case. My father-in-law, Professor Uriel Simon, likes to compare prophecy to a telegram. While the message of a letter is typically elaborate, the message of a telegram is terse enough to allow multiple interpretive possibilities. This is reminiscent of the Sages' approach to dreams, which Scripture often treats as quasi-prophecies, and which the Rabbis outright define as "one-sixtieth of prophecy":[6]

> R. Elazar said: Whence that all dreams follow the mouth? As it says, "And it happened that just as he had interpreted for us, so it was" (Gen. 41:13).
> Rava said: That is only when he interprets it for him in line with the dream, as it says, "Each man according to his dream did he interpret" (Gen. 41:12).[7]

The interpretation of a dream that emerges from the mouth of the interpreter is what gives it meaning and effect on the world. Kabbalistically, the "mouth," a metonym for language, corresponds to the *sefira* of *Malkhut*, because it perceives the divine word or efflux and expresses it in a way that gives structure to reality. This is equally true of dreams and prophecies.[8]

Like dreams, then, prophecies remain inchoate without human interpretation. "An uninterpreted dream is like an unread letter."[9] And since prophecies are comparable to dreams, without human actualizers their divine message remains folded in on itself, unable to find expression in this world.

---

6. Berakhot 57b.
7. Berakhot 55b.
8. See Zohar, I:183a.
9. Berakhot 55b.

TRANSLATION FOR CONTEMPORARY REALITIES

As partners in the instantiation of prophecy, we have the opportunity – and the obligation – to explicate the words of the prophets while being attuned to the current reality and to our understanding of God's will. The way we go about this and the circumstances we take into account will directly impact the kind of future we create.

Regarding the topic of this volume, today one must consider the nature of non-Jewish faiths. When the biblical prophecies were written down, these religions had since time immemorial been idolatrous, polytheistic, cultic. Today, the major faiths of the world are organized religions that profess monotheistic belief and encourage individual spirituality and worship. Unbelievably, most of humanity belongs to one of the Abrahamic religions that trace their origins back to Judaism itself! One cannot help but see the hand of God guiding history, growing global religions from the small seed of Judaism, religions that share its genetic code in ascribing importance to the stories of the Bible and rendering honor to the Patriarchs, Matriarchs, and other prophetic figures.

The agreement between Israel and the United Arab Emirates exemplifies a paradigm shift in this relationship, as reflected in its name. Unlike previous agreements named after the places in which they were formalized – the Camp David Accords and the Oslo Accords – the Abraham Accords are so called in reference to the shared religious heritage that unites Jews and Muslims. Religious identity all too often drives a wedge between Jews and Muslims, but here it is a stake to which two peoples have bound themselves. In the framework of the volatile Jewish-Arab relations of the twenty-first century, the narrative of shared connection to a revered and saintly forbear generates a more stable consciousness of unity that crosses religious and national lines.

UNITY WITHIN DIVERSITY

Considering the state of world religions today and the realistic possibilities before us reopens the question of religious identity in the global service of God: will it be retained or shed? There is moral value to the position that views a plurality of identities as an ideal and not a compromise. In *LiNevukhei HaDor* (*For the Perplexed of the Generation*), Rabbi

Kook explains that religious plurality suits national variability. Every nation's religious needs stem from its singular character, history, and identity. The ethos grows into and with its religion.

Jewish eschatology does not demand a reduction of this multiplicity to a monad, but aspires to unity within difference. When Zephaniah prophesies that God will transform the nations with "a pure language," he does not mean that the world will be homogenized. Rather, the dross that confuses human communication will be removed so that everyone can understand and accept one another, and assist them in their divine service. "For then I will transform peoples with a pure language, for them all to call in the name of the Lord, to serve Him shoulder to shoulder" (Zeph. 3:9).

The Seven Noahide Laws: Prerequisites for Civilization or Religious Identity?

Yakov Nagen

he starting point for investigating the relationship between Judaism and world religions is the seven Noahide laws. These constitute the Torah's basic demands of humanity. According to the Talmud, every person must observe these mitzvot, and since they are divinely legislated, some argue that they are a universal religion for non-Jews. An examination of their source and character, however, does not sustain that conclusion.

Until Noah, the story of humanity was one of gradual degeneration, which posed an existential threat to the entire world. Man ruined his relationship with the flora, fauna, and others of his own kind: "for all flesh had corrupted its ways on the earth" (Gen. 6:12). In its state of corruption, the world no longer deserved to exist, so God washed the world clean with the Flood.

The seven mitzvot are intended to preserve life by preventing such a dire state of human affairs from arising again in the world that

God recreated. The Rabbis learned: The descendants of Noah were commanded seven mitzvot: courts of judgment, blasphemy, idol worship, forbidden sexual relations, murder, theft, and [eating] a limb from a live animal.[1]

Two of these mitzvot (idol worship and blasphemy) avert damage to the relationship between man and God; two (forbidden relations and murder) prohibit the perpetration of grievous harm within human society; two (theft and courts) protect personal property; and the last (eating from a live animal) outlaws cruelty against fellow creatures.

The inclusion of this last one on the list, which seems to pale in comparison with many of the others in terms of severity and incidence in the civilized world, exposes the organizing principle behind these mitzvot. The seven Noahide laws are a bulwark against the deleterious activities of human beings on this planet. This includes the effects on members of their own species as well as on those of others. Noah himself was tasked with saving the animal kingdom from the floodwaters, and in the Flood's aftermath God made a new covenant with man and animal alike [1].[2]

This account allows us to better understand why a *ger toshav*, the "resident alien" of halakha, must observe the seven Noahide laws in order to be granted that status. A *ger toshav* is a non-Jew who wants to live among the Jewish people and share their land. These mitzvot ensure that the prospective resident will abide by the basic regulations that govern a humane society in order to live among the Jewish people.

NOAHIDE LAW AS A FRAMEWORK FOR LIVING

Time and again, the Torah demonstrates that the violation of these world-preserving directives results in expulsion from human society. The first homicide led to the permanent exile of its perpetrator, Cain. When

---

1. Sanhedrin 56a.
2. One opinion in the talmudic discourse adds the prohibition against *kilayim*, certain admixtures that mingle species. According to the rationale presented here, mixing species unnaturally is also a human corruption of nature as God made it. As the Midrash says, "Even the earth was unfaithful (*zineta*): they would sow wheat and it would produce weed grass (*zonin*)" (Gen. Rabba 28).

the Jewish people are later given their detailed penal laws, the unintentional murderer is similarly required to flee (or face death at the hand of avenging relatives). The repercussions of murder shake the world and contaminate the earth: "for blood pollutes the land, and no expiation can be made for the blood that has been spilled in it except through the blood of him who spilled it" (Num. 35:33). Murder corrupts all reality, as it did at the time of the Flood.   According to rabbinic interpretation, theft is the cardinal sin that the Torah explicitly names as the cause for the Flood. It says that "for the earth is filled with violence (*ḥamas*) because of them" (Gen. 6:13), and the Talmud translates *ḥamas* as theft.[3] In this paradigmatic case, human society itself had to be erased. The Sages also find an allusion in the Torah to forbidden sexual relationships as another offense precipitating the Flood: "for all flesh had corrupted its ways on the earth" (Gen. 6:12). The corruption here refers to sexual perversion, such as incestuous relationships and adultery.[4] Later in the Torah, the penalty given for these illicit liaisons, which like murder render the Land impure, is the loss of the right to live on it. This applies equally to Jews and non-Jews: "For all these abominations did the men of the Land who were before you do, and the Land was defiled. So let the Land not spew you out for defiling it, as it spewed out the nation that was before you" (Lev. 18:27–28). The offense is so grave that it pervades reality.

The establishment of a judicial system is likewise necessary to prevent the world from descending into anarchy and chaos. In his commentary on the Mishna, Rabbi Yonah Gerondi describes judgment in a way that lines up with our characterization of the seven Noahide laws here, namely that they are the glue that holds the world together:

> "Rabban Shimon ben Gamaliel said: The world is sustained
> by three things: judgment, truth, and peace" (Avot 1:18).

---

3. Sanhedrin 108a. In his commentary on this passage, Nahmanides writes that theft is against the natural ethic imprinted in humanity, and, as such, does not require a heteronomous command: "The reason is that it is a rational commandment that does not require a prophet's warning" (commentary on Gen. 6:13). See further Rabbi Nissim Gaon's preface to the Talmud [7], and the selection from *Ḥovot HaLevavot* [8].

4. See Rashi ad loc.

> Rabbeinu Yonah explained that it doesn't mean that the
> world was created for these three things, because at the
> beginning of the chapter it says, "The world stands on three
> things" (Avot 1:2), and they are not the same ones men-
> tioned here. Rather, first it said that the world is created
> for three things: Torah, divine service, and acts of kind-
> ness. [...] Now it says that the world is sustained, meaning,
> after it was created it continues to exist, by virtue of these,
> because through the judges who adjudicate between a man
> and his fellow the world is sustained. If not for judgment,
> might would make right.[5]

While underscoring the necessity of adjudication to prevent human
civilization from running off the rails, Rabbeinu Yonah distinguishes
between the *teloi* of all existence and the necessary conditions for that
existence. The world needs the administration of justice to exist; the
world does not exist to enrobe judges or elevate them to a lofty bench.

The fact that one of the seven Noahide laws, the establishment
of a judicial system, is treated as a global preservative corroborates our
contention that the rest of them are also in place to avert disaster. God
did not have theft in mind, as it were, when He decided to bring the
world into existence from nothing. The forbidding of theft sustains God's
handiwork so that Creation can achieve its true ends. The context in
which the seven mitzvot were given, after the Flood and at the establishment of a new pact between God and humankind, indicates their true
purpose: to avert a repeat cataclysm. If they are breached again, the world
will be corrupted and once more be unworthy of continued existence.

This characterization of the seven mitzvot also draws our attention
to a lopsidedness in the list. It is mainly a list of don'ts, with no corresponding dos. It says nothing about developing one's relationship with
other human beings or deepening one's connection to God. Beyond
refraining from thieving and murdering, how should one interact with
one's fellow? There is no command to love others like yourself, as we find
in the Torah (Lev. 19:18). A non-Jew who has abandoned idol worship is

---

5. *Arbaa Turim, Ḥoshen Mishpat* 1.

nowhere enjoined to love God, another positive commandment in the Torah (Deut. 6:5). The omission of such commands is glaring when the rabbinic list is compared to a parallel list in the ancient, extracanonical book of Jubilees, composed approximately in the second century BCE [2]. That text includes directives to improve one's relationship with God by blessing Him, and to treat other human beings properly by doing what is right, loving them, and honoring one's parents. The absence of anything similar from the rabbinic list is the clincher: the mitzvot on the rabbinic list are not the building blocks of an ideal society, but the dam walls holding back the next Flood. They are not the substance of non-Jewish religiosity.[6]

THE RELIGIOUS LIMITATIONS OF THE SEVEN MITZVOT

I am convinced that the above account is the simplest understanding of the Noahide laws, but others believe that these seven mitzvot exhaust the religiosity of the non-Jew. Structurally speaking, the seven are likened to the full complement of 613 mitzvot accepted by the Jewish people at Mount Sinai. This position has been attributed to Maimonides, since he stresses that the bindingness of these mitzvot stems not from human reason or instinctive morality, but from the divine revelation at Sinai. The non-Jew accordingly has only two options: remain a non-Jew and keep seven mitzvot, or become a Jew and keep all of them.[7]

Many have adopted this position because halakha is predisposed to work with unambiguous and rigorous definitions. The seven Noahide laws present a clear and effective gauge and guide for relations between

---

6. Various attempts have been made to account for the seemingly anemic character of the list. They typically argue that the mitzvot are general rules or categories that subsume many more laws and details. This could explain why the Talmud mentions thirty mitzvot that the Noahides accepted [9]; on this see *Sefer HaḤinnukh* [13] and Rabbi Menahem Azarya of Fano's *Sefer Asara Maamarot* [11]. But even if we widen the scope of these mitzvot, they remain too narrow to provide an answer to the nature of divine service for non-Jews.

7. See *Mishneh Torah, Hilkhot Melakhim* 10:9. Maimonides's innovative position on this issue, which derives from his philosophy and has its own problems, is discussed later in this volume.

Jews and non-Jews. This only heightens the problem, though. The hala-khic classifications of the Torah are filtered through the lived realities of the Jewish people and the particular insights of its religious leaders. The Oral Torah lives and breathes with the Jewish people. When it comes to other nations of the world, such categories are strange and foreign, since they do not emerge from their national or ethnic experience. They should be defining these laws for themselves.

Another reason for the acceptance of this view is that after but a few chapters, our holiest text, the Torah, takes its leave of humankind and zooms in on one man and his progeny. It is only natural that this influences the Jewish people's view on the rest of the humanity.

Be that as it may, it is exceedingly difficult to accept that a non-Jew's religious aspirations are reduced to accepting the seven Noahide laws, and only then because they were revealed to Moses at Sinai. Beyond the fact that the textual source for Maimonides's position is elusive, he pins the entire religious fulfillment of humankind on a historical event that is not documented in any earlier Jewish text.

Owing to these difficulties and the preceding analysis, the reason-able conclusion to reach is that these seven mitzvot are not a religion for non-Jews. By reining in man's destructive tendencies, they preserve the world from obliteration. They join all human beings in a stewardship that protects the fabric connecting man with God, man, animal, and plant. By following the ground rules, we are worthy of walking God's good earth. But these mitzvot do not fill – nor were they ever intended to fill – the profound need to find and worship God throughout our lives. They are a prerequisite for living and should not be mistaken for a full-blown religion.

SOURCES[8]

[1] Genesis 9:1–11 – The postdiluvian covenant
God blessed Noah and his sons and He said to them, "Be fruitful and multiply and fill the earth. The dread and fear of you shall be upon all

---

8. These sources concentrate on the primary rabbinic sources, as the medieval and modern treatments of the issue are discussed at length in the continuation of this

the beasts of the earth and all the fowl of the sky, upon all that crawls on the ground and upon all the fish of the sea. Into your hand they are delivered. Every moving thing that is alive shall be food for you; like the green plants, I have given you all. But flesh with its lifeblood still in it you shall not eat. And just so, your lifeblood I will requite, from every beast I will requite it, and from humankind, from every man's brother, I will requite human life. He who sheds human blood, by man shall his blood be shed, for in the image of God did He make man. As for you, be fruitful and multiply, swarm through the earth, and multiply on it."

And God said to Noah and to his sons with him, saying, "As for Me, I am about to establish My covenant with you and with your off-spring after you, and with every living creature that is with you, the fowl, cattle, and every beast of the earth with you, all that have come out of the ark, every beast of the earth. And I will establish My covenant with you, that never again shall all flesh be cut off by the waters of the Flood, and never again shall there be a Flood to destroy the earth."

[2] *The Book of Jubilees*, Chapter 7 – An ancient list of the Noahide laws[9]

During the twenty-eighth Jubilee, Noah began to prescribe for his grandsons the ordinances and the commandments – every statute that he knew. He testified to his sons that they should do what is right, cover the shame of their bodies, bless the One who had created them, honor father and mother, love one another, and keep themselves from fornication, impurity, and from all injustice.

[3] Sanhedrin 56a–b – The rabbinic list of Noahide laws[10]

The Rabbis learned: The descendants of Noah were commanded seven mitzvot: courts of judgment, blasphemy, idol worship, forbidden sexual relations, murder, theft, and [eating] a limb from a live animal.[11]

---

volume.

9. James C. VanderKam, *Jubilees* 1–21 (Minneapolis: Fortress Press, 2018), 330.
10. The list also appears in the Tosefta (ed. Zuckermandel), Avoda Zara 8:4.
11. Sanhedrin 56a.

R. Ḥanania ben Gamla says: Also [consuming] blood from a live animal.

R. Ḥidka says: Also castration.

R. Shimon says: Also sorcery.

R. Yose says: A Noahide is forewarned about everything said in the passage about sorcery: "There shall not be found among you one who passes his son or his daughter through the fire, a diviner, a soothsayer, an enchanter, a sorcerer, a charmer, one who consults a necromancer and a sorcerer or directs inquiries to the dead" (Deut. 18:10–11) "…for it is on account of these abomination that the Lord your God drives them out from before You" (18:12) – and God would not have punished unless He had forewarned.

R. Elazar says: Also *kilayim* (forbidden admixtures).

Noahides are permitted to wear *kilayim* and sow *kilayim*; they are only prohibited from breeding and tree grafting.

[4] Sanhedrin 56b – The source of the Noahide laws
Whence do we know this?

R. Yoḥanan said: For the verse says, "And the Lord God commanded the man saying, 'From every tree of the garden you may surely eat'" (Gen. 2:16).

> "And…commanded" – these are the courts of judgment, and thus does it say, "For I have known him, that he may command his children etc." (Gen. 18:19).
>
> "The Lord" – this is blasphemy, and thus does it say, "Whoever blasphemes the name of the Lord shall surely be put to death" (Lev. 24:16).
>
> "God" – this is idol worship, and thus does it say, "You shall have no other gods" (Ex. 20:2).
>
> "The man" – this is murder, and thus does it say, "One who spills the blood of man etc." (Gen. 9:6).
>
> "Saying" – this is forbidden sexual relations, and thus does it say, "…saying, if a man sends away his wife and she goes away from him and becomes another man's" (Jer. 3:1).

"From every tree of the garden" – and not from what is stolen.

"You may surely eat" – but not a limb from a live animal.

When R. Yitzḥak came he recited it in the reverse:

"And...commanded" – this is idol worship.

"God" – this is courts of judgment.

"'God (*Elokim*)' – this is courts of judgment" fits well, for it is written, "the master of the house shall approach the judges (*Elokim*)" (Ex. 22:7). But "'And...commanded (*vaytzav*)' – this is idol worship," what proves this?

R. Ḥisda and R. Yitzḥak bar Avdimi:

One said: "They have strayed rapidly from the path that I commanded them (*tzivvitim*), they have made, etc." (Ex. 32:8); the other said: "Ephraim is oppressed, crushed in justice; because he willingly walked after filth (*tzav*)" (Hos. 5:11).

[5] *Sefer HaKuzari*, 3:73 – The talmudic source is an *asmakhta*

[...] An *asmakhta*...is only a mnemonic device for something known from tradition. In this way they explained the verse, "And the Lord God commanded the man saying, 'From every tree of the garden you may surely eat'" (Gen. 2:16), as alluding to the seven mitzvot the descendants of Noah were commanded. "And...commanded" – these are the courts of judgment. [...] How remote these matters are from the verse. They must have had a tradition about these seven mitzvot and placed it on this verse as a mnemonic device, to facilitate their recall of the mitzvot.

[6] Bava Kamma 38a – Non-observance of the Noahide laws

R. Mattena said: "He stood and shook the earth; He beheld [and made the nations tremble]" (Hab. 3:6). What did He behold? He saw the seven mitzvot the descendants of Noah were commanded but did not fulfill. He arose and exiled them from their land. [...]

R. Yosef said: "He stood and shook the earth; He beheld [and made the nations tremble (*vayyatter*)]" (Hab. 3:6). What did He behold?

He saw the seven mitzvot the descendants of Noah were commanded but did not fulfill. He arose and permitted (*vehittiran*) them to them.

Did they profit? If so, we have found a sinner who is rewarded!

Mar son of Rabbana says: It is to say that even if they fulfill them, they do not receive reward for them.

Is that so? But it is taught:

R. Meir says: Whence that even a non-Jew who studies Torah is like the High Priest? It teaches, "Which man shall do and live by them" (Lev. 18:5). It does not say priests, Levites, or Israelites, but "man." You have learned that even a non-Jew who studies Torah is like a High Priest.

They said: They don't receive reward like someone who is commanded and performs but like someone who is not commanded and performs. As R. Ḥanina says: Greater is the one who is commanded and performs than the one who is not commanded and performs.

[7] The Preface of Rabbi Nissim Gaon to the Talmud – :
Noahide laws as rationally binding
One can object as follows: If someone whose mind is sound is obligated in mitzvot, why did the Holy One single out the Jewish people to give them alone, and no other nation, the Torah, and to place its mitzvot upon them? Should they not all be equally obligated?

One can further object: How is it possible to punish them for what they were not obligated in and which was not given to them? They can claim, "Had we been commanded, we would have performed them! Had we been cautioned, we would have been careful and accepted it as they did!"

We can resolve these objections as follows: Everyone has been obligated, from the day that God created man on the earth and for all generations, in all the commandments that accord with human reason and intuition.[12]

---

12. This idea already appears in the Midrash: "'You shall fulfill My laws' (Lev. 18:4) – these are the things written in the Torah that had they not been written, logic would have dictated writing them. For example, theft, forbidden sexual relations, idol worship, blasphemy, and murder – had they not been written, logic would have dictated writing them" (*Sifra, Aḥarei Mot* 9:13).

[8] *Ḥovot HaLevavot*, 3:6 – The Noahide laws as rational mitzvot

[...] [T]hey are obligated in a universal service of the Creator, which consists of all the dictates of the intellect, which were practiced by Adam, Enoch, Noah and his sons, Job and his friends, until the time of Moses. Whoever adheres to all of them in the divine service will be treated by God more favorably than everyone else, and He will grant them an exceptional advantage in this world and great reward in the next. Abraham is an example, to whom God said, "Fear not, Abram: I am a shield for you; your reward will be very great" (Gen. 15:1). [...]

[...] Corresponding to the way that He dealt kindly with the Israelites when He took them out of Egypt and brought them to Canaan, He obligated them in an additional service beyond the first one, namely, the revelational mitzvot, after warning and cautioning them about the rational mitzvot.

[9] Ḥullin 92a-b – Thirty Noahide laws

[...] "And I took thirty pieces of silver and cast them into the treasury, in the House of the Lord" (Zech. 11:13) [...]

R. Yehuda says: These are the thirty righteous people among the nations of the world, in whose merit the nations of the world are sustained.

Ulla says: These are the thirty mitzvot that the descendants of Noah accepted upon themselves, but they fulfill only three: one is that they do not write a marriage contract for males; one is that they do not weigh the flesh of the dead in butcher shops; and one is that they honor the Torah.

[10] Jerusalem Talmud, Avoda Zara 2:1 – Thirty mitzvot that the Noahides will accept in the future

R. Huna said in the name of Rav: "So they weighed out my wages, thirty pieces of silver" (Zech. 11:12) – these are thirty mitzvot that the descendants of Noah will accept in the future. [...]

R. Ḥiyya bar Julianus in the name of R. Hoshaya: The descendants of Noah will accept all of the mitzvot in the future. On what basis? "For then I will transform peoples with a pure language" (Zeph. 3:9). But in the end, they will renege on it. On what basis? "Let us break their bands of their yoke and cast away their cords" (Ps. 2:3) – this is the mitzva of tefillin and the mitzva of tzitzit.

[11] Rabbi Menahem Azarya of Fano, *Sefer Asara Maamarot, Maamar Ḥikkur Din* 3:21 – An enumeration of the thirty Noahide mitzvot

[...] There are seven general mitzvot whose elaboration yields thirty, according to chapter *Gid HaNashe*. These are they:

(1) Idol worship and its subsummations: One who makes pass through the fire, a diviner, a soothsayer, an enchanter, a sorcerer, a charmer, and one who consults a necromancer and a sorcerer or directs inquiries to the dead. [This is] like the opinion of R. Yose, who said: "A Noahide is forewarned about everything stated in the passage about sorcery." This yields ten mitzvot.

(2) Prohibited sexual relationships and their subsummations: "Be fruitful" – one; "and multiply" – two, as positive commandments. There is a prohibition against homosexual relations, even if one has an exclusive relationship using a *ketuba*. Interspecies breeding, castration, and tree grafting. Thus [we have] seven; see below [about "be fruitful and multiply"].

(3) Murder: Striking a Jew on the cheek is subsumed under it. This yields two.

(4) Blasphemy: Honoring the Torah is subsumed under it, and so is learning the Torah that was given to them. After all, the Noahide who learns it is like the High Priest. This yields three.

(5) Theft: Not learning Torah, which is our inheritance, is subsumed under it. This yields two.

(6) Judicial system for the settlement of the world: That they may not rest [on Shabbat] is subsumed under it. This yields two.

(7) [Eating] a limb from a live animal: And subsumed under it are [consuming] blood from a live animal, an unslaughtered carcass, and flesh of the dead. This yields four, and the total number is thirty.

Even though "be fruitful and multiply" is a single mitzva for us in our count of 613, one should not find it difficult that it is split into two for this [purpose], because we do not learn from the Torah of Moses to the Torah of the Noahides. Alternatively, "be fruitful and multiply" is actually counted as one for both us and them, and it is the courts of judgment that are split in two, as a positive commandment and a negative one. As it says in the Talmud according to Rashi's commentary, administer judgment and do not pervert it.

The animal sacrifices for all the early generations were performed like one who is not commanded and performs [the mitzva anyway].

This is how I think one can maintain all the opinions of the Sages, and all those related in chapter *Arba Mitot* aside from the three that appear in chapter *Gid HaNashe*, and the passages accord with all of *Tanna'im* and *Amoraim*. Each stated their opinion but none was disagreeing.

[12] Nahmanides's Glosses on Maimonides's *Sefer HaMitzvot*, Shoresh 14 – The Noahide laws

I have a further doubt and question based on their statement, "The descendants of Noah were commanded seven mitzvot" (Sanhedrin 56a). They count all the forbidden sexual relationships as a single mitzva, all the civil and criminal laws as a single mitzva, and everything pertaining to foreign worship as a single mitzva. In these they are no different from Jews – they are obligated in whatever a court would execute a Jew for. It seems that Noahides were cautioned about their mitzvot in a general manner without specifics. For instance, they were told something like, "None of you shall come near any of his own flesh: mother, maternal sister, someone's wife." That is why they are all counted as a single mitzva. With regard to the Jewish people, negative commandments and prohibitions are multiplied; and since each one receives a separate command, many mitzvot are counted. [...] Regarding civil and criminal laws, they said in the *Mekhilta*: "'And judgment' (Ex. 15:25) – these are the laws of rape, the laws of fines, and the laws of injury." They have counted all of these as one, but there is no one category that can contain all of them at once; rather, they are all included under one name, which is "judgment."

[13] *Sefer HaḤinnukh* 416 – Noahide mitzvot as general categories

Not to desire anything that belongs to our Jewish brethren. [...]

Everyone else in the world is obligated in it, too, because it is a subcategory of the commandment against theft, which is one of the seven mitzvot everyone in the world is commanded. Do not err, my son, regarding the well-known accounting of the seven Noahide laws in the Talmud, because truthfully those seven are like general categories, which contain many details. For example, you find that the prohibition against sexual relationships are considered generally for them as one mitzva that contains many details: the prohibition against a sexual relationship with one's mother, with one's maternal sister, with someone else's wife, with one's stepmother, with another man, with an animal.

PART II:
WORLD RELIGIONS
IN MEDIEVAL JEWISH THOUGHT

Rabbi Nathaniel b. Rabbi Fayyumi: Prophetic Revelation Outside of Judaism

Yakov Nagen

Of the Jewish thinkers who have accorded great respect to non-Jewish religiosity, Rabbi Nathaniel b. Rabbi Fayyumi (ca. 1090–ca. 1165) is one of the most important. Rabbi Nathaniel occupied the position of *nagid* in medieval Yemen and was one of its leading rabbinic lights. Rabbi Nathaniel's main work is *Bustān al-Uqūl*, a Judeo-Arabic work of theology and ethics, which he himself says was composed to counter Rabbi Baḥya ibn Paquda's *Al-Hidāya ilā Farā'iḍ al-Qulūb*, better known as *Ḥovot HaLevavot*, with which he fundamentally disagrees. Rabbi Nathaniel's work was translated into Hebrew as *Gan HaSekhalim* (*Garden of the Intellects*) by Rabbi Joseph Kapach in the twentieth century. In the introduction to his translation, Rabbi Kapach writes that Rabbi Nathaniel's book was very influential for Rabbi Moses Maimonides. Indications of this influence can be found in the latter's *Iggeret Teḥiyyat HaMetim* and his *Moreh HaNevukhim*. More explicitly, Maimonides himself refers to Rabbi Nathaniel with the honorific "our master and teacher" in his

Iggeret Teiman, written about a messianic pretender in Yemen, which was addressed to none other than Rabbi Nathaniel's son Rabbi Jacob.

In the sixth chapter of *Gan HaSekhalim*, Rabbi Nathaniel presents a comprehensive approach to world religions. He not only argues that Judaism allows for them, but he even asserts that they originate in divine revelation. In the same way that the one true God of Judaism sent prophets to the nations before the giving of the Torah, so it is possible – necessary, even – that He sent others after it, "so that the world would not remain without religion" [1]. Without any equivocation, Rabbi Nathaniel declares that world religions are essential to the world, a realization of God's will, and of divine origin. Every nation, according to Rabbi Nathaniel, must follow the prophecy that it has received [5].

Rabbi Nathaniel's argument proceeds logically. The Torah attests that God sent prophets to the non-Jews, and He has the ability to do so again at any time. Since, for the good of humankind, God desires that all humanity has religion, it logically follows that God sends different nations prophecies attuned to their *Volksgeist*: "for He knows what is most beneficial for His creatures and what is fit for them" [5]. Rabbi Nathaniel concludes that other religions are not only legitimate but represent the realizations of prophetic revelations tailored by God to suit their particular addressees: "It is incumbent, then, upon every nation to conduct itself according to what has come into its possession, and to emulate its prophets, priests, and leaders." This generates an obligation for the Jewish people to tolerate and respect these religions: "Consequently, we ought to observe what is already in our possession, and on which we have been raised, and not contradict anyone of another faith."

Rabbi Nathaniel's position appears similar to Maimonides's famous opinion, discussed later in this volume, that religion must be grounded in revelation. The difference is that as we will see, Maimonides limits true legislative revelation to Moses at Sinai, so that even the non-Jew's obligation to observe the Noahide mitzvot is solely because they were revealed at that historic assembly. For Maimonides, this is the essence of non-Jewish religion. In contradistinction, Rabbi Nathaniel uses revelation to arrive at nearly the opposite conclusion. Since God does not want a world devoid of religion, there must have been real revelations to other nations, upon which their national religions are founded.

Chapter 6 of *Gan HaSekhalim* is filled with additional fascinating points. Naturally, the main religion Rabbi Nathaniel had to come to terms with was Islam, so a significant portion of the chapter is dedicated to proving from the Quran itself that the Torah was not superseded and remains binding on the Jewish people. Islam belongs to those additional revelations to other peoples that bind them to their own religious systems [3]. Many scholars of religion consider this to be the straightforward reading of the Quran,[1] and various Islamic scholars have tried to reinstate it.[2] Rabbi Nathaniel's construal of the Quranic position is a remarkable precursor to Rabbi Jacob Emden's interpretation of the New Testament, which he argues did not intend to supersede the Torah.

One source that supports Rabbi Nathaniel's reading is *Sura 5, Al-Mā'ida* ("The Table Spread"), which affirms the veracity of pre-Islamic revelations:

> Truly We sent down from on high the Torah, which provides guidance and a light by which the prophets who submitted [unto God] judged those who are Jews. The sages and rabbis also judged in accordance with God's Book, which they were bidden to preserve.... [...]
>
> And We have sent down from on high unto you the Book to reveal the truth, and to confirm the Books that came before it and protect them faithfully. So judge between them in accordance with what God has sent down from on high, and do not follow their caprices away from the truth that has been revealed before you. For each among you We have given a law and a way. And had God wished, He would have made you one nation, but

---

1. Joseph Lumbard, "The Quranic View of Sacred History and Other Religions," in *The Study Quran: A New Translation and Commentary*, ed. Seyyed Hossein Nasr (New York: HarperOne, 2015), 1765–1777.

2. One such scholar claims that given the fact that Islam views itself as an offshoot of the Jewish story, to undermine Judaism or the Torah is to harm Islam, and, conversely, to legitimate them strengthens it. See Tamer Mohamed Metwally, *Bias Against Judaism in Contemporary Writings: Recognition and Apology*, trans. Ben Abrahamson (Alsadiqin Press, 2020).

He wished to test you regarding all that He has given you.
So strive to be first in good deeds, because you return all
together to God, and then He will inform you of everything
on which you disagree. Judge between them in accordance
with what God has sent down from on high....[3]

Since Rabbi Nathaniel considers Islam to be of divine revelatory
origin, the Quran is a divinely inspired work. In a strange but interesting turn, the very principle that God deliberately revealed Himself to
different peoples, which is the basis for their religions, comes from the
Quran! Although he describes it as a rational deduction – if God wants
a world brimming with religion, he must have sent His messengers to
the ends of the earth – the Quran states it outright. Rabbi Nathaniel
ends by asserting that if one traces the rainbow of religions, one finds
that it originates and terminates in the all-encompassing unity of God:

> [A]ll of them are from one God and unto Him they
> all return. All pray to Him and turn to Him, and every
> righteous soul is transferred to Him, as it says, "and the
> spirit returns unto God who gave it" (Eccl. 12:7). (*Gan
> HaSekhalim*, ch. 6, p. 115) [5][4]

Here, too, one detects affinity to the Quran, as this language seems to
echo the quote above: "You return all together to God."

Despite this pluralistic scheme, Rabbi Nathaniel assigns the Jewish people a singular role:

> God, therefore, chose us, gave us His Torah and com-
> mandments, and imposed upon us immense obligations
> that He did not impose upon any nation before or after us,
> to increase our reward. (*Gan HaSekhalim*, ch. 6, p. 111) [2]

---

3. *Sura, Al-Māʾida* ("The Table Spread"), vv. 44 and 48. Translations of the Quran
are taken from the *The Study Quran*, with stylistic and occasionally substantive
modifications.
4. *Gan HaSekhalim*, ch. 6, p. 115.

Rabbi Nathaniel's unique view of the Quran as containing true prophecy is reflected on this issue as well, because it establishes the special status of the Jewish people. As he puts it:

> The Law of the Arabs[5] mentions how God favored us and raised us above all other mortals: "children of Israel, remember My favor that I have bestowed upon you, and that I have raised you above all other mortals." (Ibid.)

One final aspect of Rabbi Nathaniel's thought bears on the relationship between Noahide law, Mosaic law, and the foundational revelations of non-Jewish religions. Neither the Torah nor the Quran abrogate the seven Noahide mitzvot; they are additions and not revisions [4].[6] The pre-Abrahamic mitzvot are deeply-buried foundations on whose rock-solid foundation other religions are built. Like the layers of an archaeological tell, each new revelation builds upon earlier ones, and the new religious construction takes on the form appropriate to the epoch. In Rabbi Nathaniel's account, the advent of Abraham did not negate the value of Noahide religion, nor did the giving of the Torah at Sinai render obsolete the commandments given to Abraham.

The theology of Rabbi Nathaniel gives monotheistic world religions seats next to Judaism at the head table, because it considers them the product of revelation and the fulfillment of the divine will, to guide all of humanity to worship the one God.

---

5. The *Quran*.
6. This is intended to deflect the polemical charge that the Quran abrogates the Torah. The assertion that the seven Noahide laws were not negated yields a rule: new revelations do not dissolve prior ones.

SOURCES

[1] *Gan HaSekhalim,*[7] Chapter 6, p. 110 – Prophets have been sent to the nations to bring religion to the world

Know, my brother, that nothing prevents God from sending to His world whomever He wishes whenever He wishes. Emanation is unceasingly drawn forth from the world of holiness, and the noble matter [proceeds] from the rarefied world to the gross world constantly, to rescue souls from the hylic sea and the world of nature from obliteration and the flames of hell. Even before the giving of the Torah, He sent prophets to the nations, as our Sages said: "Seven prophets prophesied to the nations of the world before the giving of the Torah: Laban, Jethro, Balaam, Job, Eliphaz, Bildad, and Zophar."[8]

Similarly, after its giving, nothing prevented Him from sending them whomever He wished, so that the world would not remain without religion. The prophets declared that the other nations would serve Him from the rising of the Sun to its setting: "For from the rising of the sun to its setting My name is great among the nations." (Mal. 1:11), and it says, "To Me shall every knee bow, every tongue swear" (Is. 45:23). He chose and exalted us among the nations, not because of our prior righteousness but because of His regard for our forefathers Abraham, Isaac, and Jacob, as it says, "Not because you are the most numerous of all the peoples did the Lord desire you and choose you, for you are the fewest of all the peoples. But because the Lord loved you and He kept the oath that He swore to your forefathers, etc." (Deut. 7:7–8).

---

7. *Bustān al-Ūqūl* was translated into Hebrew by Rabbi Yosef Kapach as *Gan HaSekhalim,* 2nd ed., 3 vols. in 1 (Kiryat Ono: *Agudat Halikhot Am Yisrael,* 1983–1984). Though outdated and less accurate, the English translation by David Levine, *The Bustan al-Ukul by Nathanael Ibn Fayyumi* (New York: Columbia University Press, 1908), was helpful in rendering a few formulations.
8. Bava Batra 15b.

[2] *Gan HaSekhalim*, Chapter 6, p. 111 – The chosenness of the Jews according to the Quran

God, therefore, chose us, gave us His Torah and commandments, and imposed upon us immense obligations that He did not impose upon any nation before or after us, in order to increase our reward. [...]

The Law of the Arabs[9] mentions how God favored us and raised us above all other mortals: "children of Israel, remember My favor that I have bestowed upon you, and that I have raised you above all other mortals."[10] When it says, "I have raised you," it is an absolute statement, not a historical one. [...]

Our Creator is just in imposing responsibilities upon us that He has not imposed upon others, being more exacting with us than with them, and punishing us while not punishing them. It is out of His love for us, in order to ennoble us.... Our Law and their Law both attest to it, so that they cannot deny it whatsoever, especially since it was already promised to our forefathers Abraham, Isaac, and Jacob, as it says, "In order to establish you for Him today as a people" (Deut. 29:12).[11]

We shall explain this by means of an analogy. An expert physician visiting two patients observes that one of them is on the verge of death and the other has a chance of recovery. The physician says to the relatives, "Watch this one," referring to the patient who has a chance of recovery, "carefully: make sure he adheres to a specific diet, and eats and drinks a regulated amount rather than his fill." He then says to them, "Let the other patient do as he pleases. He may eat and drink what he wants without any restrictions. Withhold nothing from him. Because his case is incurable." Thus God ... has forbidden us much in the way of food, drink, garments, marriage, and other things, but did not in like manner restrict other nations ....

---

9. The Quran.

10. See *Sura 2, Al-Baqara* ("The Cow"), vv. 40, 47, and 122.

11. The relevant continuation of the verse reads: "And He will be for you a God, as He spoke to you and swore to your forefathers – to Abraham, to Isaac, and to Jacob."

[3] *Gan HaSekhalim*, Chapter 6, pp. 111–112 – The Quran
indicates that it does not abrogate the Torah

[The Quran also indicates] that the Torah was not abrogated, which they
imagine because of the power they exercise over us, their denigration
of us, and the absence of our succor. Concerning that it said, "And [I
come] affirming that which was before me from the Torah...."[12] And it
said, "How do they judge you, when they have the Torah, wherein are
the Lord's laws, and the Lord's laws will never be forgotten?"[13] And it
said, "You shall find no change in the word of God,"[14] by which it means
the Torah. How, then, can we change His law and His religion which
Moses brought down? Our pious forefathers did not see fit to change
God's law and religion received from Moses, His messenger, and so
we are following in their footsteps and adopting their upright practice
when we cling fast to the Torah and fulfill its mitzvot and precepts, for
its exchange or alteration is forbidden. And it said, "The Lord desires
to make [this] clear for you and to guide you in the laws of those who
went before you."[15] That is proof that he [the context makes it clear that
this refers to Mohammed] was a messenger to them but not to those
who preceded them. And it said, "You people of the Book, no act shall
be received from you until you observe the Torah."[16] And it said, "So if
you are in doubt about what has been said to you, ask those to whom
the Book was given before you."[17] This implies that He would not have
commanded him to ask concerning the Book had He abrogated it. [...]

Similarly, if disputants who are not of our faith insist that our
Torah has been abrogated, we give them a silencing reply: "What do
you say about what was received by the prophet Moses – is it foolishness or wisdom?" They must perforce answer not "foolishness" but
"wisdom." This answer suffices for them, for wisdom is never altered,
changed, abrogated, or replaced by something else. God would never
give a command through a prophet with signs, proofs, miracles, and

---

12. *Sura* 3, *Āl 'Imrān* ("The House of 'Imrān"), v. 50.
13. See *Sura* 5, *Al-Mā'ida* ("The Table Spread"), v. 43.
14. *Sura* 35, *Fāṭir* ("The Originator"), v. 43.
15. See *Sura* 4, *Al-Nisā'* ("Women"), v. 26.
16. *Sura* 5, *Al-Mā'ida* ("The Table Spread"), v. 68.
17. *Sura* 10, *Yūnus* ("Jonah"), v. 94.

supernatural manifestations in the heavens and on the earth, and then change His mind to abrogate and annul it. But it is possible for Him to give additional commands to whomever He wishes, and to send whom He wishes to whomever He wishes, since all the worlds are His possession and creation. Proof that He sent a prophet to every people in their own language is in the Quran: "And We have sent no messenger except in the language of his people."[18] Consequently, had he been sent to us, it would have been in our language. And again, had he been for us, He would not have said to him, "You are among those sent to warn a people whose ancestors were not warned."[19] He intends the people who worshipped gods and idols. As for us, our ancestors had warnings in every generation and were never without prophets. His prophecy was to a people whose ancestors had not been warned and who had no Law through which to be led aright; therefore, he directed them to his Law since they were in need of it. Others had something to lead them aright. Accordingly, it is not proper for anyone to oppose the other nations, for their law and punishment are in the hands of the praised and exalted One. Rather, it is our duty to fear and trust in Him, as He commanded us in the Torah given through our prophets, which mentions covenants made regarding them and us, as we have said above.

[4] *Gan HaSekhalim,* Chapter 6, p. 112 – The Torah did not abrogate but added to the laws of Noah and Abraham

And if they say, "Our Book abrogates your Book, just as your Book abrogated the Book of Abraham," we reply: "That is not true. On the contrary, we uphold the teaching of our forefather Abraham ...." [...] When God sent Moses with the Torah of the children of Israel ... He added to the commandment of Abraham according to the need of the times. But He did not annul the commandment of Abraham. [...] This is no abrogation. Likewise, He obligated the descendants of Noah in only seven laws. This was because they were few in number and because that era could not bear more. When Abraham appeared, God enjoined upon him the observance of additional commandments.

---

18. *Sura 14, Ibrāhīm* ("Abraham"), v. 4.
19. *Sura 36, Yā Sīn* ("Yā Sīn"), vv. 3, 6.

[5] *Gan HaSekhalim*, Chapter 6, pp. 113–115 – Every nation must serve God via its land

Know that God ordered that every people should worship Him according to their law. He permitted to each people things that he prohibited to others, and He prohibited to them things that He permitted to others – for He knows what is most beneficial for His creatures and what is fit for them. This is akin to how a skilled physician knows his patients... and accordingly withholds from or permits to whomever he wishes eating and mixing [of foods]. They dare not contradict him in anything, because they yielded themselves to him in good faith, sincerity, and justice. [...] Consequently, we ought to observe what is already in our possession and upon which we have been raised, and not contradict anyone of another faith, because then the verse would be fulfilled through us: "They made me a keeper of the vineyards; my own vineyard I have not kept" (Song. 1:6).

There is a fine analogy for God's command to His creations and how He wishes it to be carried out. A king ordered his subjects to build a palace. Some of them were architects, some were carpenters, some decorators, some smiths. Of these, some zealously carried out the king's orders, while others were lax, and still others deserted the king's service. The king provided for all of them. News of their service reached the king, but he waited until he sent for them and called them to account for how they had carried out his orders. For what they had done, he recompensed double those practitioners of each craft who worked well. [And] for what they had done, he recompensed in kind those practitioners of each craft who worked poorly. At that point, repentance was of no avail to the penitent, since he had not set out to do good.

Similarly, the Creator has authorized the destruction of the world and the construction of the afterlife. He has sent prophets in every age and period that they might urge the creations about divine service and good deeds, and to guide them on the path of the upright. Both salvation and obliteration occur on account of matters that are clear. It is incumbent, then, upon every nation to conduct itself according to what has come into its possession, and to emulate its prophets, priests, and leaders. Not one [people] remains without a law, for all of them are from one God and unto Him they all return. All pray to Him and turn to Him, and every righteous soul is transferred to Him, as it says, "And the spirit returns unto God who gave it" (Eccl. 12:7).

[6] *Gan HaSekhalim*, Chapter 2, pp. 43–44 – The secret of the Shahāda (Islamic Profession of Faith)

[T]he seven planets and the twelve constellations are the foundation of the potencies, and every prophet and giver of Law alludes to them. [...] So they established for us a prayer by which we approach the King of kings, articulate our needs before Him, ask of Him that which we desire, confess our sins, and petition Him to vindicate us and guide us aright. They formulated it in eighteen blessings, which, together with the first one, the principal one, add up to nineteen – corresponding to the seven and the twelve.

[...]

Even that of the Arabs came to them only according to the combination of [these numbers]. He bound them to mention four words, which incorporate the nature of the seven and the twelve within the Arabic orthography. Only those versed in this subject grasp it, while the uninitiated are not aware of it nor its meanings. He told them that whoever says, "There is no God but Allah," and appends his name to it is like a prophet. They believe that they already have attained this by uttering these words and that they will be admitted into Paradise. Had he intended the formula to have that meaning, not a single person of intelligence would have heeded him. Instead, it means that after a person acknowledges God, he should do that which is proper, that which God has commanded every people through its prophet. If a person could go about stealing, killing, committing adultery – doing whatever displeases God – and be admitted into Paradise by uttering these words, no rational person would accept this and consider it sane. Rather, the words possess significance within their characters and orthography, which allude to the science of the seven and the twelve, which underlie all creations and are the foundations of all existents.

When a person arrives at this realization and understands this, and so acknowledges God's unity and transcendence, he becomes worthy of admission to Paradise, to attain eternal bliss. What is special about these words is the number of letters: לא אלה אלא אללה is twelve, and the number of syllables is seven, yielding nineteen.[20] לֹא is one syllable, אלה is two syllables, אלֹא is two syllables, and אללה is two syllables – adding up to seven.

---

20. The Judeo-Arabic uses Hebrew characters. The number of characters in Arabic is the same: لا اله الا الله. The transliteration – *Lā ilāha illā (A)llāh* – produces letters because some of the Semitic vowels have consonantal values and others do not.

Rabbi Judah HaLevi and the *Kuzari*: The Importance of World Religions

*Assaf Malach**

Rabbi Judah HaLevi's (1075–1141) magnum opus is typically referred to by the Hebrew title *Sefer HaKuzari*, but this name was the invention of its translator, Judah Ibn Tibbon. The original Judeo-Arabic title is *Kitāb al-Radd wa-'l-Dalīl fī 'l-Dīn al-Dhalīl* (*The Book of Refutation and Proof on Behalf of the Despised Religion*), which attests to the polemical atmosphere in which it was composed. The final decades of the eleventh century were an important stage in the history of the Reconquista, the multi-century Christian venture to win back territory on the Iberian Peninsula that had been conquered by Muslims of North

* Dr. Assaf Malach is the Steward Harris fellow of the Beit Midrash for Judaism and Humanity, head of the Jewish Statesmanship Center, Professor of Political Philosophy at Shalem College and headed the Citizenship Studies Committee at Israel Education Ministry from 2015-2022. His book *From the Bible to the Jewish State* was published in 2019.

African origin. The Jewish population was, as it often is, caught in the middle; they were persecuted by the fanatical Almoravids. HaLevi witnessed the suffering of his coreligionists firsthand, and he dedicated his book to lifting the spirits of a demoralized Jewry by arguing for their unique role in human history.

The book is organized as a dialogue between the King of the Khazars, who, in the wake of a dream, is searching for the one true religion, and a Jewish scholar who articulates the Torah's philosophy. The oppressive polemical atmosphere in which HaLevi was writing explains his focus on advocating the demonstrable superiority of the Torah over other religious creeds and spiritual philosophies, and of the Jewish people over the rest of humanity. Although the dialogical form superficially obscures it, the book contains a coherent theory of the importance of non-Jewish belief and religion, both in the unredeemed present and in the redeemed future, when all humanity will worship God according to Torah law. The scattered discussions coalesce into a multifaceted perspective on the major religions influenced by Judaism.[1]

HaLevi conceptualizes the religiosity and religions of non-Jews in two distinct ways over the course of the book, which ultimately cohere into a single theory. The first approach is that world religions are desirable because they engage the rationality of human beings, although Judaism occupies a unique pedestal because it relates to the prophetic faculty that accesses the divine. The second approach conceives of Judaism as spreading the seeds of belief and morality across the world by way of its daughter religions: Christianity and Islam. As conduits for the teachings

---

1. Like other major works of philosophy, the *Kuzari* includes statements on this issue that seem at odds with one another. Many have tried to resolve these conundrums by speculatively reconstructing its textual development. They argue that the kernel of the work, part 3, originated as a dedicated polemic against the Karaites, and as HaLevi worked out his thought further in later parts, he related to those earlier positions; see Yochanan Silman, *Philosopher and Prophet: Judah HaLevi, the Kuzari, and the Evolution of His Thought*, trans. Lenn J. Schramm (Albany: SUNY Press, 1995). Others view the *Kuzari* as an organic whole and the contradictory positions as deliberate stages of a philosophical argument; see Micah Goodman, *The King's Dream* [in Hebrew] (Or Yehudah: Dvir, 2012), 137–211. This chapter makes no attempt to decide this important issue, but it does note the discordant voices and presents a possible way to harmonize them.

of Judaism, it would seem that HaLevi thereby envelops all humanity within the higher religiosity associated with the Jewish people.

Let us begin by analyzing HaLevi's first argument. It differentiates Jewish Scripture, founded on revelation, prophecy, and manifest providence, from other belief systems. HaLevi describes the Jews as having a "godly, angelic" stature, on whom the "divine matter" (*ha'inyan haEloki*) and prophecy rest.[2] Other religions and nations are not privy to this experience of the divine. Time after time, HaLevi stresses that proper, pure intention to grow close to God is insufficient to achieve that goal; the revelation of the divine matter is the only way to it. This point is conveyed at the very beginning of the *Kuzari* through the king's dream, in which he is informed, "Your intent is worthy in God's eyes, but your deeds are not." And this is not for a lack of trying: "He was exceedingly careful in the commandments of the Khazar religion, to the point that he himself would serve in their Temple and offer sacrifices with sincerity."[3] HaLevi reinforces this point when he describes the essence of the mitzvot: they are not a distillation of human wisdom or of the optimal means to order society or perfect morality, but operate on the divine plane that corresponds to the special spiritual stature of the Jewish people. The mitzvot cannot be deduced through human reason, and one who attempts to arrive at them in this way is like a patient who walks into a pharmacy, goes behind the counter, and makes his own medication: "A person cannot reach the divine matter except through the divine command, by which I mean, those deeds that God commands upon them."[4] The only people to possess the divine religion, accordingly, must be the Jewish people. They alone received the "essence" (*segulla*) from Adam, who passed it down, son after son, to Jacob, from whom an entire people emerged as a vessel for it.[5] According to this genetic approach, no faith or people outside of the Jews possesses the divine religion [1].[6]

---

2. *Sefer HaKuzari*, 1:42.

3. *Sefer HaKuzari*, 1:1.

4. *Sefer HaKuzari*, 1:98. See the continuation in 1:99 and also 1:35–41, and variations thereof, passim.

5. *Sefer HaKuzari*, 1:95.

6. Silman and Goodman point out that there are other places in the *Kuzari* where the distinction between Jews and the rest of humanity is grounded in belief and not in

This essentialist position is central to the *Kuzari*, and it raises the question of what exactly is the point of other religions. If they are not quite the "divine religion" and in the same league as Judaism, are they beneficial for non-Jews or are they a terrible mistake?

HaLevi's anthropology prizes the actualization of the human intellect, so the founding of rational-intellectual religions that shape a harmonious society and polity holds great importance for him. While this religious function is to be categorically distinguished from the prophetic-religious dimension of Judaism, human beings still have an obligation to realize their humanity. On the most basic level, HaLevi is sure that this behavior receives a divine reward: "In our opinion, every human being, whatever their nationality, receives reward for their good deeds."[7] There is another level beyond this, where people of faith have an advantage over the questing philosopher: "the religious seek out God for benefits that go beyond knowing Him" [5]. In a number of places, he further commends "religion founded on logic and directed toward governance."[8] Though he reminds his readers that this religion is inferior to one founded on revelation and prophecy, it is still vital to humanity.

In a long passage where the Sage contrasts the innovativeness of the Torah in its non-rational, divine mitzvot (Shabbat, circumcision, animal sacrifices) with the rational, societal laws that also exist among the nations of the world, it is clear that Jews are human beings first and an "angelic" caste second. They may not forsake their humanity, and the prophets reproach them for it: "If only you would observe the commandments that even the lowliest society accepts, namely acting justly, dealing kindly with others, and thanking God for His kindness." The divine

---

natural ability. One example for Silman: "To this the pious profess those fundamental religious principles that complete the Jewish belief.... Whoever acknowledges all of these with every fiber of their being is a true Jew who can look forward to being attached to the divine matter, which cleaves only to the Jewish people, of all the nations" (*Sefer HaKuzari*, 3:17). According to his textual theory, such statements belong to the first recension of the *Kuzari* and HaLevi's earlier thought; see Silman, *Philosopher and Prophet*. Goodman points to 5:20 to show that this line of thinking is not limited to part 3, as Silman claims. Either way, the exclusiveness of the mitzvot to the Jewish people is incontestably a major theme of the *Kuzari*.

7. *Sefer HaKuzari*, 1:111.
8. *Sefer HaKuzari*, 1:13 and 1:81.

Torah can only be properly fulfilled after the societal, rational law has been first fulfilled, and the latter already encompasses acts of justice and gratitude for divine kindness. (*Sefer HaKuzari*, 2:48) [2]

The conclusion to be drawn from all these passages is that other religions should be appreciated for their critical work in forming human beings into moral agents.

In multiple places, HaLevi asserts: "One should not criticize the philosophers, because they did not receive wisdom or religion as their inheritance."[9] Morever, in the fifth and final part of the *Kuzari*, he is unstinting in his praise for the rational laws they legislate to order society:

> To the contrary, one should praise them for their attain-
> ments through their speculative abstractions, and for their
> pursuit of the good, for which they founded rational laws,
> spurning this-worldly pleasures. They certainly have an
> advantage since they are not obligated to accept our opin-
> ions…. (*Sefer HaKuzari*, 5:14) [3]

Into this scheme that bifurcates religion into divine legislation and rational invention, HaLevi must determine where to place the great monotheistic religions of Christianity and Islam. The King ventures that the two are quite close to Judaism because they deem the Land of Israel spiritually superior, they believe in the Torah's narratives, and they profess monotheism. The Sage counters this by utterly rejecting any comparison. He asserts: "By changing the site to which prayers are directed, by seeking the divine matter where it is not to be found, and, even worse, by abrogating most of the non-rational mitzvot, they are at many a remove from us" [5]. The fact that they adopted monotheism does not mean that much, as their belief is "like the belief of Abimelekh's men, the citizens of Nineveh, and the philosophers." The moment they had the gall to take their rational, social religion for a divine one, they became blinded by their error. HaLevi compares them to someone who tries to bring people to the Sun and instead brings them to one of the poles, pretending that it is the Sun. In another analogy, he refers to

---

9. *Sefer HaKuzari*, 1:63. See also 4:13, 16 and 5:14.

them as "dead nations that tried to imitate the living one" and "at best achieved a superficial likeness" [4]. Islam's practice of ritual circumcision and Christianity's observance of a day of rest are pale imitations of the original mitzvot, "like idolatrous icons imitating living, breathing human beings."[10] He summarizes his attitude toward these two religions by saying, "As close as they are, they are equally far" [5]. Since they are not the product of genuine revelation, they cannot shepherd their faithful to the plane of divine religion.

In this account of religions, note that the Jewish people embody the essence of all creation: "everything has come into being, therefore, for this essence, so that the divine matter can cleave to it."[11] The Jews are more than a herald to the nations or a vanguard revealing the special essence to all humanity. They are the means, but also the end: "This essence exists for the purest essence of all, namely, the prophets and the pious."[12] This illuminates an infamous line in the *Kuzari* that smacks of xenophobia: "Israel among the nations is like the heart among the organs – the most vulnerable and the most robust."[13] HaLevi does not intend by this simile that the Jews, like the heart, serve the rest of humanity, the other limbs of the body. He means that Jews exist at the highest spiritual level that is marked by hypersensitivity, in the same way that the heart responds readily to stress.

Now let us turn to the second approach to non-Jewish religion. The Sage describes the Jewish people as spreading knowledge of God among the nations of the world, about which God is said to declare, "Israel, by whom I will be glorified" (Is. 49:3). The King finds this statement an exaggeration, so the Sage explains his meaning. Until the Israelites became a nation, the world was a stew of beliefs. Some denied the existence of God, others observed the dictates of reason, still others worshipped deities of all shapes and sizes. None, however, believed in a divine "judge and provident overseer...who dispenses reward for good and punishment for evil" [6]. It was the Jews who introduced this

---

10. *Sefer HaKuzari*, 3:9.
11. *Sefer HaKuzari*, 2:44.
12. Ibid.
13. *Sefer HaKuzari*, 2:36.

belief to the world, and spread it to the four corners of the earth through Christianity and Islam, which supplanted polytheism with monotheism:

> This congregation became a spiritual guide for everyone, and every subsequent religion cannot depart from these roots. Today, the entire citizenry of the civilized world professes that God is eternal and the universe created.... (*Sefer HaKuzari,* 2:54) [6]

The King finally concedes to his interlocutor, "There is definitely what to be glorified by, and your explanation is wonderful." He then adds his own scriptural proof texts for this idea.

This account of the Jewish mission to spread monotheism dovetails with HaLevi's idea in part 4 that God has a "hidden design" in keeping the Jews in exile [7]. He draws an extended analogy to a seed that must rot in the soil to prepare the earth for the production of a new sprout. Judaism is this seed, to which "every subsequent religion truly assimilates...even if it appears to be quite dissimilar." In this passage, HaLevi criticizes his Christian and Muslim contemporaries: "Even the most faithful of these religions veer into heresy in their belief in divine providence, which they spread among the masses."[14] Still, they are the leading edge of progress, "a preparation for the expected Messiah, who is the fruit, and at the end of days, when they acknowledge him, they will become his fruit, and the tree will become one."

HaLevi ascribes vast import to the major non-Jewish religions. All of them participate in the ultimate goal of Creation, the revelation of God's name in this world by humankind, by which God is glorified. Christianity and Islam in particular move humanity closer to the true

---

14. Cf. *Sefer HaKuzari,* 3:11, where HaLevi classifies belief in divine providence as part of the rational mitzvot but also as an innovation of the Torah: "The belief emerges from the Torah that God intimately knows a person's innermost thoughts and certainly their actions and words, and that he repays their good and wicked deeds in kind." The idea of divine providence lies somewhere between the rational and the revealed, between contemporary religious belief and future belief. This characterization requires further examination, as many schools of medieval Christianity and Islam did believe in divine providence.

belief, softening the world for the messianic era, when they will rejoin Judaism and the tree will be made whole. Notably, HaLevi does not go into detail about the relationship between the Jews and the nations in the eschaton, so one cannot evaluate the strength of the graft for any potential differences between stock and scion.

This conceptualization of non-Jewish religion has the power to explain seeming inconsistencies in HaLevi's thought. In an unusual passage, HaLevi mentions a story attributed to Plato, in which a non-Jewish prophet tells a philosopher that his intellectual pursuit of God will not result in revelation. The only way to God is through the Jewish people and their prophets [8]. But how can a non-Jew be privy to prophecy, when HaLevi says that only Jews attain to the prophetic degree? Apparently, the answer is embedded in the prophet's own words. HaLevi does not believe in real prophecy among the non-Jews to develop their own religions, but he does allow for it when it points non-Jews to the one nation that does possess legitimate prophecy: the Jews.[15]

With this insight, we can resolve another well-known problem with the *Kuzari's* frame story. If non-Jews do not receive real prophecy, not even converts,[16] how can the King merit "the repetition of the same dream multiple times"?[17] After all, for HaLevi, dreams are a kind of revelation.[18] The answer is, again, that he is being directed to the Jews. The angel may not guide him to Judaism immediately, but in the end, the King ends up face to face with the learned Sage. At the beginning of part II, the King has another dream in which he is beckoned to the mountains of Warsān, where he encounters a group of Jews that gather

---

15. This is structurally similar to another problem generated by HaLevi's absolutism and its solution. He makes the exclusivist claim that prophecy can only occur in the Land of Israel. What of the explicit contradictory evidence from Scripture itself? All of those prophecies, he explains, remain tethered to the Land, because they are in some way about the Land itself; see *Sefer HaKuzari*, 2:14.

16. A convert can achieve the sublime degree of the pious or wise, which is only "one degree lower than the prophetic degree" (3:11), but cannot raise that additional degree to true prophecy (1:115).

17. *Sefer HaKuzari*, 1:1.

18. On the importance of dreams in HaLevi's thought, see *Sefer HaKuzari*, 3:53 on "veridical dreams" being a type of Holy Spirit, and 3:11 on "faithful dreams" as a source of Bible interpretation.

there on Shabbat. They facilitate his own conversion and that of his entire kingdom. The connection between this dream and being steered to Judaism is obvious.

When HaLevi writes about the exclusive Jewish hold on prophecy, he must deal with Balaam, the most famous non-Jewish prophet. HaLevi has this to say: "The Torah likewise reports the prayer of a non-Jew, prophesying by God's leave, who seeks for himself the death of the righteous and sharing the fate of the Jewish people."[19] In this paraphrase of the biblical verses, HaLevi reconceptualizes Balaam's entire prophecy as being about the spiritual superiority of the Jewish people. The center of gravity for divine prophecy rests among the Jewish people, so to them must all prophecy return.

This understanding of prophecy aligns with HaLevi's second treatment of Judaism and the other religions. The Jewish people disseminate knowledge of God, and other religions are their instruments in this sacred mission. But as they go forth into the world, they are constantly bidden to look back to the Jews, who possess the true beliefs and teachings directly from the mouth of God and know best how to serve and grow close to Him.

HaLevi's approach to non-Jewish religions and religiosity can be summed up as follows. There is religion that accords with human reason and optimally manages the tangled webs of human beings. All people, regardless of the epoch in which they are thrust into this world or the continent they happen to call home, ought to adhere to this religion, which includes social justice and gratitude to God. And when they do so, they should be praised for it. This religiosity fully realizes the humanity of the human being, but there is another, transcendent level of religiosity that exists above human reason and its practical applications. This religion is bound up with God, and it is communicated to human beings through prophecy. As of now, only the Jewish people possess this religion, having merited prophetic revelation of the precise methods to worship God – the mitzvot. Other religions, Christianity and Islam most prominently, assert that their own religions are divinely revealed, so they replace the Land of Israel or Shabbat with their own sacred sites and

---

19. *Sefer HaKuzari*, 1:115.

times. But they are mistaken. Despite this religious particularism, the *Kuzari* exhibits a thematic streak of universalism that is forward-looking. In the future, God will be glorified by the symphony of nations exalting him. This grand production will be run through the Jewish people, who will have spread their positive influence throughout the world to reform all religions in order to worship God properly. Christianity and Islam are primary channels for imparting this monotheistic message of Judaism, although their life-giving waters are contaminated with the detritus of error. This is reminiscent of the position taken by Rabbi Moses Maimonides, who – perhaps having been influenced by HaLevi himself – described a long-term plan similar to HaLevi's "hidden design." Granted that Christianity and Islam are gravely wrong, "man does not have the ability to fathom the thoughts of the Creator," and His hidden hand has placed them in the right place at the right time "to pave the way for the King Messiah."[20]

This universalist orientation receives support from rare revelations to the non-Jews, which are either prophetic or, as in the case of dreams, quasi-prophetic. These instances of revelation nudge non-Jews to seek out the Jewish people, who in their lofty spiritual stature know the true ways to access God. This is the case for Balaam, Plato's prophet, and the dreams of the Khazar King. In all these instances, the recipient's attention is drawn to Judaism and the Torah revealed prophetically to Moses, which teach them about their glorious future living a life as close to God as possible, together with the Jewish people.

SOURCES

[1] *Sefer HaKuzari*, 1:102–103 – **The true religion pertains to Jews who have attained the divine matter**

The Khazar said: Why wasn't the Torah given as instruction to all of humanity? Would that not have been more appropriate for the divine wisdom?

The Sage said: Would it not have been more appropriate for all animals to speak? If you are saying this, you must have forgotten what

---

20. *Mishneh Torah, Hilkhot Melakhim* 11:4.

I have already told you about the [spiritual] inheritance of Adam's descendants. Earlier I said that the divine matter (*inyan haEloki*) rests on one member of every family: the kernel among his brothers and the essence (*segulla*) of his father. He was the one who received that light; all the others were like husks and did not receive that light. This was until the sons of Jacob, who were all kernel and essence. They differed from all other human beings by divine properties that made them, as it were, into members of a separate, angelic species. All of them sought and many attained the level of prophecy, and those who did not still got very close through pious acts, self-sanctification, self-purification, and drawing close to the prophets.

[2] *Sefer HaKuzari*, 2:46–48 – Intellectual-social religion is a *sine qua non* for human society and for divine religion

The Sage said: It pains me to see you have forgotten the foundational principles that I told you earlier and that you acknowledged. Have we not agreed that one cannot draw close to God except by deeds that He has commanded? Do you think that closeness to God is attained through feelings of submission, humility, and so on?

The Khazar said: Yes, and rightly so! I read as much in your books, as it says: "What does the Lord your God ask of you but to fear the Lord your God, etc." (Deut. 10:12); "And what the Lord demands of you, only doing justice, loving kindness, and walking humbly with your God" (Mic. 6:7), and so forth.

The Sage said: These and similar statements are the rational laws that naturally and chronologically precede the divine Torah, and without which no human society can function. Even a band of thieves must have some code of justice for their bond to last. It was only when the Israelites rebelled and relaxed their observance of the rational mitzvot and the kind of behavior vital to the continued existence of society (in the same way an individual cannot subsist unless they meet their vital needs of food and drink, movement and rest, sleep and wakefulness), while maintaining the sacrificial cult and other divine, non-rational mitzvot, that God informed them that He would be satisfied with less: "If only you would observe the commandments that even the lowliest society accepts, namely, acting justly, dealing kindly with others, and thanking God for His kindness." The divine Torah can only be properly fulfilled after the societal, rational law has been first fulfilled, and the latter already encompasses acts of justice and gratitude for divine kindness. Why would anyone who does not perform these bring sacrifices and observe the mitzvot of Shabbat, circumcision, and the like, which the intellect neither requires nor rejects? These are the particularistic mitzvot of Judaism that are additions to the rational mitzvot, by which one reaches the divine matter (*ha'inyan haEloki*), without knowing their reason. [...] Regarding this and the like was it said to them, "What the Lord demands of you," "Add your burnt offerings to your sacrifices" (Jer. 7:21), and similar statements. But how can a Jew possibly attain perfection by being satisfied with "doing justice, loving kindness" and forsaking the mitzvot of circumcision, Shabbat, Passover, and all the rest?

[3] *Sefer HaKuzari*, 5:14 – One should not criticize philosophers but praise them for their independent attainments

The philosophers can justify themselves because they must rely on logical reasoning, given that they possess no prophecy nor divine light. That is why they perfected the arts of logic and dedicated themselves completely to them. [...]

They have other such views, which are less proven than those in *Sefer Yetzira*, but doubt plagues all of them and there is no consensus among philosophers. One cannot fault them for that, though. To the contrary, one should praise them for their attainments through their speculative abstractions, and for their pursuit of the good, for which they founded rational laws, spurning this-worldly pleasures. They certainly have an advantage since they are not obligated to accept our opinions, whereas we are obligated to believe in whatever our own eyes have seen and in the tradition, which is tantamount to eyewitness testimony.

[4] *Sefer HaKuzari*, 2:32 – The similarity between the major religions and the Jewish people is like a mannequin and a human being

The Sage said:

The dead nations that tried to imitate the living one at best achieved a superficial likeness. Their descendants also established temples to God, but no sign from God was forthcoming in them. They retreated from the world and practiced asceticism for prophecy to descend upon them, but it did not. Neither did their corruption, through sin and transgression, bring hellfire or sudden contagion upon them, so that they might take it to heart as divine punishment for their rebellion. And when their heart – the site to which they directed their prayers – was destroyed, nothing about them changed except their being many or few, strong or weak, divided or united – all according to nature and happenstance. But when our heart, our Temple, was destroyed, we became sick. And when our heart is restored to its strength, we will be healed, whether we will be strong or few, whatever our state will be at that time, for our Creator, the Living God, is our King, and He gives us strength even in our current state of dispersion and exile.

[5] *Sefer HaKuzari*, 4:10–13 – The major monotheistic religions and the difference between religion and philosophy

The Khazar said: Even the religions that arose after you that acknowledge the truth attribute distinction to that place. They say it is the place of prophetic ascent, the gate of heaven, and the place of ultimate judgment to which the souls of the dead will be gathered on the day of judgment. They further admit that prophecy only ever occurred among the Jewish people. They also revere the Patriarchs and acknowledge the account of Creation, the story of the Flood, and most of what is written in the Torah. Adherents of these faiths even make pilgrimages to that noble place.

The Sage said: I would compare them to those converts who accepted the roots of the mitzvot but not their ramifications, were it not for the fact that their deeds contradict their words. On the one hand, they verbally honor this site of prophecy; on the other hand, they direct their prayers to places previously associated with specific gods and where no divine sign was seen, simply because most of them happen to live in that area. Moreover, they retain all the ancient pagan practices, holidays, and sacrifices; they have rid themselves only of the idols, not the practices. [...] While it is true that they are monotheists, their belief in God's interaction with the world is like that of Abimelekh's men, the citizens of Nineveh, and the philosophers. The founders of these two religions claimed to have attained divine illumination at their place of origin, namely, the Land of Israel, whence they were lifted to Heaven and ordered to guide the people of the world on the right path. At the beginning, that Land was in fact the only place to which the faithful directed their prayers, but this lasted only a short time. Quickly enough they began praying toward wherever the majority of them lived. To what can this be compared? To someone who is to bring everyone to the Sun, since they all have weak eyesight and cannot see the Sun to know the arc of its movement. Instead, he leads them all to the South or North Pole and exclaims, "Here is the Sun! Look at it up close!" But, of course, they cannot see it. [...]

The Khazar said: But aren't members of these religions closer to you than the philosophers?

The Sage said: Indeed, the distance between a religious person and a philosophizer is great. The former seeks out God for benefits that go beyond knowing Him, whereas the latter seeks Him out only to describe Him as He actually is, the same way one tries to describe the Earth as, for example, being situated at the center of the largest sphere instead of the zodiacal sphere. For the philosophizer, ignorance regarding God is no more injurious to a person than ignorance regarding the Earth is to a flat-earther. The only benefit is to apprehend the true nature of things, because such knowledge assimilates the knower to the Active Intellect, to the point of their unification. [...] As far as philosophers are from apprehending God through prophecy, one should not fault them for this. Their sole entrée to theology is via logical reasoning, which can only lead them to the aforementioned. The honest among them would say to the followers of the Torah what Socrates said: "My fellow citizens, I do not reject your theology, but I also do not acknowledge it, because I know only human wisdom." As for the two religions, as close as they are, they are equally far. This should come as no surprise. Even Jeroboam and his cronies, who were closer to us, being circumcised Jews who observed Shabbat and all other mitzvot, barring those their government duties prevented, and who even acknowledged the God of Israel ... we consider idolaters. Member of these two religions are better than they in outlawing graven images, but by changing the site to which prayers are directed, by seeking the divine matter where it is not to be found, and, even worse, by abrogating most of the non-rational mitzvot, they are at many a remove from us.

[6] *Sefer HaKuzari*, 2:50–55 – The Jews bring the world to true belief

The Sage said: [...] Moreover, He said, "Israel, by whom I will be glorified" (Is. 49:3).

The Khazar said: This is an undue statement; the poetry goes too far in saying that God is glorified by flesh and blood.

The Sage said: If the statement were about the creation of the Sun, would you find it easier to accept?

The Khazar said: Of course, because of the immensity of its effects. [...] According to our understanding, how could its creation not bring glory to its Creator?

The Sage said: But isn't the light of spiritual sight more rarified and worthy of praise than the light of the eyes? Was not all of humanity, aside from the individuals discussed above, blind and confused before the advent of the Jewish people? Some said there is no creator, reasoning that there is no part of the universe more worthy of being created than of being creator, so everything must be eternal. Others said that only the celestial sphere is eternal. [...] But all agree that they have not seen the slightest indication of anything supernatural. Philosophers with the finest minds and sharpest thinking conceded the existence of a *sui generis* first cause, but in their logical reasoning they inclined to opine that this cause does not act upon the universe, especially not on individual existents.... This state of affairs persisted until that congregation was purified enough for the light to descend upon it and to have miracles wrought for it, for the natural order to be broken on its behalf. People see with their own eyes that the universe has a judge and provident overseer, who knows what is and is not important, who dispenses reward for good and punishment for evil. This congregation became a spiritual guide for everyone, and every subsequent religion cannot depart from these roots. Today, the entire citizenry of the civilized world professes that God is eternal and the universe created, and their proof is the Jewish people – the favor God showed them and the punishment He meted out for them.

The Khazar said: In this there is definitely what to be glorified by, and your explanation is wonderful. It similarly says, "to make Himself an everlasting name" (Is. 63:2), "You made Yourself a name as on this day" (Neh. 9:10), and "for praise, acclaim, and glory" (Deut. 26:19).

[7] *Sefer HaKuzari*, 4:23 – The hidden design of the Jewish exile is the gradual purification of non-Jewish beliefs

God has a hidden design in keeping us in exile, which can be likened to the design embedded in a seed. The seed falls to the earth, where it seems to break down into dirt, water, and mud, and the observer sees no tangible sign of its previous form. After some time, though, one understands that it is the seed assimilating the water and dirt and gradually refining them into the elements so that they can be transformed into its substance, from which it produces husks, leaves, and more. This continues until the seed becomes so purified that it is ready to bear the divine matter (*ha'inyan haEloki*) and the form of the original seed. At that point it grows into a tree that bears fruit, like the fruit from which that very seed came.

The same is true of the Mosaic religion. Every subsequent religion truly assimilates to it, even if it appears to be quite dissimilar. These religions are but a preparation for the expected Messiah, who is the fruit, and at the end of days, when they acknowledge him, they will become his fruit, and the tree will become one. Then they will revere the root that they had formerly disparaged, as we explained in our interpretation of "Behold, My servant shall prosper" (Is. 52:13).

Do not praise these religions for the way they spurn idolatry and strive to unify God and find fault with the children of Israel, who worshipped idols during the monarchic period. Instead, focus on the fact that even the most faithful of these religions veer into heresy in their belief in divine providence, which they spread among the masses. They even compose poetry in this vein, declaring that there is no provident hand over man's deeds that rewards good and punishes evil, and their words are published and savored. This has never happened among the Jewish people. Although our people have had those who believed that their idols and the celestial spirits could bring them blessings, swayed by the common belief of their time that such worship is efficacious, this was only in addition to the religious law that they observed in full. If it were not so, why would they not have converted to the religions of the non-Jews among whom they were exiled?

[8] *Sefer HaKuzari*, 4:27 – Prophecy to a non-Jewish philosopher to learn from Jews who bear God's revelation

The Sage said: You have spoken well, King of the Khazars! This is the truth, the true belief; all else should be abandoned. It might have been this very logical reasoning in *Sefer Yetzira* that brought our forefather Abraham to recognize God's unity and sovereignty before having merited any revelation. After receiving this revelation, though, he left behind all this logical reasoning and sought only to win God's favor, having learned its nature and how and where to attain it. The Sages expounded the verse, "'And He brought him outside' (Gen. 15) – leave your astrological speculation," meaning, abandon astrology and all other natural philosophy that is speculative. Plato also related that a certain prophet in the time of King Marinus received a revelation and conveyed the following to a philosopher who devoted his life to attaining revelation through philosophical inquiry: "You will not reach Me via this path, but only by those whom I have placed as intermediaries between Me and My creations" – i.e., the prophets and true laws.

Rabbi Moses Maimonides: Noahide Law as the Exclusive Revelation to the Nations

Yakov Nagen

R abbi Moses Maimonides has a unique stature as an authoritative theologian and halakhist. His understanding of Judaism's evaluation of other faiths and religiosity, therefore, carries serious weight. We must explore his various works in depth in order to grasp the subtleties and implications of his position.

Maimonides's point of departure is the talmudic discussion of Noahide law in Tractate Sanhedrin. An important question, already touched upon in the chapter on Noahide law, flows from this *sugya*: Do these seven mitzvot comprise the entirety of the eschatological religion of non-Jews? Does Judaism intend to guide the nations in establishing a Noahide religion, and is that all there is to their religiosity? One can discern three major approaches to this issue, the third of which is that of Maimonides.

NOAHIDE LAW AND GENTILE RELIGION

The first approach believes that other religions are a legitimate expression of God's will. The seven Noahide laws provide the vital substrate for human flourishing. Once those foundations have been poured, though, the various nations are expected to build their own religious identity upon it, in consonance with their national and cultural characters.

This limitation of the scope of Noahide law emerges from an analysis of the full list of mitzvot. As I have argued, the essence of these mitzvot is the mandate to do no harm, in the absence of which human civilization cannot exist. It is no coincidence that the seven commandments do not positively outline the proper relationship with God or other people. This corpus of law assumes a religious identity that exists beyond it. If that is true, one must still answer a crucial question: What is the legitimating source for a religion that advocates relationships between man and man and between man and God that diverge from those found in Judaism?

Over the centuries, multiple answers have been proposed. One presented in a previous chapter is that of Rabbi Nathaniel Fayyumi, which claims that there are religions that arise from genuine revelation. When prophecy ceased among the Jewish people, other nations took up the mantle. A better-known position, to be presented in the next chapter, is articulated by Rabbi Menahem Meiri. The legitimacy of these non-Jewish religions stems from their commitment to ethical behavior, which finds practical halakhic expression in his innovative category of "peoples bound by religious morals and laws." Further chapters examine the thought of Rabbi Joseph Albo and of Rabbi Abraham Isaac HaKohen Kook on this issue.

These answers all support our basic contention: the seven Noahide laws are for all of humanity, and beyond that God wants man to seek Him out in such a manner that religions coalesce out of his grassroots efforts. This approach, the variations of which define certain religions as legitimate, enables cooperation and mutual respect while honoring differences of identity.

The next line of thinking assumes that the elaborate religions of the non-Jews serve to ensure observance of the seven Noahide laws. Like the previous approach, this one also allows for interfaith cooperation, but unlike it, the world religions are not evaluated on their own terms. They are gazed at through the prism of Judaism, refracted through our own system of values. Noahide law is a thin concept internal to Judaism that is used a yardstick to measure other religions. Members of these faiths have a much richer self-definition, an acknowledgment of which is lacking within this approach.

Finally, a third approach, the one seemingly espoused by Maimonides, does not grant legitimacy to other religions. Even the Noahide laws must be observed out of the belief that they were revealed to Moses on Mount Sinai. Just as Jews are obligated in the full complement of the Torah's mitzvot by dint of their revelation, so too must non-Jews vis-à-vis the Noahide laws.

To highlight the differences between these approaches, let us apply them to Islam, a monotheistic religion whose observance incorporates the seven Noahide laws. The first approach would consider Islam a legitimate religious mode of divine worship on its own terms. The second would legitimize Islam by virtue of the fact that its faithful fulfill the seven Noahide laws. Approach number three would place Muslims outside the category of idolaters, but would hope that ultimately they would adopt the identity held out to them by Judaism: the Noahides who keeps their mitzvot out of sincere belief in their having been revealed to Moses at Sinai.[1]

NOAHIDE LAW AS REVEALED RELIGION

In *Hilkhot Melakhim*, Maimonides rules that "the pious of the nations of the world" are those who accept the seven Noahide laws "because the Holy One commanded them in the Torah and informed us through our teacher Moses that the descendants of Noah had been commanded them." But if they observe them because doing so seems rational, they are instead considered "one of their sages" [1].[2]

---

1. As both Christianity and Islam acknowledge revelation at Sinai, there are those who include both even in this strict definition of Noahism. See Rabbi Zvi Hirsch Chajes (1805–1855), *Tiferet LeMoshe*, 489–490.

2. This is according to the version of the text that reads *ella meḥakhmeihem*, which

Maimonides's ruling has three implicit assumptions. First, Noahide law constitutes an entire religion for non-Jews; it is the equivalent of their Torah. Second, real religion must be grounded in revelation to Moses at Sinai, and its observance must include awareness of this fact. Third, the theophany at Sinai was not only for the Jewish people but for the entire world. The Jewish people received 613 mitzvot, and the nations of the world received seven.

Notably, these assumptions demonstrate great respect for non-Jews. Just like the Jews, Maimonides is saying, non-Jews merited a revelation from God at Sinai, almost as if they were standing with the Israelites at the foot of the mountain. This accords with another egalitarian position of Maimonides, which does not locate the difference between Jews and non-Jews in race or the nature of the soul.[3] Nevertheless, Maimonides believes that adherents of all religions should ideally accept the one true religion that Judaism provides them: the seven Noahide laws.

THE PRINCIPLES UNDERLYING MAIMONIDES'S OPINION

Rabbi Yosef Karo in his *Kesef Mishneh* writes that Maimonides's ruling has no source [2], a point that will be discussed in the next section. If one analyzes his restrictive position carefully, several underlying theological and philosophical tenets, expressed elsewhere in Maimonides's writings, become evident.

(1) *There is only one truth.* Maimonides insists that only one truth exists and all disagreement, even in halakha, is the result of human error. As a result, pluralism indicates the corruption of tradition, and understandably he searches for a uniform religious identity. His fervent desire to restore religious law to a unitary, undisputed state is concretized in his monumental code *Mishneh Torah*, in which dissent rarely appears.

(2) *The revelation at Sinai was a unique moment in world history.* According to Maimonides's theory of prophecy, only Moses possessed

---

manuscript analysis confirms as the original. Most printed texts erroneously have *velo meḥakhmeihem*, which would mean that such a person is neither pious nor wise.

3. See Menachem Marc Kellner, *They Too Are Called Human: Gentiles in the Eyes of Maimonides* [in Hebrew] (Ramat Gan: BIU Press, 2016).

the prophetic capacity to convey eternal commands in God's name. Other prophets paled in comparison to him, as he alone was the exclusive conduit for God's legislation. As Maimonides writes explicitly in his commentary on the Mishna: "Everything we do or do not do today is only because of God's command through Moses, not because God commanded it to prophets who preceded him" [10]. Moses is extraordinary, the instrument of divine, absolute Truth. What of the other prophets? They were not charged with legislating in God's name. Either their spiritual attainments led them to prophesy in God's name, or they were exhorting the people to observe the mitzvot transmitted by Moses. Moses alone was the lawgiver.[4]

> If this principle underlies Maimonides's evaluation of world religions, he is not really invalidating those religions due to their substance but on the grounds of their pedigree. No prophet aside from Moses – not even a Jewish one – has the ability, and therefore the legitimacy, to transmit a divine book, body of law, or order.[5] What made the revelation at Sinai singular was not the people, the Israelites, who experienced the revelation, but the identity of the prophet on the summit where heaven kissed earth.

(3) *Mitzvot must be performed because God commanded them.* In Maimonides's thought, one receives a share in the World to Come by fulfilling divine commands because they are divine commands. This intention apparently imbues the act with metaphysical significance that allows one to enter the metaphysical reality of the next world.

(4) *Insistence on theological precision.* More broadly, Maimonides stands out from other medieval thinkers and authorities in his insistence on theological precision. For example, in his list of heretics who have no portion in the World to Come, he includes "one who says that

---

4. See *Moreh HaNevukhim*, 2:39.
5. Rabbi Kook addresses and clarifies this in his *Shemona Kevatzim* [11].

there is one Master but He is a body with an image."[6] The Raavad adds a sharp gloss:

> Why did he call this person a heretic, when men greater and more virtuous than he followed this line of thinking, based on what they saw in the verses, and, even more so, based on what they saw in the aggadic statements that confound people's minds?

Maimonides's exceptional rigor regarding theological matters helps explain his ruling on non-Jewish religious observance. The seven mitzvot must be fulfilled while their divine origin and prophetic messenger are borne in mind.

THE DIFFICULTY WITH MAIMONIDES'S OPINION

Rabbi Yosef Karo finds Maimonides's ruling to be sourceless but declares it a "sound" opinion [2]. Moses Mendelssohn vociferously objects to this characterization:

> I find these words impossible to swallow. Can it be that all the denizens of the planet, from the Far East to the West, will descend to the abyss? [...] What are the nations, upon whom the light of Torah never dawned, supposed to do? [...] Does the Holy One deal tyrannically – perish the thought – with His creatures, to obliterate them and blot out their name for no wrongdoing? Can this be called a "sound" opinion?[7] (Letter to Rabbi Jacob Emden) [3]

Mendelssohn finds this ethically unconscionable, and his critique is similar, *mutatis mutandis*, to one leveled at Christianity. Since it holds that there can be no salvation outside the Church, it damns everyone else to

---

6. See *Mishneh Torah, Hilkhot Teshuva* 3:7–8.
7. Part of the sharpness of this critique is based on the fact that Mendelssohn had the erroneous text of Maimonides; see footnote 2.

hell.[8] In fact, Maimonides's position is even more problematic. Christianity explicitly demands belief in Jesus, about whose life and teachings there are entire libraries, whereas Maimonides requires non-Jews to believe in something – the revelation of the seven Noahide mitzvot at Sinai – that is not documented in any source.

In a responsum [5], Maimonides appears to cite *Mishnat Rabbi Eliezer* [6] as a source for his opinion. This only deepens the problem, however. *Mishnat Rabbi Eliezer* is a late aggadic Midrash whose halakhic authority is doubtful. It is also hard to see it as Maimonides's source, because nowhere does it say that non-Jews must perform the Noahide mitzvot in the belief that they were revealed to Moses at Sinai. What the Midrash does do is insist on observance out of the desire to obey God's will, and not due to some other motivating factor, like human reason or idolatrous association. According to this source, so long as a monotheistic religion believes that the Noahide laws are God-given, its adherents also receive reward in the next world for their fulfillment, which is the highest level.[9] Moses and Mount Sinai, so critical to Maimonides's ruling, are not part of the equation here.

Beyond the problem of Maimonides's source, his requirement is not echoed by others. It is absent from the writing of his fellow medieval authorities, and, what is more, some of them explicitly allow for the observance of Noahide law due to their rationality. Rabbeinu Bahya ibn Pakuda, for example, posits that rationality is the defining factor of Noahide law and what sets it apart from the Mosaic Torah. The former derives from reason and the latter from revelation.[10]

---

8. It bears noting that in recent years the Church has grappled with this ethical problem. See at length in John Hick, *God Has Many Names* (Philadelphia: Westminster Press, 1980).

9. Due to the difficulty with Maimonides's position, Rabbi Kook [4] explains that performing the mitzvot out of intellectual conviction is greater than doing so based on their revelation from on high. "The World to Come" that Maimonides promises the non-Jew who observes the mitzvot due to their revelational origin is actually a lower level. Recently, Rabbi Eugene Korn has passionately argued for this reading in his *Israel and the Nations: The Bible, the Rabbis, and Jewish-Gentile Relations* (Brookline, MA: Academic Studies Press, 2023), 80–88.

10. Ḥovot HaLevavot, 3:6. Rabbi Nissim Gaon has a similar formulation in his introduction to the Babylonian Talmud. Also see Maimonides's own opinion on acts that

NOAHIDE LAW AS NON-JEWISH RELIGION

As noted above, when Maimonides requires the seven mitzvot to be performed out of belief in their revelation, he conceives of them as a full-fledged religion. Indeed, Maimonides refers to them as the "their Torah," the main implication being exclusivity – this and nothing else. Non-Jews may not practice even the monotheistic faiths:

> The general rule is that they are not allowed to invent a religion and to make themselves mitzvot as they see fit. They must either convert and accept the mitzvot or uphold their Torah – neither adding to nor taking away from it. (*Mishneh Torah, Hilkhot Melakhim* 10:9) [7]

To confirm the parallelism between *the* Torah and "their Torah," Maimonides extends the prohibition against altering the number of mitzvot in the Torah (Deut. 13:1) to the seven mitzvot: "neither adding to nor taking away from it." For Maimonides, the Noahide laws are a kind of distillation of Judaism to provide a religion and Torah for the non-Jew.[11]

---

go against one's moral instinct in his *Moreh HaNevukhim* [14]. In this connection, Rabbi Abraham Isaac HaKohen Kook (*Orot HaTorah*, ch. 11) says that "*derekh eretz* precedes the Torah" refers to mitzvot that our intellect tells us to follow naturally. A halakhic source that omits Maimonides's requirement is Rabbi Eliezer of Metz's *Sefer Yere'im* (233): "It is learned: Isi ben Yehuda says, 'Before a hoary head you shall rise' (Lev. 19:32) – every hoary head is implied.'Meaning, even a gentile, so long as they fulfill the seven mitzvot that Noah's descendants were commanded, that is, the pious of the nations of the world. 'And R. Yoḥanan says, The halakha accords with Isi ben Yehuda. Abbaye would rise before Aramean elders.' Meaning, one who fulfills the seven mitzvot that the descendants of Noah accepted upon themselves. And according to the opinion in Tractate Avoda Zara (64b) that it refers to a *ger toshav*, it is no difficulty, for the Talmud still refers to him as Aramean. But if they do not perform [the mitzvot], such as idolaters in the era of idolatry, illicit sexual relations, and murder, Isi would not say to rise before and honor him." *To'afot Re'em* ad loc. infers that Rabbi Eliezer of Metz does not affirm Maimonides's conditions and maintains that so long as a non-Jew observes Noahide law, regardless of intentions, that is enough to define him or her as "the pious of the nations" and as a *ger toshav*.

11. Maimonides's treatment is based partly on the prohibition for a non-Jew to keep Shabbat (Sanhedrin 58b). In his understanding, the problem is that the non-Jew is inventing a new religion. Later in this volume, we will argue that the simple

GENTILE PERFORMANCE OF ADDITIONAL MITZVOT

If a non-Jew wishes to fulfill a mitzva in the Torah that is not part of his mandate of seven, Maimonides permits it: "A Noahide who wishes to perform one of the other mitzvot of the Torah in order to receive reward is not to be prevented from performing it according to halakha" [8]. The Noahides may have only received seven mitzvot in the revelation at Sinai, but they still enjoy a connection to the other mitzvot of the Torah revealed there. This widens the circle of non-Jewish religiosity a bit more, so that it can encompass other mitzvot. This allowance may flow from Maimonides's universalist view of the assembly at Mount Sinai discussed above.[12] While some later authorities restrict Maimonides's position to the example of charity that he cites,[13] the straightforward reading applies it to any mitzva that a non-Jew wants to perform, as Maimonides writes explicitly in a responsum about circumcising a non-Jew [5].

Maimonides's view of the inclusion of non-Jews in the revelation at Sinai is complex. In one direction, the uniqueness of the event prevents non-Jews from developing their own religions. In the other direction, the universality of the revelation tucks non-Jews under the wings of the Torah. This is important. Maimonides's opinion is neither the

---

understanding of the prohibition is that Noah is told after the deluge that the natural order of day and night and the progression of the seasons will not be disrupted. The reasoning behind the prohibition is local rather than general.

It is worth mentioning the historical context of Maimonides's ruling. His was a time when Jews across the world experienced harsh religious persecution at the hands of Muslims: under the Almohads in North Africa and Spain, and under various rulers in Yemen. Many Jews were faced with the choice of martyrdom or forced conversion. His reluctance to validate the religion of those pressuring his people to convert and reject their own faith is understandable.

12. The connection of Noahides to the Torah's mitzvot can be likened to the connection of women to time-bound mitzvot: they are exempt but can still say *vetzivvanu* ("and we were commanded") in the blessing over the mitzva. The Rashba explains: "Women may make a blessing on time-bound mitzvot despite the fact that they are only optional for them, because they are ultimately involved in a mitzva. It is only that the Loving One did not obligate them in it on the same level as men; instead, if they wish to, they may perform it, and they are considered obligated vis-à-vis *vetzivvanu*" (*Ḥiddushei HaRashba*, Rosh HaShana 33a).

13. See *Iggerot Moshe, Yoreh De'ah* 2:7: "It is clear that it applies only to the mitzvot of consecration and *tzedaka*."

consensus nor is it binding, but even within his own view that rejects other religions, he offers non-Jews a more varied and satisfying religious diet instead of the same seven mitzvot every day.

WORLD RELIGIONS: A MISTAKE?

It is true that Maimonides rejects other religions and does not permit non-Jews to practice them, but that does not mean that they have no value at all. In the grand scheme of things, they have a role to play. He views the success of the monotheistic faiths as evidence of God's hand in history, "to pave the way for the King Messiah and to prepare the entire world to serve God together." These religions lay the groundwork for the Jewish Messiah and ultimately will be victims of their own success: "When the King Messiah truly arises ... they will immediately realize that their fathers fed them lies and their ancestors and prophets led them astray" [9]. At the end of days, the nations will recognize that they have been perpetuating religious mistakes. Understandably, it would require the determination of a Messiah to awaken such a dramatic change in the whole world.

Owing to the fact that most of the world population today belongs to religions that worship the one God, each in their own way, some by default observing Noahide law, it should be emphasized that Maimonides's opinion is not shared by other rabbinic authorities of the Middle Ages. Other weighty figures, from his own and later eras, delineate paths to a redeemed world in which there is spiritual cooperation across humanity in serving God, either through world religions as they are or after some reformation. On these accounts, God did not allow these religions to arise so they can be tools to be disposed of but because they have intrinsic value, "for them all to call in the name of the Lord, to serve Him shoulder to shoulder" (Zeph. 3:9).

THE POSSIBLE RELIGIOUS ATTAINMENTS OF NON-JEWS

Maimonides indeed restricts the scope of religious activity for the halakhic category of Noahides, yet all of humanity, even those who have not accepted the seven mitzvot, can reach sublime religious attainments. He writes:

> ... [A]ny inhabitant of this world whose spirit generously moves him and whose intellect enlightens him to separate himself, to stand before God in order to minister to and worship Him, to know the Lord... such a person is sanctified as holy of holies, the Lord shall be His portion, his inheritance shall last forever and ever.... (*Mishneh Torah, Hilkhot Shemitta VeYovel* 13:13) [12]

"Any inhabitant of this world" obviously includes non-Jews, making sanctification, the Lord as one's portion, and other spiritual rewards available to Noahides. To reap these rewards, must one perform the mitzvot with the Maimonidean intention? He does not add any such condition here.

Furthermore, if one reads Maimonides's formulation in *Hilkhot Melakhim* carefully, one notices that the phraseology focuses on the positive, namely, that one who fulfills the mitzvot with his required intention receives a portion in the World to Come. Maimonides never says that one who fails to do so will never receive such a portion:

> Whoever accepts the seven mitzvot and is careful to perform them is considered one of the pious of the nations of the world and has a portion in the World to Come. [...] But one who performs them due to intellectual conviction is neither a *ger toshav* nor one of the pious of the nations of the world, but one of their sages. (*Hilkhot Melakhim* 8:11) [1]

The fact that Maimonides does not clearly state the negative provides an opening for the religiosity described in *Hilkhot Shemitta VeYovel*. If we combine the two accounts, Maimonides appears to offer two avenues to the next world. *Hilkhot Melakhim* discusses the fulfillment of the seven Noahide mitzvot in obedience to the divine command at Sinai. *Hilkhot Shemitta VeYovel* is describing a parallel path of sanctity through divine service.

Rabbi Sarel Rosenblatt has proposed that these paths were blazed by two key figures in Maimonides's thought: Abraham and Moses.[14] Moses's greatness was his capacity to receive unique revelation, whereas Abraham's was his rational investigation of the cosmos that brought him to divine worship: "He began interrogating with his mind [...] he had no teacher nor anyone to inform him [...] his heart would interrogate and understand until he arrived at the path of truth."[15] *Hilkhot Shemitta VeYovel* presents the Abrahamic model, in which the individual dedicates one's life to seeking out and serving God. This is bottom-up and limited to the individual aspirant. *Hilkhot Melakhim* codifies the Mosaic approach, in which revelation for the Jews and the rest of the humanity is the be-all and end-all. This is top-down and is for communities of the faithful.

The individual's path to the World to Come, through spiritual attainment and knowledge of God, brings us to Maimonides's relatively famous conception of the next world in *Hilkhot Deot*. He posits that it is a spiritual reality, in which the soul – the "divine image" of a person – persists "forever and ever" on account of its knowledge of God [13]. The wording there accords perfectly with what we find in *Hilkhot Shemitta VeYovel* [12].

In Maimonides's eyes, Abraham does not represent religion per se but an individual's path to God that can also merit the World to Come.[16] Seemingly, this path should be only available to the few, because humanity today is almost totally divided into the organized religions that Maimonides deems illegitimate. However, even if Maimonides would not consider most of them to be formally observing Noahide law, if they obtain sufficient knowledge of God and perfect their character, they too fulfill God's will and enjoy a portion in the World to Come, to endure "forever and ever."

---

14. These two figures also figured prominently in Maimonides's personal life. He himself was named Moses and was popularly compared to the biblical Moses: "From Moses to Moses none arose like Moses." He named his only son Abraham.

15. *Mishneh Torah, Hilkhot Avoda Zara* 1:2–3.

16. My friend Professor Abdulla Galadari pointed out to me that this is the conception of Abraham found in the Quran. There, he is not called a Jew or Christian but a *ḥanif*, a monotheist who worships God outside the formal context of any religion.

SOURCES

[1] *Mishneh Torah, Hilkhot Melakhim* 8:10–11 – Observance of Noahide law due to Sinaitic Revelation

Our teacher Moses gave the Torah and mitzvot as an inheritance only to Israel – as it says, "An inheritance of the congregation of Jacob" (Deut. 33:4) – and to anyone from the other nations who wishes to convert – as it says, "you and the convert (*ger*) alike" (Num. 15:15). Whoever does not wish to do so, though, is not compelled to accept the Torah and mitzvot. Moses further commanded from the mouth of the Almighty to compel every inhabitant of the world to accept the mitzvot that the descendants of Noah were commanded, and whoever does not accept them is to be executed. Whoever does accept them is the one everywhere called a *ger toshav* (resident alien), and they must accept [them] upon themselves in front of three Torah scholars. Whoever accepts upon himself to circumcise himself and twelve months pass without him having done so is considered like someone of the nations.

Whoever accepts the seven mitzvot and is careful to perform them is considered one of the pious of the nations of the world and has a portion in the World to Come. This is provided that one accepts and performs them because the Holy One commanded them in the Torah and informed us through Moses that the descendants of Noah had been commanded them. But one who performs them due to intellectual conviction is neither a *ger toshav* nor one of the pious of the nations of the world, but one of their sages.

[2] *Kesef Mishneh, Hilkhot Melakhim* 8:11 – Maimonides's source is reasoned opinion

It seems to me that when our master writes, "This is provided that one accepts, etc.," it is his own opinion. And it is sound.

[3] A Letter from Rabbi Moses Mendelssohn to Rabbi Jacob Emden – An ethical objection to Maimonides's opinion[17]

I find these words impossible to swallow. Can it be that all the denizens of the planet, from the Far East to the West, will descend to the abyss and be a horror to all flesh? [...] What are the nations, upon whom the light of Torah never dawned, supposed to do? [...] Does the Holy One deal tyrannically – perish the thought – with His creatures, to obliterate them and blot out their name for no wrongdoing? Can this be called a "sound" opinion?

[4] Rabbi Abraham Isaac HaKohen Kook, *Iggerot Re'iya*, 1:89 – Piety versus wisdom among the nations

I am inclined to think that by "has a portion in the World to Come" Maimonides intends an inferior level, indeed. Although it is a wonderful good, even wicked and boorish Jews merit it, so that in the scheme of spiritual states, it is inferior. Maimonides thinks that intellectual attainments accomplish far more for man than righteous behavior. As a result, "has a portion in the World to Come" is specifically assigned to "the pious of the nations of the world," whose intellectual attainments are not great, having come to their belief through pure movements of the heart, and who behave uprightly by accepting that their mitzvot were given as such from God. But someone who is able to arrive at the seven Noahide laws by intellectual conviction is truly wise and full of understanding. It is he who is considered "one of their sages," for the level of wisdom is very high; it goes without saying that he has a portion in the World to Come. Such a person is at the level of holiness, and their standing deserves fuller expression than "has a share in the world to come."

But even if Maimonides's words are to be taken at face value, it would not be an imposition to say that the degree of the World to Come, which he speaks about in his book, is that selfsame degree that the divine superiority of our Holy Torah grants to its keepers. There exist other levels that every good thing can grant, but they are not called "the World to Come." That superiority comes from the power of the Torah, and it

---

17. Cited in Jacob S. Levinger, *Maimonides as Philosopher and Codifier* [in Hebrew] (Jerusalem: Bialik Institute, 1989), 22.

uniquely suits whoever accepts it with the holiness of its faith. It does not at all negate other levels imagined by each philosophical system.

[5] *Teshuvot HaRambam* (ed. Blau) 148, p. 282 – A midrashic source for Maimonides's opinion

Question: Regarding the circumcision of the non-Jews and of the uncircumcised, may a Jew accept it upon himself? Is there any distinction between the Muslims and the Christians in this? And what is the meaning of the *Baraita*: "The Rabbis learned, A Jew who circumcised a non-Jew for the sake of conversion – to exclude for the sake of a worm, which is not permitted. And a non-Jew should not circumcise a Jew, etc."?[18] What does "A Jew who circumcised a non-Jew for the sake of conversion" come to teach?

Answer: A Jew may circumcise a non-Jew if the latter wishes to cut and remove the foreskin, because a non-Jew receives a reward for any mitzva that they perform.

Nevertheless, he is not tantamount to one who is commanded and performs it. This is only if he performs it while acknowledging and believing that it is the prophecy of Moses that commands it from God, and he does not perform it for some other reason or idea that he finds correct. This is clarified in the *Baraita* of Rabbi Eliezer ben Yaakov, and I have explained it myself at the end of my great composition.[19] [...] Whenever someone comes to us to be circumcised to fulfill the mitzva, we may do so, even though he will remain a non-Jew.

[6] *Mishnat Rabbi Eliezer* 6 – Fulfilling the Noahide laws because they are divinely commanded

The difference between the pious of Israel and the pious of the nations of the world:

The pious of Israel are not called pious until they fulfill the entire Torah, whereas the pious of the nations of the world are called pious so long as they fulfill the seven mitzvot that the descendants of Noah were commanded with all their particulars.

---

18. *Avoda Zara* 26b.
19. *Mishneh Torah, Hilkhot Melakhim* 8:10.

Under what conditions? When they perform them and say, "We perform them since our forefather Noah commanded us from the mouth of the Almighty." If they do it this way, then they inherit the World to Come like a Jew. This is the case even though they do not keep Shabbat or the festivals, because they were not commanded about them. But if they perform the seven mitzvot and say, "We heard it from so and so," or "It is of our own accord since the intellect dictates it," or if they associated it with an idolatrous name – [even] if they fulfill the entire Torah, they receive their reward only in this world.

[7] *Mishneh Torah, Hilkhot Melakhim* 10:9 – **Non-Jews must convert or be Noahides**

An idolater who learns Torah is liable for execution; they may only learn their seven mitzvot. Likewise, an idolater who rests, even on a weekday, is liable for execution if they made it like Shabbat for themselves. Needless to say [this applies] if they made a holiday for themselves. The general rule is that they are not allowed to invent a religion and to make themselves mitzvot as they see fit. They must either convert and accept the mitzvot, or uphold their Torah – neither adding to nor taking away from it. And if one learns Torah, rests, or invents something, they lash and punish him, and inform him that he is liable for execution for it, but such a person is not killed.

[8] *Mishneh Torah, Hilkhot Melakhim* 10:10 – **A Noahide can receive reward for performing the Torah's mitzvot**

A Noahide who wishes to perform one of the other mitzvot of the Torah in order to receive reward is not to be prevented from performing it according to halakha. If he brings a fire-offering, it is accepted; [if he] gives *tzedaka*, it is accepted. It seems to me that it is given to poor Jews, since he is sustained by the Jewish people and it is a mitzva upon them to sustain him. But if an idolater gives *tzedaka*, it is accepted and given to poor idolaters.

[9] *Mishneh Torah, Hilkhot Melakhim* 11:4 (uncensored) –
Christianity and Islam pave the way for the Messiah
If a king of the Davidic line arises who is learned in the Torah and pre-
occupies himself with mitzvot according to the Written and Oral Torah
like his forefather David, compels all of Israel to follow it and strengthens
its observance, and wages God's wars, he is presumed the Messiah. If
he successfully defeats all the surrounding nations, rebuilds the Temple
on its site, and gathers in the exiles of Israel, he is certainly the Messiah.
But if he is not successful to such an extent or is killed, evidently he is
not the one whom the Torah has promised, and he is like all the other
perfect and righteous kings of the Davidic dynasty who died. The Holy
One caused his rise only to test the masses, as it says, "And some of the
wise men will stumble, to purge them, to refine, and to purify until the
appointed time, because the set time is in the future" (Dan. 11:35)....

All the events surrounding Jesus of Nazareth and the Ishmael-
ite who arose after him were only to pave the way for the King Messiah and to prepare the entire world to worship God together. As it
says, "For then I will transform peoples with a pure language, for them
all to call in the name of the Lord, to serve Him shoulder to shoulder"
(Zeph. 3:9)." How? The entire world has already been filled with talk
of the Messiah, the Torah, and the mitzvot, such that it has spread to
faraway lands and many spiritually obtuse peoples who discuss them.
Concerning the Torah's commandments, some say they are true but no
longer apply and have not been practiced for generations, while others
say they contain mysteries and are not as they sound, that the Messiah
has already come and revealed their mysteries. When the King Messiah truly arises and succeeds, and he is uplifted and exalted, they will
immediately realize that their fathers fed them lies and their ancestors
and prophets led them astray.

[10] *Commentary on the Mishna,* Ḥullin 7:6 – **Performing
mitzvot only because God commanded them through
Moses**
[...] Pay attention to the important rule brought in this mishna, in
their statement, "It was prohibited from Sinai." You must understand
that everything we do or do not do today is only because of God's

command through Moses, not because God commanded it to prophets who preceded him. For example, we do not eat a limb from a live animal not because God forbade the descendants of Noah from doing so, but because Moses prohibited us from doing so, when he was commanded at Sinai to let the prohibition remain in place. Similarly, we do not circumcise because Abraham circumcised himself and the men of his household, but because God commanded us through Moses to be circumcised in the way Abraham circumcised. Additionally, when it comes to the sciatic nerve, we are not following the prohibition of our forefather Jacob but the command of Moses. After all, you see their statement, "613 mitzvot were said to Moses at Sinai,"[20] and all of these are included in the count of mitzvot.

[11] Rabbi Abraham Isaac HaKohen Kook, *Shemona Kevatzim, Kovetz* 2:54 – The uniqueness of Mosaic prophecy according to Maimonides

For Maimonides, the eternity of the Torah is rooted in the state of the world at the time of its giving. Nothing budges from the Torah even as the affairs of the world change. The prophecy of Moses does not belong to the natural spirit of reality, unlike the rest of prophecy, whose absence from those worthy of it is confounding and whose appearance is natural. But the prophecy of the master prophet is a miracle, akin to *creatio ex nihilo*. Just as the moment of bringing existence into being lies beyond the tides of time and the foundation of this process is not subject to change, so the Torah is immutable.

[12] *Mishneh Torah, Hilkhot Shemitta VeYovel* 13:13 – The level of someone who serves God from their own intellect

Not only the tribe of Levi, but any inhabitant of this world whose spirit generously moves him and whose intellect enlightens him to separate himself, to stand before God in order to minister to and worship Him, to know the Lord; who goes upright like God made him; and who removes from his neck the yoke of the many reckonings people seek of him – such a person is sanctified as holy of holies; the Lord shall

20. Makkot 23b.

be His portion, his inheritance shall last forever and ever, and He shall meet his needs in this world, as He did for the priests and Levites. For David of blessed memory says, "The Lord is my portion and my cup; You maintain my lot" (Ps. 16:5).

[13] *Mishneh Torah, Hilkhot Yesodei HaTorah* 4:8–9 – Meriting the World to Come through knowledge of God

The soul of all flesh is the form that God gave it. The superior intellect found in the human soul is the form of the human being whose intellect is perfect. About this form is it said in the Torah, "Let us make man in our image, like our semblance" (Gen. 1:26), meaning, that he should have a form that knows and apprehends the intelligible things....

The form of this soul is not composed of the elements, such that it would decompose into them...it is from God, from Heaven. Therefore, when the matter decomposes...this form is not obliterated...for it knows and apprehends the intelligible things that are separate from matter, and it knows the Creator of all, and it endures forever and ever. That is what Solomon said in his wisdom, "Dust returns to the earth as it was, but the spirit returns to God, who gave it" (Eccl. 12:7).

[14] *Moreh HaNevukhim*, 3:17 – Natural forewarning

Justice is an absolute necessity with respect to Him: He rewards the righteous for all their deeds of kindness and uprightness, even though they were not commanded about it through a prophet, and He metes out punishment for every wicked deed that man does, even if they were not warned about it through a prophet, because one is naturally forewarned against it.

[15] Letter from Maimonides to Rabbi Ḥisdai HaLevi in Alexandria – Meriting the World to Come through knowledge of God and refinement of character[21]

Regarding your question about the nations, you know that "the Loving One desires the heart,"[22] and words follow the intention of the heart. That is why the true Sages, our Rabbis of blessed memory, said, "The pious of the nations of the world have a portion in the World to Come."[23] If they apprehended what ought to be apprehended of the knowledge of the Creator and refined their soul with good character traits, there is no doubt about it: whoever has refined their soul with virtue and fitting wisdom for belief in the Creator is definitely destined for the World to Come.

---

21. *Iggerot HaRambam* (ed. Shailat), p. 681. Some doubt the attribution to Maimonides, but Nahmanides, among others, assumes it is authentic.
22. Sanhedrin 106b.
23. Sanhedrin 105a.

Rabbi Menahem Meiri: Moral Behavior and Theological Belief as the Basis for Fellowship with Non-Jews

Sarel Rosenblatt

Rabbi Menahem ben Shlomo Meiri (1249–1315) was one of the most important leaders of Provençal Jewry during one of its most vigorous, albeit difficult, periods.[1] Provence lay at the crossroads of the distinct culture spheres of European Jewry, with Spain to the southwest, France to the north, and Italy to the east. Its Jews were exposed to a range of halakhic traditions and customs, intellectual and philosophical currents. They also witnessed the persecution of these surrounding communities by the Church, much of it originating in the kingdom of

---

1. There is no evidence that Meiri held an official rabbinic position, but historical documentation indicates that he was one of the leaders and representatives of the Jewish community. See Richard W. Emery, *The Jews of Perpignan in the Thirteenth Century: An Economic Study Based on Notarial Records* (New York: Columbia University Press, 1959), 28.

France and the kingdoms of Spain, and calamities like the burning of the Talmud in Paris (1242), the disputation in Barcelona (1263), and the expulsion of French Jewry (1306). Many refugees ended up in the cities of Provence.

Within southern France itself, Jews had a complicated relationship with their Christian neighbors. The Church repeatedly tried to enforce a separation between Jews and Christians and eventually saw some success on the streets of Provence, but many communities remained mixed. There was civic cooperation, extensive business connections, and even ties between the intellectual elite – so much so, that there was even a trend of conversion to Judaism that greatly worried the Christian clergy.[2] When Rabbi Menahem Meiri was working out how to formulate his halakhic attitude toward non-Jews, he undoubtedly had this robust coexistence in mind.

Meiri's views of the halakhic status of non-Jews and Christianity (as well as Islam) are scattered across his voluminous commentary on the Talmud, *Beit HaBeḥira*. In dozens of places, Meiri redefines the halakhic categories of "the non-Jew" and "idolatry" that were minted by the rabbis for the non-Jews of antiquity. By analyzing the conceptual and legal foundations underlying the rabbinic positions – as we will see at length below – Meiri is able to restrict the vast majority of the Sages' harshest sentiments toward non-Jews, which strongly discourage most types of meaningful interaction and set forth a host of legal inequalities with regard to the ancient idolaters of the Middle East. He argues that they would never have been said about most of the non-Jews and non-Jewish faiths of his own time and place. In building these halakhic bridges to members of other monotheistic faiths, Meiri uses the morality and theology common to all of them as the thick cords from which to suspend them. Even if those faiths get it wrong on certain points of theology, in his eyes they are far closer to Judaism than others that do not rest on this shared foundation of ethics and belief. Practicing these

---

2. For more on Jewish life in medieval Provence, especially the different kinds of interaction with non-Jews, see Ram Ben-Shalom, *Jews of Provence and Languedoc: Renaissance in the Shadow of the Church* [in Hebrew] (Raanana: The Open University, 2017), 12–14, 150–169, 213–285.

religions is also preferable to observing the bare minimum of the seven Noahide mitzvot. Meiri's goal is to generate a sense of fraternity with non-Jews of these religions and to treat them as primary partners in creating a life filled with morality and faith.

Given the widespread mistreatment of Jews in Meiri's lifetime, one might argue that Meiri is engaging in apologetics to protect his coreligionists. The less antagonistic Jewish sources and practices are to the Christian majority, the better for the Jews. However, when one considers the sheer span of Meiri's argument across his commentary, its absolute consistency, and its appearance even in areas of halakha that have no practical application, it seems far more reasonable that Meiri was so convinced of the correctness of this position, that he stood by it steadfastly even when the storms of anti-Semitism swept across European kingdoms and principalities.

Meiri was primarily a talmudic commentator and a halakhist, so to grasp the full extent of his position on non-Jews and non-Jewish religion, we now embark on a journey across the sea of Talmud.

"PEOPLES BOUND BY RELIGIOUS MORALS AND LAWS"

The proper relationship Jews should maintain with their non-Jewish neighbors has exercised the minds of Jewish leaders and thinkers for the last two thousand years. The common political arrangement before modernity, in which Jews lived under Christian or Muslim rule, generated an inherent tension between the desire to be good citizens and prosper, and the halakhic limitations on interacting with non-Jews and idolaters.

Medieval Jewish authorities held different views on how and when Jews may cultivate personal or commercial relationships with non-Jews, if at all. Most of the permissive authorities tried to police the border of religious identity while permitting financial dealings necessary for the Jewish community's solvency. Meiri went in a different, much more ambitious direction. For him, there was much more at stake than the local Jewish economy. Instead of minting his own brand of halakhic license, as it were, to narrowly permit the conduct of business with non-Jews, he argued that Judaism should fundamentally respect non-Jews and their monotheistic religions, and that the daylight between us and them is not as great as people think.

In *Beit HaBeḥira*, Meiri invents a novel conceptual category that shifts the binary from Jew versus non-Jew to moral monotheist versus immoral polytheist. The way he sees it, medieval Christianity is categorically different from the "polytheistic religions" of old. The legal, economic, and social sanctions that the talmudic Rabbis imposed on the non-Jews of their time never envisioned the Christians of the Middle Ages as a target.

An examination of Meiri's writings demonstrates that Meiri applied his reconceptualization in three discrete areas: (1) the legal rights and obligations of a non-Jew in areas of personal status, finances, and torts; (2) the prohibitions and restrictions on activity that directly or indirectly abets idol worship; and (3) the institutions intended to enforce social separation and prevent intermarriage.[3]

The first area includes a wide range of laws: remuneration for damage caused by one's animal, the obligation to return a lost object, the obligation to save a life, the prohibition against price gouging, and the punishment for killing a person. In all of these cases, halakha formally distinguishes between a Jew's responsibility to another Jew and responsibility to a non-Jew. Meiri erases this distinction when he characterizes the non-Jews of his time as "peoples bound by religious morals and laws."

For instance, the Mishna states that if a Jew's animal causes damage to a non-Jew's animal, the Jew is exempt from payment. In the reverse situation, the non-Jew would be obligated to pay.[4] In his commentary on the relevant talmudic passage, Meiri stresses that this law was only formulated by the Sages for the non-Jews of their day, so it does not apply to the Christians of medieval Europe. The non-Jews of antiquity were "peoples not bound by religious morals and laws," that is, morally degenerate barbarians, and the law's logic is predicated on

---

3. See Moshe Halbertal, *Between Torah and Wisdom: Rabbi Menachem HaMeiri and the Maimonidean Halakhists in Provence* [in Hebrew] (Jerusalem: Magnes Press, 2001), 82–83.

4. Mishna Bava Kamma 4:3. There is no distinction between whether the damage must be paid in full or only in part (where the animal had no track record of violent tendencies).

this very fact: "Since they pay no consideration to the money of others, they are fined so that they do not accustom themselves to cause damage" [1]. The discrimination in tort law is justified by injustice. Meiri believes that such non-Jews exist in his day at "the edges" of the civilized world.[5] Perhaps this is a reference to the pagan tribes in the northeastern reaches of Europe. The local Provençal Christians, by contrast, are "bound by religious morals and laws," so "the law for them is the same as it is for us." In this novel conceptualization, medieval non-Jews have more in common with Jews that then they do with ancient non-Jews. This bifurcation of non-Jews recurs in many other areas of halakha, like returning a lost object.

"BROTHERLINESS"

The Torah qualifies the mitzva of returning a lost object by describing its owner as "your brother" (Deut. 22:3). According to the Talmud, not only is there no obligation to return such an item to a non-Jewish owner, but there is even a prohibition against it.[6] Even so, the Talmud itself and later halakhists like Rabbi Moses Maimonides clarify that there are circumstances in which one *must* return a lost object to its non-Jewish owner: to preserve peaceful relations and avoid a desecration of God's name.[7] Here too, Meiri stakes out his own position. He thinks that the above prohibition only pertains to "the irreligious," not to "peoples bound by religious morals who worship God in some respect" [5]. The obligation to return the lost object applies to the latter under all circumstances. Meiri expands the biblical designation of "your brother" to include his non-Jewish contemporaries. Meiri has a similar formulation regarding the prohibition against price gouging: "The Sages stated a rule: 'No person shall wrong their fellow (*amito*)' (Lev. 25:17) – do not wrong the one who is with you (*im she'ittekha*) in Torah and mitzvot." This sounds limited to Jews, but Meiri explicitly includes "whoever is bound by religious morals" in this category of fellowship [2].

---

5. *Beit HaBeḥira*, Avoda Zara 6b, s.v. *lematta*.
6. See Bava Kamma 113b and Sanhedrin 76b.
7. See *Mishneh Torah, Hilkhot Gezela VaAveda* 11:3.

The extension of brotherhood beyond the Jewish community also appears in an area of law that is not strictly economic, so the preservation of Jewish livelihoods does not seem to be a motivating factor. It is a pure specimen of Meiri's warm feelings toward his Christian neighbors. The Talmud states that one should not greet non-Jews on one of their holidays.[8] On a regular day one may inquire after their welfare to promote amicable relations, but even then one may not "double a greeting." What does this mean? Meiri explains that it entails using "words of affection and familiarity" that might lead to them "liking each other and becoming overly friendly" [3]. The ultimate concern is that it might lead to idolatry, which "was very attractive because of the many advantages produced through its worship." At a time when non-Jews are no longer pagan idolaters, there is no prohibition against really investing oneself in the welfare of non-Jews and becoming genuine friends with them. It ought to be noted, though, that there is a small number of prohibitions governing relations between Jews and non-Jews that morality does not suspend or negate: eating food cooked by non-Jews, drinking wine handled by non-Jews, and marrying non-Jews.[9] In these cases,

---

8. See Gittin 62a.
9. *Beit HaBeḥira*, Avoda Zara 26a, s.v. *harbe*. As for the non-Jew who rests on Shabbat, Meiri's position requires further analysis. On the one hand, in this source he includes this prohibition on a list of institutions intended to prevent intermarriage. On the other hand, elsewhere (Sanhedrin 59a) he seems to say that the prohibition is only if the non-Jew rests in a way that is similar to our laws of Shabbat or the festivals, and their holiday is being construed as a superior interpretation of our mitzva of Shabbat. Since the latter does not seem to be the case with the Christian or Muslim days of rest, it would follow that he did not view non-Jews resting as forbidden.
  Meiri also addresses the prohibition of a gentile learning Torah (Sanhedrin 59a). He opines that this has nothing to do with non-Jews qua non-Jews and is instead a potential problem of mistaken identity. A Jew might mistake a learned non-Jew for a Jew and accept his erroneous interpretations of the Torah. Meiri goes on to permit non-Jews learning Torah for two reasons: basic Torah study is necessary to fulfill those mitzvot that a non-Jew must perform, and advanced Torah study is allowed if it concerns the seven Noahide laws in some way or another, since "most of the fundaments of the Torah are subsumed under them." Not only may the non-Jew engage in this study, but "they are to be respected even like the High Priest, because given that they are studying what pertains to them, there is no concern that others will be misled."

though, they have the very direct goal of preventing assimilation and intermarriage. None of them is intended to isolate us from non-Jews or sour our relations with them.

Meiri's expanded definitions of the Torah's "brother" and "fellow" to include non-Jews reshapes the Jewish perception of the world. Instead of distinct Jewish and non-Jewish spheres, the world is divided between moral, law-abiding people who worship God, and barbaric, lawless people who worship many gods. In Meiri's worldview, the Jews and Christians of Provence stand shoulder to shoulder in the struggle of the civilized world against paganism and barbarity.[10] A series of halakhic positions fills out this expanded fraternity. Not only is it forbidden to cause harm or injury of any kind of non-Jews,[11] but one must even violate Shabbat to save their lives.[12] Not only is it forbidden to financially extort them [2], but one must "sustain them," that is, look after their poor.[13] On a holiday, the Torah says to us that you may cook "for yourselves" (*lakhem*), and the Talmud excludes non-Jews from this allowance. Since, according to Meiri, "the unspecified 'non-Jews' mentioned in the Talmud are adherents of ancient pagan beliefs,"[14] the Christians of medieval Provence do not fit this definition. One may cook for them on a holiday.

THE CRITERION OF MORALITY

The concept of "peoples bound by religious morals and laws" runs like a thread throughout the fabric of *Beit HaBehira*. It is worked into disparate areas of religious law across many tractates. While it chronologically distinguishes medieval non-Jews from their pagan predecessors, more importantly, it binds Jews, Christians, and Muslims together

---

10. A similar argument was made in the last century by Rabbi Abraham Joshua Heschel, who pitted Judaism and Christianity against the materialism of Western society; see his "No Religion is an Island," *Union Theological Seminary Quarterly Review* 21:2:1 (Jan. 1966): 117–134.

11. *Beit HaBehira*, Horayot 11a, s.v. *kol shehu*.

12. *Beit HaBehira*, Yoma 84b, s.v. *pikkuah nefesh*.

13. *Beit HaBehira*, Avoda Zara 26a, s.v. *hagoyim*, and 64b, s.v. *af al pi*.

14. *Beit HaBehira*, Beitza 21b, s.v. *mimma*.

under a single rubric. On what basis did Meiri invent and justify such a far-reaching category?

Apparently, Meiri tried to get to the bottom of the many rabbinic ordinances and laws that put distance between Jews and non-Jews. What value did the Sages hold so dear that they required Jews to break off, avoid, or minimize contact with non-Jews, in situations where finances are at stake and lives even in jeopardy? Meiri did not think this lies in abstract matters of faith but in practical areas of moral behavior. So far as one can tell, Meiri was familiar enough with Christian theology to assess that "their belief is distant from ours" [5] and that "they have gotten some things wrong according to our beliefs" [3]. On the normative plane, theological incorrectness is not what is determinative for him. What matters are obedience to the law and the pursuit of justice. So long as non-Jews have a proper moral code, "they have the same law as actual Jews" in many areas of halakha [5]. The litmus test of morality is whether a given society or religion deems violence, murder, or harm of the innocent as a moral injustice.

For the Sages, the seven Noahide laws were the determining factor. They are the necessary foundation for human civilization, for a society of human beings to live together in mutual respect and fellowship. When Meiri looked around him at his fellow Christian burghers, he saw more than men and women who kept the seven mitzvot in which non-Jews are obligated. He saw people whose religious identity raised them to another level altogether: "So long as they keep the seven mitzvot, the law for them is the same as it is for us, and we have no advantage. Needless to say, this certainly applies to peoples bound by religious morals and laws" [1].

THE THEOLOGICAL FOUNDATION

The reader should not form the mistaken impression that moral behavior is all that matters for Meiri, and that it can paper over even the most glaring errors of theology. A deeper look at his writings, including those outside his talmudic oeuvre, reveals that it is his conviction that theology and faith are what produce the kind of morality he so deeply values.

In a few places, he explains that the line dividing the barbarous pagans from the moral monotheists has its origins in their beliefs.

The moral turpitude of ancient paganism was an outgrowth of its conception of divinity. Its pantheism identifies the forces of nature as gods: "In antiquity, incorrect beliefs were rampant. They only believed in what is perceptible, in what is common knowledge and the first intelligibles" [10]. Polytheists did not believe in some abstract God who is ontologically distinct form the world, who providently manages it and calls it to judgment. "On account of this they denied the existence of God, the existence of any transcendental being, and all religious rules" [11]. This theological error led to the breach of "religious morals," that is, moral norms. These beliefs persisted into Meiri's time but only among small groups "in some places at the edge of the civilized world." Neither Christianity nor Islam subscribe to this fundamentally flawed theology, and so their religious societies produce "peoples bound by religious morals and laws." Meiri knows of Judaism's detailed criticisms of the religious doctrine of other faiths, including Christianity. Still, to label an entire religion as idolatrous – resulting in all the halakhic ramifications discussed above – requires a thorough evaluation of its theology. Regarding Christianity, Meiri states that its adherents belong to those "peoples bound by religious morals who believe in the existence, unity, and omnipotence of God, even if they have gotten some things wrong according to our beliefs" [3]. He does not demand pure monotheism, a bar Christianity would not meet, but awareness of a transcendent God that engenders fear of Him.[15] Hence, even on a theological level Meiri places Christianity and Islam in the same category as Judaism, all of them being distinct from polytheistic and more threatening religions that deny "the existence of God and the existence of anything transcendental" [10].

---

15. It is interesting to compare Meiri's position to one taken by Rabbi Abraham Isaac HaKohen Kook. In a later chapter dedicated to Rabbi Kook's thought, we will see that he thinks that the abrogation of the mitzvot and the doctrine of original sin necessarily lead to an immoral society. While this is undoubtedly true for a Jew, Meiri would counter that for a Christian, Christianity's dogmas are sufficient to move the faithful to lead a moral life. It is not up to us to decipher how exactly this works within the Christian religious experience.

Understanding that for Meiri there is a theological foundation for his criterion of morality adds another dimension to his legal doctrine that accounts for additional halakhic rulings of his. Recall that one discrete area of halakha in which Meiri implements his reconceptualization governs activity that directly or indirectly abets idolatrous practices. In this context, notably, Meiri does not justify distinguishing ancient from medieval religions on moral grounds but by reason of theology.

Meiri permits, for example, doing business with non-Jews on their holidays, because the prohibition in the Talmud "was said with respect to pagans with their images and idols, but nowadays it is completely permitted" [4]. Why? Because the polytheists "would worship the heavenly host, the Sun, and the Moon, the trees and the stones," which is not true of Christian worship.[16] When the Talmud forbids commercial dealings with non-Jews on Sundays, its reference to *notzerim* is ostensibly a reference to Nazarenes, the term for Christians.[17] While Rashi states this outright,[18] Meiri dissents: "I interpret it based on a verse in Jeremiah (4:16): '*Notzerim* are coming from a distant land,' where the people called them *notzerim* after Nebuchadnezzar. There was an idol of the Sun in Babylonia, and all of Nebuchadnezzar's people would worship it" [4].[19] This pagan worship "ceased ... from most places, so there is no need to be exacting about them."[20] That does not mean that Meiri is completely comfortable with facilitating Christian rituals. He is uneasy about selling wine and bread to priests for mass: "It seems to me that all of them can be permitted, but it would be best for a scrupulous, self-disciplined person to refrain" [9]. In other words, it is praiseworthy to refrain from supplying, even for a price, non-Jewish worshippers with the actual objects of a religious ritual.

Turning to another prohibition, the Talmud rules that one may not transmit "secrets of the Torah" to non-Jews. Once again, Meiri limits this to "someone who worships gods and the heavenly host"; it is

---

16. *Beit HaBeḥira*, Avoda Zara 6b, s.v. *lematta*.
17. See the uncensored text of Avoda Zara 6a.
18. See the uncensored text of Rashi ad loc., s.v. *notzeri*.
19. See Lawrence Zalcman, "Christians, Noṣerim, and Nebuchadnezzar's Daughter," *The Jewish Quarterly Review* 81 (1991): 411–426.
20. *Beit HaBeḥira*, Avoda Zara 13a, s.v. *yarod*.

not aimed at the faithful of Christianity or Islam [6]. In another place,[21] Meiri clarifies that the "secrets of the Torah" are theological notions that pertain to belief in an abstract, transcendental God, a belief that is shared by Christianity and Islam.[22]

This soft view of Christianity and Islam leads Meiri to take an even more radical one on churches and mosques, the physical centers of worship and ritual in these religions. The Talmud records blessings that hope for and celebrate the destruction of temples of idolatry.[23] The ideology behind them is that these structures are antithetical to the Jewish people's divine mission of spreading belief in the one God. Meiri places mosques and churches beyond the scope of these blessings, because they apply only to "the temples of idol worshippers and of adherents of other ancient beliefs who are not bound by religious morals, consistently referred to by the Talmud as 'nations of the world'" [8].

We have now seen the entire sweep of Meiri's complex position on non-Jewish religions. He finds the disagreements between Judaism and Christianity to be primarily about matters of faith. He recognizes Christian dogma to be far from correct, yet he also sees "no need to be exacting about them."[24] It is too easy to carve up the world absolutely on the basis of gross simplifications. We must look at every religion in all its complexity, and decide which of its many components are halakhically determinative.

Meiri makes two key moves regarding non-Jewish religiosity. First, he underscores the positive theological advances of the major medieval religions, especially as compared with pagan beliefs. Second, he minimizes the impact of the disparity in theology; in normative terms, it is marginal. Instead of shining a spotlight on the gap between faiths, Meiri chooses to illuminate the commonalities. Instead of denouncing other

---

21. *Beit HaBeḥira*, Avot, ch. 3, s.v. *vehinneni*.
22. A comparison between the passages in Avot, on the one hand, and *Ḥibbur HaTeshuva* and *Peirush LeTehillim*, on the other, shows that in all three Meiri uses the story of the Tower of Babel as a paradigm of pagan heresy and of the kinds of people who may not be taught the secrets of the story. Along similar lines, see Nahmanides's Bible commentary on Ex. 20:2.
23. See Berakhot 58b.
24. *Beit HaBeḥira*, Avoda Zara 13a, s.v. *yarod*.

faiths as fundamentally wrong, he finds where they are fundamentally right. He does not do this to score points with his Christian overlords or to ensure working relations with his fellow townsmen – "to promote peaceful relations" – but because he sees the goodness in Christianity and Islam. These faiths bring people to recognize a transcendent, incorporeal God who is fully involved with and judges this world, and as a result they build societies founded on justice and morality. Meiri wants us all to recognize that we are kindred spirits.

CONCLUSION

This chapter has explored the way Rabbi Menahem Meiri thought about non-Jewish religions and religiosity. His talmudic commentary and other writings exhibit a high estimation of them, at least in their potential. Not only is adherence to a non-Jewish religion compatible with the demands of Noahide law, but a full-bodied religion is superior to this lean body of law so long as it includes faith in a transcendent, provident God and a fear of that God that inculcates moral behavior. Christianity and Islam qualify for both.

Our analysis of Meiri's many comments on the issue reveals a two-tiered position. In the top tier, theology does not directly determine Judaism's stance on another religion. The relevant factor is moral behavior, as produced by the legal norms and cultural framework of a religion, which maintains a civilized society. That is why there is no normative dissonance between declaring a religion's beliefs incorrect and treating its followers as partners, fellows, and even extended family.

Undergirding the criterion of morality, though, is the bottom tier, which is theological through and through. There is a required set of beliefs, according to Meiri, that gel together to moral behavior. Meiri teaches us something important here about how to approach interfaith relations. There is a danger to dichotomous thinking about religions, because it caricatures them based on select elements. Perusing the data allows one to tease apart the good from the bad, and to acknowledge both for what they are. Christian and Islamic theology, for Meiri, contain the necessary theological ingredients for forming a monotheistic brotherhood. Note that he doesn't mean this in strictly moral terms;

the nexus of morality and theology implies a larger community with a religious identity as well. In the same way that Meiri resisted oversimplified theology and chose a more penetrating, nuanced account, so in the real world of Provence, in which Jews and Christians lived side by side, he refused to make generalizations about non-Jews based on the bad apples among them. In place of an us versus them mentality, Meiri took a good look around at the fine men and women living moral lives and created a new halakhic category into which upstanding human beings – Jews and non-Jews both – could be comfortably placed

If Meiri were alive today, he would likely deem significant segments of contemporary Christianity and Islam as partners of great promise for a broader brotherhood. The criterion of morality, without which meaningful partnership between Jews and non-Jews is impossible, is met by them, as is the sharing of fundamental theological tenets. Some use Meiri as an example of "religious tolerance." While this characterizes the practical outcome of his position, it does not do justice to the depth of his thinking on the issue. It is not simply that he values the Other as a human being. He interrogates religions to find their points of goodness and correctness, justice and morality, and then, with analytical adroitness and critical coherence, demarcates a new halakhic space for them.

What was the fate of Meiri's halakhic position? It was adopted in practice by Rabbi Betzalel Ashkenazi, a rabbinic luminary living in the Land of Israel in the sixteenth century, in his *Shita Mekubbetzet*.[25] In

---

25. *Shitta Mekubbetzet*, Bava Kamma 113a. Some Orthodox Jews, including Torah scholars, claim theḤazon Ish said not to rely on Meiri's position because his writings were unavailable to the vast majority of halakhic decisors until relatively recently. This is difficult to sustain for two reasons. First, we ourselves see that earlier authorities did have access to his writings, considered him on par with other authorities of his time, and even ruled like him. In *Mishna Berura*, Meiri is mentioned hundreds times and the halakha accords with him in many instances. Second, some attribute the Ḥazon Ish's position to a certain passage in his eponymous work, where he argues in favor of older printed editions, which Torah scholars used for centuries, over "improved" ones based on newly discovered manuscripts. He explains his reasoning: "The halakhic codes have been passed down to us in an unbroken chain of tradition, and they have been pored over by the great scholars of every generation to preserve and purify their language, so they should be considered the most accurate" (*Ḥazon Ish, Moed* 67:12). This logic applies to the publication of a new edition of Rabbeinu

the twentieth century, which witnessed the return of the Jewish people to their Land, the Holocaust, and the founding of the State of Israel, the issue of the proper relationship between Jews and non-Jews again became a burning one. Many halakhic decisors followed Ashkenazi's ruling and considered Meiri's stance the right one. Rabbi Abraham Isaac HaKohen Kook wrote in 1904: "The halakha accords with Meiri, for all the peoples that are bound by proper interpersonal laws already have the status of *gerim toshavim* (resident aliens) in all our obligations toward them."[26] Sixty years later, Rabbi Jehiel Jacob Weinberg, a Holocaust survivor and the author of the responsa collection *Seridei Esh*, wrote:

> In my opinion it is fitting to put an end to the hatred of the religions for each other. […] We must solemnly and formally declare that in our day this does not apply. Meiri wrote as such, but the teachers and *ramim* whisper in the ears of the students that all this was written because of the censor.[27]

Rabbi Hayim David HaLevi also reads Meiri this way and rules like him. He ends by saying:

> Since non-Jews today do not have the status of idolaters, even if Jews were to regain sovereignty in halakhic and practical terms, we would not have to treat them that way. In all our relationships with non-Jews, in the Land or outside it, as a Jewish state with non-Jewish citizens, as individuals with non-Jewish neighbors or friends, one should not maintain good relationships merely to promote peaceful

---

Hananel's commentary on a talmudic tractate based on an unearthed manuscript fragment, but not to Meiri's massive and wide-ranging *Beit HaBeḥira*. Moreover, Meiri's comments were indeed known to "great scholars of every generation."

26. *Iggerot Re'iya*, vol. 1, 89, p. 99.

27. Quoted in Marc B. Shapiro, "Scholars and Friends: Rabbi Jehiel Jacob Weinberg and Professor Samuel Atlas," *The Torah U-Madda Journal* 7 (1997): 118. The original was published in Rabbi Zvi Yisrael HaLevi, *Israel and the Nations* [in Hebrew] (Jerusalem: Mekhon Daat HaTorah, 2009): 24–25.

relations but because they are not halakhically idolaters. Sustaining them, visiting their sick, visiting their dead, comforting their mourners... and more, all should be done out of a moral obligation as human beings, not specifically to promote peaceful relations.[28]

Based on this chapter, I would add that, according to Meiri, the fact that a non-Jew today is not halakhically considered an idolater does more than dictate our moral posture toward them in halakhic terms. It also enables us to see them as a potential brother or sister in spirit, with whom we can join hands to expand the brotherhood of humanity that the Torah envisions, and to view their religion as a partner for spreading the divine in the world.

SOURCES

[1] *Beit HaBeḥira*, Bava Kamma 37b

If a Jew's ox gored a non-Jew's ox, they are exempt from the law of "one's fellow" (Ex. 21:35). If a non-Jew's gored a Jew's, whether [the owner] had been forewarned or not, they pay full damages. Since they pay no consideration to the money of others, they are fined so that they do not accustom themselves to cause damage. Based on what the Talmud says, this is only for peoples that are not bound by religious morals and laws, as it says: "He saw the seven mitzvot the descendants of Noah were commanded but did not fulfill. He arose and permitted their money whenever the law finds them liable" – the implication being that so long as they keep the seven mitzvot, the law for them is the same as it is for us, and we have no advantage. Needless to say, this certainly applies to peoples bound by religious morals and laws.

[2] *Beit HaBeḥira*, Bava Metzia 59a

Whoever is bound by religious morals is included in [the prohibition against] price gouging, but idolaters are not part of this brotherhood

---

28. Rabbi Hayim David HaLevi, "The Promotion of Peaceful Relations in Relationships between Jews and Non-Jews" [in Hebrew], *Teḥumin* 9 (1988): 71.

to include them in price gouging. The Sages stated a rule: "'No person shall wrong their fellow (*amito*)' (Lev. 25:19) – do not wrong the one who is with you (*im she'ittekha*) in Torah and mitzvot."

[3] *Beit HaBeḥira*, Gittin 62a

One need not refrain from greeting idolaters, but it is inappropriate to make small talk longer than usual and beyond the customary greeting. This is what I call doubling a greeting, for when a person makes their greeting unusually long, it demonstrates extra affection and a sense of kinship. You know that idolatry was very attractive because of the many advantages produced through its worship.... [A Jew] would initiate the customary greeting so that [the idolater] would respond in kind, and the former would not foster too much of a sense of kinship. But if [the Jew] would wait for [the idolater] to initiate the greeting, the latter might do so with words of affection and familiarity, and the former would need to respond in kind, resulting in them liking each other and becoming overly friendly. Others would then learn from their behavior and follow their lead. [...] But this has no bearing on peoples bound by religious morals who believe in the existence, unity, and omnipotence of God, even if they have gotten some things wrong according to our beliefs.

[4] *Beit HaBeḥira*, Avoda Zara 2a

Furthermore, concerning the non-Jews outside the Land, it is only permitted before the holiday, while on the holiday itself it is prohibited. And yet the custom is to permit it even on the holiday itself! Based on this it seems to me that all of this was said with respect to pagans with their images and idols, but nowadays it is completely permitted. As for the Talmud's statement, "[Doing business with] a *notzeri* is always forbidden," I interpret it based on a verse in Jeremiah (4:16): "*Notzerim* are coming from a distant land," where the people called them *notzerim* after Nebuchadnezzar. There was an idol of the Sun in Babylonia and all of Nebuchadnezzar's people would worship it. You already know that the Sun rules the first day of the week according to the count of the daily rulers. For that reason, they would call that day *notzeri*: due to the rule of the Sun on that day, it was dedicated to Nebuchadnezzar. This seems plainly correct.

[5] *Beit HaBeḥira,* Bava Kamma 113b

One may not steal even from idolaters who are not bound by religious morals. And if a Jew is sold to one, it is prohibited to leave their domain without a ransom payment. Likewise, one may not cancel their loan. Nevertheless, one is not obligated to go searching for their lost object to return it to them. Furthermore, even if one finds their lost object, one is not obligated to return it to them. Finding a lost object is a partial acquisition, so returning it is a supererogatory act, and there is no impetus to be extra pious for the irreligious. Similarly, if they make a mistake of their own accord, not on account of some ploy or confidence scheme, it is not necessary to make them whole. But if they find it, one must make them whole. Similarly, even a lost object must be returned if keeping it will cause a desecration of God's name. It follows that whoever belongs to peoples bound by religious morals that worship God in some respect, even though their belief is distant from ours, they are not included in all this. Rather, they have the same law as actual Jews in these matters, even with regard to a lost object or mistake or anything else, without any distinction whatsoever.

[6] *Beit HaBeḥira,* Ḥagiga 13a

One may only disclose secrets of the Torah to a worthy person, and one may not disclose secrets of the Torah to a non-Jew – someone who worships gods and the heavenly host. Since they reject the foundation [of monotheism], how can they be taught Torah? About this does it say, "He relates His words to Jacob... He did not do so to every nation" (Ps. 147:19–20).

[7] *Beit HaBeḥira,* Ḥullin 114b

Any unslaughtered animal carcass is prohibited to eat but permitted to derive benefit from, except for the stoned ox, as will be explained in the appropriate place. For it says about the carcass, "To the stranger within your gates shall you give it so that he may eat, or sell it to a foreigner" (Deut. 14:21). Giving to a stranger and selling to a foreigner is not the final word – even the opposite is permitted – it is only that there is a mitzva to give to a stranger before selling to a foreigner. The stranger has been taken under the wings of the Divine Presence, and so is one of our brothers whom you are commanded to sustain. The foreigner, by contrast, so long as they are an idolater, you are not commanded to sustain.

[8] *Beit HaBeḥira*, Berakhot 58b

Whoever sees synagogues in Israel in use says, "Blessed…who establishes the border of the widow"; in ruins one says, "Blessed…the true Judge." As for the temples of idol worshippers and of adherents of other ancient beliefs who are not bound by religious morals, consistently referred to by the Talmud as "nations of the world," whoever sees them in use and at peace says, "The Lord will destroy the house of the proud" (Prov. 15:25); in ruins one says, "God of vengeance, the Lord" (Ps. 94:1).

[9] *Beit HaBeḥira*, Avoda Zara 14b

These things are prohibited out of concern for an [idolatrous] offering, for whatever they offer to their gods is prohibited, be it bread, wine, or anything else. But that which is not itself an offering but is used to render honor – like candles for lighting, a silver or gold object that houses an offering, or vestments that worshippers wear for incense-burning or service – both its purchase and use as collateral is permitted. Thus did the rabbis of northern France write, too. Some of them even permitted what could be an actual offering, like bread, if given to priests as part of their wages. The same applies to books made for chanting. Some are exacting and prohibit some of these in places where idolatry still remains, as we have explained. It seems to me that all of them can be permitted, but it would be best for a scrupulous, self-disciplined person to refrain. In chapter four, these matters will be further clarified.

[10] *Ḥibbur HaTeshuva*, ed. Avraham Sofer (Jerusalem: Ḥemed, 1976), pp. 255–256

In antiquity, incorrect beliefs were rampant. They only believed in what is perceptible, in what is common knowledge and the first intelligibles. This belief is attributed to the Generation of the Dispersion. Anything transcendental was considered non-existent. This led them to deny the existence of God and the existence of anything transcendental. They would worship the celestial bodies. If they had seen a ladder set on the ground and its top reaching to heaven, they would not have seen the

Lord of Hosts upon it, nor would they have believed in His holy ones. [...] The Generation of the Dispersion could not imagine anything imperceptible; only the objects of their senses or common knowledge existed. The philosopher went further by daring to believe in whatever reason or logical reasoning could demonstrate to exist, which led to conviction about some cornerstones and foundations of the Torah, like the existence of God and the existence of transcendental existents.

[11] *Peirush Tehillim*, ed. Yosef HaKohen (Jerusalem: n.p., 1974), p. 47 (Ps. 19:8)

The objects of faith should be believed through one of three[29] means: sense perception, common knowledge, or tradition. In antiquity, there were terrible beliefs. They only believed in what is perceptible, meaning what is apprehended by the senses, and what is common knowledge, meaning that which is well known via the first intelligibles. [...] On account of this they denied the existence of God, the existence of any transcendental being, and all religious rules. Some of them are still around in some places at the edge of the civilized world. [...] A person's faith is incomplete without the inheritance of the Torah, and one who accepts it accepts upon themselves the yoke of Heaven, to believe whatever the religion requires him to believe in so that the belief is perfect, without any lacuna.

---

29. The text reads "four" but based on the continuation has been emended to "three" (per note 5 in the critical apparatus ad loc.).

Rabbi Joseph Albo:
A Noahide Law for Every Nation

Yakov Nagen

Rabbi Joseph Albo (1380–1444) lived in Spain during a period that saw intense persecution of the Jews by the Christian populace and clergy. In 1391, when Albo was only a boy, waves of anti-Jewish fervor rippled across the Iberian Peninsula, and Jews across its Christian kingdoms were murdered and forcibly converted. In 1413, now a mature scholar, Albo was one of the Jewish delegates to the Disputation of Tortosa, one of the most protracted Jewish-Christian disputations of the Middle Ages. Organized and run by the Church, the debate was rigged, since Jews were straitjacketed in what they could and could not say. To make their argument they were not allowed, for example, to express criticism of Christianity. The goal was to make Christianity the clear winner and to win converts. In this regard it was quite successful.

Albo's monumental work, *Sefer HaIkkarim*, presents Judaism's fundamental principles of faith, along the way polemicizing explicitly and implicitly against Christianity. In the book, Albo distinguishes between "conventional religion and "divine religion": the first aims to create a stable and flourishing sociopolitical order, and the second brings about the perfection of character and intellectual opinions, so that the soul can enter the World to Come [1]. Divine religion, in Albo's thought, requires three principles of faith: the existence of God, the divine origin of the Torah, and divine recompense. Christianity cannot be a divine religion, because belief in the trinity impinges on the belief in God's existence. Albo also critiques the conception of predestination in Islam, which he understood as denying free will, which would in turn conflict with the principle of divine reward and punishment [5].[1] Another claim lodged against Christianity and Islam is that "the giving of a divine religion" – meaning, the original event of its divine revelation – "must be spread far and wide, and that any religion that does not enjoy such broadcasting is not truly divine" [2].

In spite of this seeming restriction on divine religions, Albo allows for a plurality of religions. Moreover, he seems to consider this ideal:

> What ought to be philosophically investigated now is whether there must necessarily be one divine religion for all of humanity or multiple. [...] Upon further consideration, one finds that although it is necessarily so with respect to the giver, it is not necessarily so with respect to the recipient. Human temperaments vary, whether due to the diversity of parental temperament or other factors, to the point that it is impossible for two people to have the same temperament or nature. [...] People are also different based on where they live, because the nature of lands differs based on the air, mountains, waters, and the like. [...] Since this diversity is inherent to the recipient and not the giver, it must concern matters pertaining to the recipient, namely, the presumptions and conventions that prevail between people of certain localities regarding good and bad, for what is good to some is bad to others. But regarding the general principles and their derivatives, which are

---

1. Just as Judaism has many theological and philosophical approaches to the apparent contradiction between divine foreknowledge and free will, so does Islam.

all dependent upon the giver, it is impossible to conceive of any variability. (*Sefer HaIkkarim*, 1:25) [3]

Recall how for Rabbi Nathanel Fayyumi, religious pluralism is sourced to multiple revelations, and for Rabbi Menahem Meiri it is a product of the morality is the major religions. Albo locates the roots of plurality in his very conception of religion. On one side, God is an immutable monad, so there is a fixed series of principles of faith with all of their logical entailments. On the other side, human beings constitute a multiplicity, with each nation having a unique character based on its natural environment and biological ancestry. To bring them together requires some allowance for variability within divine religion.

Albo then introduces a completely new idea: "Noahide law" is not a static body of laws but a dynamic religion that develops according to national temperament, ethical sensibilities, and environmental conditioning: "according to their respective national differences" [4]. The profound cultural variability between peoples determines the realization of Noahide law.

This is reminiscent of how Rabbi Abraham Isaac HaKohen Kook envisions the evolution of the Oral Torah: "We feel that the unique character of the national spirit... is what lends the Oral Torah its unique form."[2] Religions can be viewed as a kind of "Oral Torah" for the seven Noahide mitzvot. In the same way that there are seventy facets of the Torah, so the seventy nations each have their own interpretation and form of the seven mitzvot. The Jewish people do not define the mitzvot of the rest of humanity; it is the nations themselves that determine the character, parameters, and implementation of these laws.[3]

As much as he values other religions, Albo preserves the uniqueness of the Jewish people and Judaism:

---

2. *Shemona Kevatzim, Kovetz* 2:57.

3. In his explanation of the amoraic dispute about the Noahide law of *dinim* (establishing a judicial and/or legal system), Rabbi Moses Isserles (*Shut Rema* 10) explains that according to R. Yohanan, the scope of that law is established by the non-Jews themselves. It includes "observing the customary law of the land and justly judging between fellow citizens and foreigners." He emphasizes that "this is not according to the Jewish laws that Moses gave us at Sinai but is conventional law." Although

> There is no question that the nations would attain human
> flourishing through Noahide law, since it is divine, even if
> they did not flourish to the extent attained by the Israel-
> ites through the Torah. [As] our Rabbis said, "The pious
> of the nations of the world have a portion in the World to
> Come." (*Sefer HaIkkarim*, 1:25) [4]

Practically speaking, Albo does not fully legitimize Christianity and
Islam. Among other things, he theologically objects to Christianity's
belief in the trinity and Islam's belief in predestination. Even so, his
thought provides the foundation for others', especially his idea of human
diversity as the basis for religious multiplicity. Nearly half a millennium
later, Rabbi Elijah Benamozegh (1823–1900) writes about non-Jewish
religion:

> [T]his variety of forms, apart from the supreme unity
> to which it is subordinated, constitutes in its totality the
> universal religion. For the variety is not arbitrary or acci-
> dental, but something necessary and organic, with roots
> in the depths of human nature. [...] [T]he various other
> forms of religion, corresponding to differences of race and
> nationality, all participate in the Noahide Law, of which
> they form the specific varieties.[4]

The nations of the world lend their natural hues and shades to the religious spectrum, and together they comprise "Noahide law." Additionally, this religious diversity is not an ancient phenomenon but always
ongoing:

---

he limits this position to R. Yoḥanan, with whom R. Yitzḥak disagrees, and only to
one of the seven Noahide laws, they offer us a template for thinking about how the
seven Noahide laws can be defined in non-halakhic terms.

4. Ed. and trans., Maxwell Luria, *Israel and Humanity* (New York: Paulist Press, 1995),
315–316.

[Noahide law,] in its inevitable plurality, has a role which begins and ends on this earth, and has diverse variations which correspond to the diversity of race, place, and time.[5]

Another approach similar to Albo's can be found in the thought of Rabbi Kook, which will be treated in a later chapter. He attributes the differences between religions to the diversity within national identity. Conversion is problematic, in this conception, because it weakens the spirit of the people into whose bosom the person was born.

SOURCES

[1] *Sefer HaIkkarim*, 1:8 – **The difference between conventional and divine religion**
Conventional religion falls short of divine religion in various respects. The first is what we have said, that the conventional organizes human behavior to optimize the sociopolitical order, but it does not suffice to provide intellectual perfection – as we will explain in the continuation – so that the soul outlives the body. It cannot return to and repose in the land of the living from which it was taken, because [conventional religion] only covers good and bad. Divine religion does suffice for this, because it encompasses the two complements on which human perfection depends: character and intellect. It covers good and bad, and it distinguishes between truth and falsehood, which are intellectual opinions. This is what David was describing when he said, "The Torah of the Lord is perfect, returning the soul" (Ps. 19:8).[6] In other words, conventional religion is imperfect because it does not cover true opinions, but divine religion is perfect because it encompasses perfection of character and perfection of intellectual opinions, which are the two complements on which the perfection of the soul depends. For that reason, it returns the soul to God who gave it, to the place where it originally lived.

---

5. Ibid., 316.
6. *Meshivat nafesh* is usually translated along the lines of restoring life, but this translation accords with Albo's explanation in the immediate continuation.

[2] *Sefer HaIkkarim*, 1:20 – The giving of a divine religion must be widely publicized

According to our Rabbis, [the giving of the Torah at Sinai] was publicized to the entire world. They said: "'The Lord came from Sinai and shone forth to them from Seir; He appeared in Paran' (Deut. 33:2). What did He want in Seir and what did He want in Paran? It teaches that the Holy One brought the Torah around the entire world, but they didn't accept it, until the Jewish people accepted it, etc."[7] Now, there are seventy nations in the world, yet it only mentions Seir and Paran. It must not be referring specifically to Mount Seir and the Paran Desert, then, but to the entire world. That is to say, the Holy One foresaw that founders of religions would arise in Seir – the Edomites and their adherents – and in Paran – the Ishmaelites and their adherents, and these two nations from the seed of Abraham, first of the believers, encompass the entire world. He therefore publicized to them the giving of the Torah to the Jews, to demonstrate that the giving of a divine religion must be spread far and wide, and that any religion that does not enjoy such broadcasting is not truly divine.

[3] *Sefer HaIkkarim*, 1:25 – There can be multiple divine religions

What ought to be philosophically investigated now is whether there must necessarily be one divine religion for all of humanity or multiple. [...] Upon further consideration, one finds that although it is necessarily so with respect to the giver, it is not necessarily so with respect to the recipient. Human temperaments vary, whether due to the diversity of parental temperament or other factors, to the point that it is impossible for two people to have the same temperament or nature. [...] People are also different based on where they live, because the nature of lands differs based on the air, mountains, waters, and the like. [...] Since this diversity is inherent to the recipient and not the giver, it must concern matters pertaining to the recipient, namely the presumptions and conventions that prevail between people of certain localities regarding good and bad, for what is good to some is bad to others. But regarding the

---

7. Avoda Zara 2b.

general principles and their derivatives, which are all dependent upon the giver, it is impossible to conceive of any variability.

[4] *Sefer HaIkkarim,* 1:25 – Noahide law differs according to nation

For this reason you will find that although Noahide law and the Mosaic law differ on certain legal particulars – as will be discussed – they agree on the general matters from the giver's side. The two coexist: when Mosaic law could be found among the Israelites, Noahide law existed for all the nations. They varied according to geographic variability, meaning, the Land of Israel versus outside the Land, and also according to their respective national differences due to ancestry. There is no question that the nations would attain human flourishing through Noahide law, since it is divine, even if they did not flourish to the extent attained by the Israelites through the Torah. [As] our Rabbis said, "The pious of the nations of the world have a portion in the World to Come."

[5] *Sefer HaIkkarim,* 1:26 – Critique of certain Christian and Islamic principles of faith

What emerges from our discussion in this book is that the number of principles of the divine religion are three: the existence of God, the divine origin of the Torah, and divine recompense. One cannot conceive of a divine religion without them.

Under these three are derivative principles. If the fundamental principles are genera, these are only species. If one removes a derivative principle, the fundamental principle remains intact; if one removes a fundamental principle, all of its derivatives disappear, as we have explained. [...] The other religions that are called divine place other derivative principles under these fundamental ones, but if one removes any of them, their belief system collapses. Under "the existence of God" the Christians place the trinity and incarnation. These clearly contradict the principles that derive from the principle of God's existence. Under "divine recompense" they place the advent of the Messiah and resurrection of the dead, without which their religion could not exist. Likewise, under "divine providence" the Ishmaelites place fate (*al-qaḍā'*) and predestination (*al-qadar*), whose existence would remove free will and eliminate divine recompense. I do not count free will as one of the fundamental principles of divine religion despite it being necessary for it, because it does not flow from it being "divine" per se, but because it is logically presupposed by any code of conduct or law, be it human or divine. [...]

PART III:
WORLD RELIGIONS
IN MODERN JEWISH THOUGHT

Rabbi Jacob Emden: Christianity as a Positive Force of Noahide Religion

Assaf Malach

"A CONGREGATION FOR THE SAKE OF HEAVEN"

Rabbi Jacob Emden (1698–1776) was one of the greatest rabbis of the eighteenth century. As the son of the illustrious Rabbi Zvi Ashkenazi (known as *Ḥakham Tzvi*), Emden was known by the acronym Yaavetz, which stands for Jacob ben Zvi in Hebrew. His writings span the entire breadth of Torah learning and practice. Some notable, important works include: *Beit Yaakov* (originally titled *Ammudei HaShamayim*), a siddur rich with his insights on halakha, custom, and language; a work of responsa titled *She'eilat Yaavetz*; and a composition on *Shulḥan Arukh* called *Mor UKetzia*. Beyond his greatness in Torah, Emden was erudite and industrious. He owned a printing press and operated it singlehandedly, and even wrote what is considered to be the first rabbinic autobiography, and perhaps even the first autobiography worthy of the name in Hebrew.

Emden served for a few years as the rabbi of Emden in northern Germany, which lent his family their surname, but he subsequently returned to his birthplace of Altona in Prussia, where he lived until his death without holding any official rabbinic position. He is famous for his uncompromising positions on many issues, and he gave no quarter in his polemical offensives. One of his most famous running battles was with Rabbi Jonathan Eybeschütz, the chief rabbi of Altona-Hamburg-Wandsbek, whom he suspected of being a Sabbatean. He vigorously opposed any form of assimilation to the Christian majority – in dress, speech, cultural practices and pastimes, the study of philosophy, and more. Despite this, his writings have a consistently positive attitude toward Christianity and Islam. These religions, according to Emden, played a significant role in the eradication of idolatry, the dissemination of the correct theology, and the inculcation of ethical behavior. He attributes their success to them being "a congregation for the sake of Heaven," which the Mishna says "will endure in the end" [1]. They can be so characterized because they believe in and disseminate "correct religious tenets" such as divine Creation, reward and punishment, providence, prophecy, and revelation, and they adopt and teach "desirable character traits" [2–3].

Emden stands out among rabbinic heavyweights in emphasizing the positive religious foundation of these religions.[1] It is more than just searching for and finding halakhic leniencies to exclude them from the halakhic category of idolatry and lubricate the wheels of social and commercial interaction. Across his works, Emden examines these religions on their own merits, finding them meritorious. He goes so far as to call them faithful kin to Jews: "[they] are our brothers in believing in the Torah, prophecy, and other matters and in the good character traits they exhibit" [4].

The starting point for Emden is Rabbi Moses Maimonides's historical account in *Mishneh Torah*, in which Jesus and Muhammad are agents of the divine plan "to pave the way for the King Messiah."

---

1. For an expanded treatment of this, see Leeor Gottlieb, "Rabbi Jacob Emden's *Resen Matteh*: First and Second Edition with an Introduction, Textual Comparison, and Notes" [in Hebrew], in Benjamin-Ish Shalom and Amichai Berholz ed., *BeDarkhei Shalom: Studies in Jewish Thought Presented to Shalom Rosenberg* [in Hebrew] (Jerusalem: Beit Morasha, 2007), 295–321; David Sorotzkin, *Orthodoxy and Modern Disciplination: The Production of Jewish Tradition in Europe in Modern Times* [in Hebrew] (Bnei Brak: HaKibbutz HaMe'uhad, 2011), 279–348; Azriel Shohat, "The German Jews' Integration within their Non-Jewish Environment in the First Half of the 18th Century" [in Hebrew], *Zion* 21 (1956): 207–235.

Maimonides considers these religions mistakes, and it is only in God's sublime calculus that two wrongs somehow make a right. The seedlings they planted may be weeds, but they have done the hard work of loosening up the soil of humanity, so that it will be receptive to the true faith when the Messiah comes and reveals the errors of their ways. It is here that Emden breaks with Maimonides. He views Christianity and Islam as essentially positive because he argues that as they are right now, they contain many accurate beliefs and ethical traits that were learned from the Jews and then spread far and wide. He uses Maimonides's framework, but he substitutes rejection with glowing appraisal.

EARLY CHRISTIANITY AS NOAHIDE LAW

Emden's exact position is better understood through *Resen Matteh*, a unique work dedicated to exploring Christianity in depth. Published in 1758, it is based on a responsum he penned to the rabbinic leaders of the Council of the Four Lands a year prior, in which he justified turning in Frankists to the Christian authorities, even if it might endanger their lives. According to him, the spiritual affinity between Jews and Christian should bond them together in the struggle against the Frankists, who wreck the very foundations of religion and morality. This inspirational position retains its relevance to this day, when we ought to work together across religious lines against phenomena that are destructive to faith and morality. In addition to their continued applicability, Emden's words interest us as an innovative perspective on Christianity and its relationship to Judaism.

Throughout this composition, Emden analyzes passages from the Gospels and the rest of the Christian canon in great detail. His chief contention is that based on Christian Scripture, Jesus, Paul, and their disciples never intended to uproot the Torah from the Jews. In reality, they strengthened Jewish Torah observance and declared it forbidden for Jews to abrogate even a single jot or tittle from their Torah scroll. They intended to found a religion for non-Jews that was based on the seven Noahide laws, and from the point of view of the Torah their accomplishments were praiseworthy: "He had come to establish a religion for the nations going forward, and even this was not new. It is essentially the seven Noahide laws that the nations had forgotten which Christ's apostles reestablished" [5]. The idea of supersession, under which the Jewish people would be replaced by believers in the Church, was a ploy to help Christianity find a warm welcome among non-Jews, but it was not the aspirational goal of early Christianity.

Similar claims about the intentions of the first Christians were raised centuries before Emden in the environment of medieval religious polemics. Emden points out that the outstanding Algerian rabbi Simeon ben Zemah Duran (1361–1444) in his *Magen Avot* made observations similar to his. One of these was that medieval Christianity had become misaligned with the vision of its ancient founders.[2] Unlike Duran, however, Emden advances a historical argument that Jesus "brought a great deal of good unto this world" [5]. He reinforced Jewish observance in the Torah, and he ensured the instruction of the seven Noahide mitzvot to the nations of the world. While the positive portrait of Christianity that Emden paints is situated in the context of his fight against the Frankists, it is consistent with what he writes in non-polemically charged compositions, and it itself was reprinted in two editions after the polemic had subsided. His was a principled position and he stood by it. We even have his own word to take for it, because in *Resen Matteh* he says, "I regularly say [this] (not as a sycophant, because that doesn't suit me…thank God for making me a righteous Jew, creating me upright…I am of the remnant of Israel that doesn't speak falsehoods or utter deceptions)."[3]

Exactly how historically accurate Emden's account is deserves the kind of scrutiny that must be left for another forum. It has been sufficiently established, though, that in its infancy Christianity was a predominantly Jewish religious movement that viewed itself as an interpretation and fulfillment of Judaism and Jewish Scripture. Only gradually did it work itself free from the framework of Judaism, and the stages of this process are debated by scholars. But regardless of historical precision, it is a signal contribution to Jewish-Christian relations. The primary identification of Christianity with the spread of monotheism and Noahide law is an unusual position that has real-world consequences because

---

2. See *Magen Avot*, vol. 2, ch. 4 (Jerusalem: Mekhon HaKetav, 2007), 196–198.

3. *Resen Matteh*, 307.

by highlighting the positive elements Christianity shares with Judaism, it creates a basis for an affirmative Jewish attitude toward Christianity.

GENERAL ATTITUDE TOWARD NON-JEWS AND CHRISTIANITY

In other works, Emden talks about Christianity and Islam in words that complement those in *Resen Matteh*. He mentions the fact that clergymen from both faiths defended Jews over the course of history, and he points out that the holy texts of Judaism were printed in Christendom, thereby providing Jews access to them and preserving them from oblivion. Jews owe Christians a debt of gratitude on this score [1].

In a few places, Emden addresses the status of contemporary Christians, particularly owing to their belief in the Trinity. He proposes various reasons they are not considered polytheists. This brings him into accord with many halakhists who permit partnerships with non-Jews even if they might take an oath in the name of their gods, because non-Jews are not enjoined from theologically associating God with other entities.[4] Sometimes, he explicitly applies this reasoning of medieval decisors to Christians. At other times, he rejects this possibility because he reasons that theological association is only possible for a pure monotheist who associates the one God with a constellation or lower representative being during worship. Since Christianity does not have a pure monotheistic conception of God, its belief is more problematic than association. Nevertheless, he does not go so far as to call Christians idolaters, because their worldview is not fundamentally polytheistic. Even when they practice idolatrous rites, that is only as a cultural convention without any substantive identification with the pagan view of matters. As the Talmud says, "Non-Jews outside the Land are not idol worshippers but follow the customs of their parents."[5] He then adds, "It is sufficient that the Jews do not consider them idolaters" [2]. He seems to be leaning on the Tosafists' opinion that common practice is not to

---

4. See, e.g., Rema, *Oraḥ Ḥayim* 156.
5. Ḥullin 13b.

apply the laws concerning idolaters to Christians because "we are certain that the non-Jews among us do not worship idolatry."[6]

Emden declares it an obligation to preserve the physical and financial wellbeing of non-Jews and prevent any injury or loss to them, just as one must do so for Jews. He even goes so far as to declare that all non-Jews – and not only the pious among them – have a portion in the World to Come. The only ones barred entry from the heavenly gates are of a kind with Jews: the rebellious who sin with their bodies [2–3].[7] He asserts that this would even apply to the non-Jews of antiquity and when Israel was a sovereign nation in its land, so it would definitely apply today when the Christian nations are close to us in various ways, "protect us so we can observe our Torah, believe in the giving of the Torah, observe a number of mitzvot, and have desirable character traits" [3].[8] This leads him to conclude that Jews must pray for the welfare of those nations among whom we live [3, 6]. This is not to prevent anti-Jewish sentiment. It is our duty to pray even for "alien peoples," so we certainly must beseech God on behalf of "Esau's progeny, who are, after all, our brothers" [6].[9] Notably, Emden does not invoke generic sentiments about the value of all human beings and the proper attitude to the rest of humanity, nor does he appeal to the more limited logic of preventing acrimonious relations. No, he sings the praises of contemporary

---

6. *Tosafot*, Avoda Zara 2a, s.v. *asur*.

7. Emden makes this claim in a responsum to a medical student (*She'eilat Yaavetz*, 1:41), where he discusses the prohibition of profiting from a non-Jew's corpse and estate. He speaks of "correct religious tenets" professed by his fellow Christians and analyzes the issues of theological association.

8. *Derashat Hali Khetem* deals with theft from and injury to a non-Jew, both in general and specifically Christians.

9. This responsum (*She'eilat Yaavetz* 1:144) discusses a phrase from the Rosh HaShana liturgy, "mercifully remember the binding of Isaac today for his progeny." *Shulḥan Arukh* (*Oraḥ Ḥayim* 591:7) criticizes those who add two words of clarification that yield "for the progeny of Jacob," because they are altering the sagaciously crafted and accepted prayer rite. A number of modern authorities think that even the original refers only to Jacob's offspring, but Emden believes it applies even to the nations of the world, for whom we ought to always pray, and especially to Esau's descendants who are our relatives.

non-Jews, and the lyrics cover their religion and morality. That is why the faithful ought to be treated like brothers and sisters.

EMDEN'S POSITION AND THE CHURCH TODAY

Emden was neither the first nor last halakhic decisor to place Christians in a special category.[10] Three aspects of his viewpoint stand out as worthy of special attention. First, he chooses to see the good in Christianity and Islam. He maximizes the importance of their monotheistic faith and moral character. The fact that sometimes they have failed to live up to their own religious ideals does not taint their core goodness. Second, by claiming that it never intended to do away with the Torah for Jews and aimed to spread the seven Noahide mitzvot for non-Jews, he constructs a historical model of Christianity that legitimizes it from a Jewish perspective. Third, he engages Christianity deeply on the home turf of its holy books. Emden's methodology and approach set an important precedent for us today in terms of the possibilities of discourse and kinship between Judaism and the other monotheistic faiths.

Given the dramatic developments of the Catholic's Church's position on the Jewish people, Emden's views take on increased importance.[11] In 1965, Vatican II produced "the Declaration on the Relation of the Church with Non-Christian Religions" within the framework of the document called *Nostra Aetate* (In Our Time). It absolved the Jews of all blame for the death of Jesus and expressed the Church's reservations about labeling the Jews rejected or cursed. Even so, the details of this complex text became the subject of intense debate and multiple interpretations. In recent decades, the Church furthered this new approach, under which Jews are "the beloved elder brother of the Church of the original Covenant, never broken and never to be broken." Christianity did not completely supersede Judaism and invalidate the divine designation of Jews as the "chosen people." A document produced by the

---

10. For his successors, see the next chapter.

11. See Dina Porat, Karma Ben Johanan, and Ruth Braude, eds., *In Our Time: Documents and Articles on the Catholic Church and the Jewish People in the Wake of the Holocaust* [in Hebrew] (Tel Aviv: Tel Aviv University, 2015).

Vatican in 2015, titled "The Gifts and the Calling of God are Irrevocable," exemplifies this new view. Astonishingly, the current position of the Catholic Church on the founding principles of Christianity fits Emden's reading of them very well.

As a final thought, there are significant parallels between Emden's thinking about Christianity and Rabbi Nathaniel b. Rabbi Fayyumi's about Islam, discussed in an earlier chapter devoted to Fayyumi. Both engaged with these religions on their own terms, reading their sacred texts carefully, interpreting their founders' intentions historically, and observing the practices of their adherents keenly. What they discovered are forces of good that have spread Jewish beliefs throughout the world. They offer us a perch from which to identify the positive in the monotheistic faiths, without diminishing the singularity of Judaism and the Jews even one iota.

SOURCES

[1] *Leḥem Shamayim,* Avot 4:11 – Christianity and Islam as congregations for the sake of Heaven[12]

Any congregation that is for the sake of Heaven will endure in the end, etc. One can challenge this from the two sects that have increased exceedingly upon the face of the earth, filling it from one end of the earth to the other, whose congregations have flourished and endured for many years and which still take new territories to spread their rule from ocean to ocean. How can they both be right if they disagree with each other, and when they both disagree with us? Aside from them there are mighty and old nations that do not share the beliefs of our three religions, and which are spread out across the three continents of the world, where they enjoy great peace and prosperity and live securely. Surely there can be no proof from them! God divided them up on the earth when He gave the nations their inheritance and set the borders of peoples.[13] Obviously, the Tanna was not speaking of congregations that have no connection to us but to the new, distinct faiths that emerged from us and built their

---

12. Printed in *Etz Avot* (Sighet, 1912).
13. Paraphrasing Deut. 32:8.

spiritual edifice upon the foundation of our divine religion. Since each of them contradicts the other, one is of necessity untrue. One can therefore deduce that their congregation is *not* for the sake of Heaven. How, then, can I explain how they endure coterminously, and yet endure they both have, from then until now? And since the Tanna does not specify the parameters of "in the end," it isn't reasonable that he meant the end of the world, because then what would be the point? Heaven and earth will cease to exist, the fabric of existence having worn away.

Do not be perplexed by this matter, because it was orchestrated from on high; God had only good intentions (besides, the Tanna's statement does not apply to those entire nations that are not considered "congregations"). Simply understood, there is no contradiction to this mishna: vis-à-vis the nations of the world who came before them, who did not recognize the one God and worshipped wood and stone, who did not acknowledge His omnipotence in this world nor reward and punishment in the next, their congregation is also considered "for the sake of Heaven." They publicize knowledge of God far and wide, so that people know: there is a sovereign over heaven and earth who rules, manages providently, rewards and punishes (at least for what is forbidden by reason, and most of them accepted the seven mitzvot, aside from the many good attributes that they have adopted), makes those who are good, upright, and extremely self-sanctified prophesy, so that through them He gives just laws and statutes by which to live – and many other principles of faith that they received from us. Since even those in distant lands and at the end of the earth have certainly been informed, as Heaven wishes, of many of these precious matters, their congregation has endured thus far, for they have rendered glory to the Lord God of Israel and to His Torah. They have proclaimed His glory among peoples who knew Him not and had not heard tell of Him. Therefore, the reward of their having the profit of Heaven at heart shall be paid equitably, for the Loving One desires the heart.[14]

As for the two clans [among whom] God chose to humble many peoples and yoke them to the beliefs and principles necessary for civilization and a functional society, He did not make them submit to the

---

14. Sanhedrin 106b.

yoke of Torah because they did not receive it from their ancestors. They did not stand on Mount Sinai, nor were they commanded in it (they also were not slaves in Egypt, and so they are not obligated in the 613 mitzvot). If they theologically associate the name of Heaven with something else, they do not do so out of rebellion; they are continuing the practice of their parents, and the Sages have already said that they are not commanded about theological association.

They have also done the remnant of Israel a great favor. If not for them, we would not have had a chance among the people who hate the Jewish people out of religious jealousy. God has been with us and cultivated scholars of Edom and Ishmael who defend us in every generation due to the shared divine Torah, upon which they have built up their edifices. Although many of the dimwitted have tried to wipe us out without a trace and attacked us savagely through their libels, the enlightened, especially the Christian theologians who pursue the truth, have stood up to them – to all who would harm us – like lions. Since we remain steadfast in our observance of the divine Torah, they have found us blameless. They therefore protect us, and this shall be counted a kindness for them. As our Sages said, "Either in Your shadow or in the shadow of Esau's descendants."[15]

Know that the enlightened Christians not only study and expound the Written Torah, thereby spreading its glory throughout the world, but they have even defended and protected the Oral Torah, a sure pillar for those who stumble. When wicked, sinful people of ours plotted to get rid of the Talmud once and for all, fine defenders of theirs met the challenge and saved it, as is written in *Sefer HaHayyim*:

> I heard from the local elders that in days past some wicked kinsmen of ours tried to inflict physical and reputational harm upon our precious treasure (the Talmud), and they planned to consign it to the fire, on account of what their puny intellects found perplexing and consequently scorned. They nearly carried out their evil plan but God inspired

---

15. Gittin 17a.

one Christian scholar to stand before the authorities and
the public and defend the holy book....

[...] Some of their scholars spoke well of the Jewish people, their belief,
and their Torah study, especially Pope Gregory and his disciple Augus-
tine, Sextus, Justinus, Reuchlin, Bernhardus, and many others like them,
who saved the Jewish people from traps set for them by their enemies
and stopped many persecutions. Go see for yourself God's wondrous
deed on our behalf in this exile. The Torah would have been nearly forgotten if not for the many great Christian nobles who made a financial
outlay and printed all the holy books in our possession: Bible, Mishna
and Talmud, Midrash, codes, grammars, kabbalistic and ethical works,
responsa, daily regimens, maxims and riddles, wordplay and poetic writing, natural and other philosophy. In general, they have published all the
major works to aesthetic perfection, and if not for this, not even one in a
thousand would be able to access one of these holy and precious works.
We certainly owe them our gratitude, and praise the Lord for sending
them before us to sustain us. This is sufficient for our purposes here.

[2] *She'eilat Yaavetz* 1:41 – Non-Jews (Christians) today are not idolaters

This is certainly the case for these nations that possess religious beliefs
and laws, and that believe in a Creator who manages providently and
who rewards and punishes, as well as in other correct religious tenets.
Even though they desired many deities, they are not enjoined about this.
As our Rabbis said, a Noahide is not commanded against theological
association (and thus does it say, "that the Lord your God allotted for
all of the nations" [Deut. 4:19], even though the elders needed to prevent theological misinterpretation).[16]

One still needs to look into this matter more. It seems that one
who theologically associates "something else" does the following: they
leave the divine unity completely intact and acknowledge that there is
a *Cause of causes*, the King of kings, the Holy One, but they introduce
intermediaries in the running of the lower world – like a planet, angel,

---

16. See Megilla 9a.

or any of the many other agents of divine governance – into their worship by association, saying that it is the King's desire to share His glory with the servants that minister before Him, and that the servant of the King is like a king. This was the opinion of most idolaters since time immemorial. None of these increased the number of divine domains like the dualists and those like them, who speak of multiple beginnings and distinct divine domains while claiming that they comprise a unity. With their tongues they lie about Him, saying whatever they dream up – Heaven forfend! One can say that they do not meet the definition of theological associators, because those who multiply supreme gods are the worst kind of heretics. By choosing more than one, they have nothing at all, as is self-evident and cannot be elaborated further here. (Unfortunately, from the day that the Torah's secrets were disclosed to outsiders, they in their muddled thinking were able to strongly reinforce their positions. God's honor, by contrast, lies in concealment.) Nevertheless, it is sufficient that the Jews do not consider them idolaters. The Rabbis said, "Non-Jews outside the Land are not idol worshippers, but follow the customs of their parents."[17] For that reason, their lives are precious to us, even if we were to rule over them and they would be our subjects in our land. They said (even about full-fledged idolaters) that non-Jews are not lowered [into a pit].[18] Undoubtedly, outside the Land, where we take refuge in their shadow, we are also obligated to protect them to the best of our ability and to save them from death and any financial loss or injury. Even safeguarding their money must be dear to us. […] This is all straightforward. One may therefore not derive benefit from their corpse, like that of any other Noahide, because they are no worse off for observing the seven Noahide laws. And if they transgress them they are punished, but ultimately they have a spiritual rectification after they endure their punishment. They have a level and portion in the World to Come that is suited for them. They have already said that the pious of the nations of the world have a share in the World to Come. They said that the sinners of the nations of the world are judged for generations and generations only with respect to the rebellious who sin with their

---

17. Ḥullin 13b.
18. Avoda Zara 26a–b.

bodies, which is also what they said regarding Jews.[19] The rebellious sinners of neither are banished forever; they have a spiritual rectification, and are not akin to the animal whose soul is completely obliterated. [...]

[3] *Derashat Ḥali Khetem*, 27a – Stealing from a non-Jew is prohibited, especially today when world religions are reformed[20]

I must also inform you that there is no distinction between Jew and non-Jew regarding the prohibition against stealing and theft. Parenthetically, I should mention here what I myself heard this week (when I delivered this sermon). A certain non-Jew had wicked plans for the Jews, because they make the blessing every day, "that He did not make me a non-Jew." He said that the Jews do not esteem the non-Jew, but treat their life, property, and possessions as free for the taking. I said that this is utter nonsense. [...] The point of this blessing is that non-Jews are not commanded in 613 mitzvot like we, who went out of Egypt, are. They are therefore also not commanded to rest on Shabbat and the festivals, as we are. This is similar to the intent behind our blessings, "that He did not make me a slave" and "that He did not make me a woman": a slave is only obligated in mitzvot on the level of a woman, and a woman is only obligated in mitzvot that are not time-bound, as she is subsumed under her husband who rules over her. Nevertheless, they are as dear to us as ourselves. The same is true of the non-Jew. We have already concluded from the Talmud that stealing from a non-Jew is prohibited, and this refers even to those ancient peoples who did not know God, and even when they were under our thumb in our land. And these nations, under whose protection we take refuge, protect us so that we can observe our Torah, believe in the giving of the Torah, observe a number of mitzvot, and have desirable character traits, and we must pray for their welfare, as it is written, "And seek the welfare of the city to which I have exiled you [and pray for it to the Lord], for through its welfare shall you have welfare" (Jer. 29:7). For even regarding the ancient nations among whom we lived, the Sages commanded us to support their poor, visit their sick,

---

19. Rosh HaShana 17a.
20. *Derashat Ḥali Khetem* is printed in *Derush Tefillat Yesharim* (Krakow, 1921).

and accompany and bury their dead, so it is all the more true regarding these nations who are our lords (even regarding the ancient nations, who did not deal kindly with the Jews and had no commonality in Torah or character, the Torah indicated to us that they are inhabitants of that land and called them lords [...]), that we Jews are supposed to submit to them and not – God forbid – even consider stealing from them or wronging them in any way at all. If you act in this way, my brothers, I promise you that you will be successful in this world and the next one. You shall have everything you want in your lifetime. I shall watch and rejoice, and it shall be a balm for my pain. That will be my reward.

[4] *Derashat Ḥalie Khetem*, 30a – The host nations are "our brothers" who have "good character traits"

[...] All of this applies to the ancient nations that had no connection to us whatsoever. It goes without saying that regarding the nations in whose shadow we take refuge, who are our brothers in believing in the Torah, prophecy, and other matters, and in the good character traits they exhibit, and who have not wronged us but – to the contrary – defend us in our observance of the Torah, regarding them we undoubtedly have an obligation to take care and watch over their property and possessions as if they were our own.... I have elaborated on this further in other places.

[5] *Resen Matteh* – Christianity is a good religion for the world that spreads the seven Noahide laws among the nations[21]

[...] Even the nations of the world set themselves restrictions after the Flood. This is especially true of the Christians, who added additional restrictions to abstain even from that which is permitted to a Jew, even what is not considered an incestual relation for us and the Torah allowed. They do not allow polygamy, and a wife's sister and her other relations remain prohibited even after her death. They are careful not to swear that something is true and to avoid even a hint of theft. They have desirable character traits and upright morals; the pious keep themselves from revenge, hatred, and causing any harm to their enemy. How fortunate

---

21. The text is taken from Gottlieb, "*Resen Matteh,*" and the angle brackets indicate material from the earlier edition.

both they and we are, when they treat us as their religion dictates. <For they are commanded in their Gospels, "If anyone strikes you on the right cheek, turn the other also"²² [...] They have many similar practices of piety. If they would fulfill those religious mandates, they would command high praise, and then we would certainly be happy and successful to the highest degree in our exile among them; and then we would certainly not have thousands upon thousands of our holy people killed – their blood spilled like water – burned, executed in cruel and unusual ways, and buried alive. [...] If only they would do as they are bidden, which would genuinely be best for us ... > [...]

It is well established that Christ and his disciples, especially Paul, exhorted observance of the Torah, saying that all the circumcised are bound together in it. [...] Indeed, according to the authors of the Gospels, no Jew is permitted to abandon the Torah. [...] On this, they point out an internal contradiction regarding Paul, because in Acts of the Apostles (ch. 15) he mentions that he circumcised his disciple Timothy <who was Greek (Acts 16:3)>. This is a very knotty problem: his own action contradicts his statements that circumcision was a temporary commandment to last only until the advent of the Messiah, since it was performed after the coming of Christ. Realize and accept the truth no matter who says it: this clearly shows that Christ and his apostles did not come to abrogate the Torah, God forbid. It is written in Matthew (ch. 10) that Christ said:

> Do not think that I have come to abolish the Torah or the Prophets; I have come not to abolish but to fulfill. For truly I tell you, until heaven and earth pass away, not one letter, not one stroke of a letter, will pass from the Torah until all is accomplished. Therefore, whoever breaks one of the least of these commandments and teaches others to do the same will be called least in the kingdom of heaven.... (Matt. 5:17–19)

---

22. Matthew 5:39.

[...] This resolves the contradiction among the words of Christ himself, for in some parts of the Gospels, learned Christians understand that he has come to give them a new Torah in place of the Mosaic Torah. How then can he explicitly say that he has only come to fulfill it? It is as I have said: the authors of the Gospels never even entertained the thought that Christ had come to completely abrogate the Jewish religion. Rather, he had come to establish a religion for the nations going forward, and even this was not new. It is in actuality the seven Noahide laws that the nations had forgotten, which Christ's apostles reestablished. [...] For the nations of the world he set down the seven Noahide laws, in which they have already been obligated since God created humankind. That is why he outlawed idols, incestual relations, [consumption of] blood and strangled animals, and he forbade them circumcision and Shabbat, all according to the law of our Torah through rabbinic interpretation. [...] Therefore, Christ's disciples chose for those nations that are not converting to Judaism immersion in lieu of circumcision. [...] They made them a remembrance of Shabbat on Sunday <and they did all this wisely, so that they would not end up transgressing the interpretation of the Oral Torah: someone who is not Jewish nor voluntarily converting may not be circumcised nor rest on Shabbat. [...] Thus, they do not perform the immersion according to the law of immersion in the Mosaic Torah, so that they do not add on to the words of the Torah. They chose it only as a gesture of similitude. [...] Likewise, they make Sunday into Shabbat, not to rest completely but to generate a remembrance of the first day on which the world was made, to bear the Creation of the world in their consciousness and mind, to know that the palace has a Ruler who fashioned and built it as He saw fit, and that if it pleases Him he can tear it down and obliterate it in a moment. [...]

The truth is plain as day: the sole intent of the authors of the Gospels was to make more attractive the allowance for the nations to eat unclean animals, for it is assuredly permissible for them. Their aim was constructive, so that they would not find accepting part of the Torah, the seven mitzvot, too difficult, and refuse to listen to them. They stressed this so that they would believe in the Torah and prophecy and willingly accept whatever they commanded them, and leave the Jews alone and assist them in keeping the Torah, receiving joint reward for this. [...]

This is truly what the founder of their laws intended. [...] Even though the simple reading of certain passages in the Gospels sounds like they intend to vex us, this too was to appeal to the nations. [...] All this was a stratagem so that the nations would not be jealous of the Jewish people and their Torah. They made it seem as if the Torah had become obsolete with the rejection of the Jewish people as God's nation, and they would take their place through grace. They invented all of this to benefit the nations, so that they would not be like the beasts of the field and animals of the forest.... [...] Subsequently, the masses were seduced by poorly informed priests, and as time passed alien ideas became entrenched because they didn't understand the plan of their predecessors (who concealed their true intentions) nor fully grasp their intention. They are very far off the mark, so they despise the Jewish people. [...]

Based on this truthful analysis, I regularly say (not as a syco-phant...) that Christ brought a great deal of good unto this world.... He strengthened the Mosaic Torah with all his might, as explained above and which cannot be denied, and none of our sages spoke more full-throatedly about the necessary eternal existence of the Torah. At the very same time, he did much good for the nations of the world (so long as they do not upend his good intent for them, as some fanatics have done, failing to grasp what the authors of the Gospels meant and repaying good with evil).

<What I have written here is not my first foray into this matter to open people's eyes. I have already been vocal about this. [...] I spoke at length about enlightened Christians who have helped the Jewish people observe the Torah and practice their religion. [...] These are also the words of Rabbi Moses [Maimonides] at the end of *Hilkhot Melakhim*, where he writes that Christ and the prophet of the Ishmael-ites came to pave the way for the true redeemer, may he come speedily, in our days. After these words were printed, I was shown a book titled *Milhemet Hova* printed in Constantinople. It contains a quote from the responsa of Rabbi Simeon ben Zemah Duran about the Gospels. Like me, he demonstrates clearly from the Gospels themselves what I have demonstrated in this booklet by my own lights: that the Christians mis-construed Jesus's intention in this, that he never intended to abrogate Judaism for the Jews, that he and his disciples fulfilled it; that he only

wanted to strengthen it and present the seven mitzvot to the nations. He says all of this, and it aligns fully with my own conclusions. A minor prophecy was placed in my mouth and on my pen, and I am fortunate for it. He, however, goes into even more depth. [...]

[6] *She'eilat Yaavetz*, 1:144 – Praying for the welfare of the nations every day and on Rosh HaShana

Regardless, I have a question about the rule itself, as I find it perplexing: What is the definitive source that one may not include the progeny of Esau in this prayer, so that this is even a question? In fact, we recite something similar: "And you lovingly remembered Noah, etc. Therefore let his memory come before you to increase his descendants, etc." Is there anyone who says that the descendants of Noah are not non-Jews? The progeny of Esau are included, too. And this [prayer] is even more problematic, since all the non-Jewish nations are included, even those not of the Patriarchs' stock, yet the Jewish people themselves do not seem to be included, as they learned explicitly: One who said "*Konam* regarding Noahides" is permitted to derive benefit from Jews.[23] In the same way that we are not exacting regarding this formulation, since Jews are not explicitly excluded, so too we are not concerned if it sounds like Esau's progeny are part of "the progeny of Isaac."

To the contrary, it is actually better this way, because we already pray for them on a daily basis (as I have written in my glosses on *Birkat HaMinim*, see there at length), and we definitely should on the holy Day of Remembrance. Since we pray even on behalf of those unknown peoples and non-Jew idolaters who have no connection to us, we should say as much for Esau's progeny, who are, after all, our brothers. In my humble opinion, this is an unnecessary inference and the shorter version is fine in every respect. One should not alter it in any way.

[7] *Ammudei Shamayim, Birkat HaMalshinim* – More on the religious state of contemporary nations

The *minim* are Epicureans, so named after Epicurus the Greek, may the name of the wicked rot, who denied divine providence and considered

---

23. See Mishna Nedarim 3:10.

the world a free-for-all, without judgment or judge – God forbid. [...] Contemplate the wonders of the Perfect Intellect, who caused His holy spirit to rest upon the composers of our prayers, for He desires the prayer of the righteous: since that time, nearly all of these sects have disappeared from the world, to the extent that they have no known sect in the world, only individuals who hide their beliefs and act under the cover of darkness, slinking about in the gloom. Nowadays, the major nations believe in divine providence and promote monotheism. The prayer is still necessary, though, because of the wicked offshoots that remain, so that they do not strike root and spread their poison and bitterness. [...]

Modern Halakhic Authorities on Christianity as a Commendable Religion

Assaf Malach

There is a trend among medieval Ashkenazic halakhists to distinguish the Christianity of their day from the idolatry condemned by the Sages, which results in leniencies in social interaction and business relationships. The position of Rabbi Jacob Emden discussed in the previous chapter is exceptional in its innovative reading of early Christianity, but it is essentially a continuation of this medieval halakhic discourse. In the present chapter, we will look at an array of halakhic sources that predate and postdate Emden's definition of Christians and Muslims as "our brothers in believing in the Torah, prophecy, and other matters, and in the good character traits they exhibit."[1] Some of the latter reflect the actual influence of Emden's position on the major religions as fulfilling the seven Noahide mitzvot and his definition of their adherents as "the pious of the nations of the world."

---

1. *Derashat Ḥali Khetem*, 30a.

For purposes of clarity, here is a typology of lenient approaches toward Christianity:

1. Halakhic rulings that require us to seek the welfare of non-Jews and not cause them any physical or financial harm. This is for one of two reasons: they act on behalf of our welfare so we must show gratitude, or we are concerned about provoking hostility.

2. Halakhic rulings on the devotion of contemporary Christians. There are two claims here: they practice religion because it is the cultural norm rather than out of a sense of devotion, or they are not knowledgeable about their religion.

3. Halakhic rulings or statements about Christianity itself that isolate certain of its correct elements of belief in God, the Exodus, or fundamental principles of religion and morality. Sometimes these are used to characterize it (and Islam) as a force for good in the world and as essential to its ultimate redemption. This position is often bundled with the claim that non-Jews are not enjoined from theological association, so their beliefs do not cross into idolatry.

4. Avowals that Christianity and Islam fulfill Noahide law, and that their faithful ought to be considered the pious of the nations of the world or as having the status of *ger toshav* (resident alien). This exceeds the accentuation of select positive aspects, commending the entire religion for esteem.

This chapter chronologically traces positions of the third and fourth types, which go beyond loosening the strictures on non-Jewish religion and view it as essentially beneficial.

* * *

There is a serious methodological problem in interpreting the extant sources on this issue. In the Middle Ages, Jews engaged in limited self-censorship of manuscripts in the wake of the burning of the Talmud and various disputations. By the sixteenth century, however, the advent of the printing press turned this into a widespread phenomenon. In the 1550s, under papal direction, copies of the Talmud and various other Hebrew manuscripts were consigned to the flames in massive numbers – nearly 12,000 – in Venice and Cremona. After the Council of Trent (1554), a list of prohibited books that required emendation was publicized, which led to the adoption of a gamut of practices and institutions that were highly localized. To take one example, every Hebrew book published required the approbation of three rabbis and the appointment of a censor acceptable to both the relevant Jewry and the crown. As Jewish publishing shifted from Italy to Poland and Russia, censorship shifted its focus from statements perceived to be against non-Jewish rule more than against the official or majority religion. The product of all this was self-censorship or declarations of fealty to the regime in the front matter of Hebrew books.[2]

One cannot easily tell what to make of the swearing of allegiance to the government or professions of religious tolerance that preface Jewish works from modernity. Do they reflect the true position of the authors and printers, or were they included to placate the censor and avoid reprisals by the regime? There is no simple answer, so this chapter follows a general rule. Brief, pro-government pieces (half a page or less) that emphasize the need to honor the government and avoid provoking hostility, or that claim that non-Jews today are merely carrying on their traditions, have been excluded.[3] If an author has dedicated

---

2. See Amnon Raz-Krakotzkin, *The Censor, The Editor, and the Text: The Catholic Church and the Shaping of the Jewish Canon in the Sixteenth Century*, trans. Jackie Feldman (Philadelphia: University of Pennsylvania Press, 2007).

3. An example of such an excluded text is found at the beginning of *Noda BiYehuda, Mahadura Kamma*, by Rabbi Ezekiel Landau (chief rabbi of Prague in the 18th century): "The author says: Everyone knows that I would offer words of warning and reproof in most of my sermons to be exceedingly careful to respect the non-Jews of our time. We take refuge in their lands and countries and must pray for the welfare of the kings and ministers and their armies, for the welfare of the state and its citizens. We must never return their favor, when they let us live and survive in their land, with ingratitude. I also constantly warn not to rob or steal, stressing that there is no difference between the money of Jews and non-Jews when it comes to "Do

coherent thought pieces or halakhic treatments of the status of modern non-Jews, or reiterate their position in multiple places, their words have been included. Again, the focus here is on the third and fourth, more fundamental approaches to Christianity as a major contribution to the world and to the spread of monotheism among non-Jewish nations.

* * *

Below are quotations from many modern halakhists who adopted a positive outlook – to varying degrees – on Christianity. First and foremost among them is the Rema (Rabbi Moses Isserles), who followed

---

not steal" (Lev. 19:13). [...] So you see it is prohibited to rob or steal from a non-Jew. This is all the more true of non-Jews today, in whose midst we live, who believe in the fundamental principles of faith: they believe in the Creation of the world, the prophecy of the prophets, and all the miracles written in the Torah and the Prophets. It is abundantly clear to us that we must honor and revere them. I thereby declare – and this declaration applies not only to this work but to any work, wherever it may be, that denigrates idolaters, gentiles, Cutheans, or whatever other term they may use – do not make the mistake of interpreting it as about the nations of our time, for whoever does so errs, and their interpretation is not in accordance with the Torah. The intention is to the ancient nations who believed in the zodiac and stars, like the Sabean sect mentioned by Maimonides in his *Guide*, for those nations were heretics and sectarians who did not acknowledge the Creation of the world, and denied all the miracles and prophecy. Therefore, let everyone be very careful about these matters and inscribe them in their heart lest they forget them." Landau treats Christianity positively here, but the context is unambiguously apologetic.

This illuminates a passage from the *Penei Yehoshua* of Rabbi Jacob Joshua Falk (rabbi of Lvov, Berlin, and Frankfurt in the 18th century), located at the end of his talmudic novellae on Bava Metzia: "Everyone knows that whenever any of the books – the Talmud, codes, and other similar works – mentions idolaters and the like, they all intend the same thing: those nations that were actually idolatrous. But those nations among whom we take refuge are not included therein, and not only is there an absolute prohibition to steal from, financially oppress, or mislead them, but we are warned against this just as we are against doing so to a Jew, as Maimonides wrote and *Shulḥan Arukh* codified. Even more than that, we are obligated to pray for the welfare of the kingdom and the ministers. [...] Everyone in all the communities that have been under my leadership knows that I publicly warn the people about all this in my sermons." This positivity here is boiled down to the absolute minimum, so apologetics appears to have been Falk's chief consideration. There are many more texts that fit both of these molds.

medieval predecessors and even Rabbi the Yosef Karo, who ruled that the Christians of their time were not full-fledged idolaters. In one place, the Rema does more than remove the stigma of idolatry and highlights a positive element in Christianity: "Their intention is for the Maker of heaven and earth, it is only that they associate the name of Heaven with something else" [2a].

Rabbi Eliezer Ashkenazi is more expansive and states his opposition to any hostile intent directed toward Christians or Muslims. He believes that when we recite the passage in the Haggada, "Pour out Your wrath on the nations that did not know You," we are not to have them in mind. This is because "all the non-Jews among whom the Jewish nation has been scattered evidently know about the Exodus, believe in it, and understand its significance." In order to "keep ourselves from sinning to God," we must "never curse those who know His name, only idolaters and those who do not believe in the Creation of the world" [3]. Relying on this source, Rabbi Moses Rivkes writes that the prohibition to save idolaters from mortal danger does not apply to the non-Jews of his time. He implies that he considers Christians (and perhaps Muslims) of his time to be the pious of the nations of world that have a portion in the World to Come [4]. Rabbi Moses Hagiz expresses similar sentiments [5].

Among those who lived after Rabbi Jacob Emden, a good number followed in his footsteps and considered Christianity to be fulfilling the seven Noahide mitzvot. Rabbi Elazar Fleckeles describes Christians as "those who fulfill His will, i.e., the nations that keep the seven mitzvot and are called pious" [6] and states that they have a portion in the World to Come. Rabbi Israel Lipschitz writes much the same [7].

Rabbi Zvi Hirsch Chajes expands this further and includes Christians in the category of resident aliens (*ger toshav*): "There is no doubt that they have the halakhic status of resident aliens. And those who observe the seven mitzvot because they were commanded them by God through Moses are like the pious of the nations of the world who have a portion in the World to Come" [10a]. Rabbi Samson Raphael Hirsch expresses the same opinion [11]. Chajes clarifies that their validity comes from belief in the divine origin of the Torah and its revelation to Moses: "And the Christians observe the seven mitzvot and believe that the Mosaic Torah was given from God to Moses" [10a]. Elsewhere, Chajes reasons that even though they are monotheists, they should not have the status of *ger toshav*, because Rabbi Moses Maimonides prohibits the invention of new religions [10b]. From these authorities one sees that they deemed general acceptance of these mitzvot in a religious framework as enough to make someone a *ger toshav*, and that it is the equivalent of acceptance in front of three learned Jews or a rabbinical court and is valid even in the modern period. This notion was developed at length in regard to modern Christians by Rabbi Jehiel Heller [13].

Rabbi Jacob Zvi Mecklenburg presents an alternative formulation of one morning blessing: instead of "who has not made me a *goy*," he has "who has not made a *nokhri*." He claims that the former refers to the faithless and so cannot be about the Christians of his day, who accept the fundamental tenets of belief and have morals and laws. In the list of their good qualities he includes political tolerance: "[they] seek the well-being of those peoples who reside among them, without distinguishing Jew from non-Jew" [8]. He conceives of them as non-Jews who study and fulfill the seven Noahide mitzvot and as worthy of the rabbinic dictum: "A non-Jew who studies Torah is like the High Priest."

Rabbi Israel Moses Hazan distinguishes between Muslims, who denigrate the Torah, and Christians, who "through their comprehensive inquiry and profound wisdom, have found that we are blameless in remaining steadfast to observe our divine Torah" [12]. He joins the chorus of voices that esteem Christianity for its belief in the Torah. He describes the relationship between Judaism and Christianity with a striking image: "two saplings nurtured from the same cistern."

Rabbi Elijah Guttmacher contends that we must seek the welfare of non-Jews in this day and age. He claims that the utilitarian reason for praying for the non-Jewish government stated in the Prophets, "for through its welfare shall you have welfare" (Jer. 29:7), was only applicable to the "savage" peoples of antiquity, whereas today one should "beseech God on their behalf, even when it produces no benefit [for us]" [9]. It bears contemplating what precise halakhic definition he employs, which would dictate the extent to which it can be expanded beyond Christians to other religious groups.

THE SIXTEENTH CENTURY

Rabbi Yosef Karo

An exile from the Iberian Peninsula, the eminent halakhist and kabbalist Rabbi Yosef Karo (1488–1575) was active mainly in Safed. He authored the authoritative halakhic code *Shulḥan Arukh*, in addition to his foundational commentaries *Beit Yosef* and *Kesef Mishneh*.

In section 148 of *Yoreh De'ah*, Karo codifies the laws governing interaction with non-Jews on and around their holidays.

[1] *Shulḥan Arukh, Yoreh De'ah* 148:12

Some say that these applied only during that period; today they are not well-versed in the intricacies of their religious rituals.[4] It is therefore permissible to do business with them on their holiday, to give them loans, and everything else.

* * *

Rabbi Moses Isserles (Rema)

As the greatest Ashkenazi halakhic decisor of his generation, the Rema (1530–1572) wielded great influence, and his positions in *Mapa*, his addendum to Karo's *Shulḥan Arukh*, were treated as authoritative.

In two glosses, the Rema articulates his position that Christians of his era should not be viewed as idolaters for purposes of forming business partnerships. Whereas Karo gives the reasoning that Christians are not really polytheists, in the first gloss [2a], the Rema goes a step further even though it is not strictly necessary for halakhic leniency. He claims that Christians in fact have the one Creator in mind and merely associate "something else" with Him. In the second gloss [2b], though, when he lays out a series of halakhic permits, he completely omits this more positive understanding of Christianity. In fact, he goes on to cite

---

4. Hebrew *elilim*, literally "gods." The intent is that even if certain aspects of worship were at one point considered idolatrous, by the sixteenth century the halakhist would take into account the contemporary understanding ascribed to rituals by worshippers.

authorities who recommend that "a scrupulous, self-disciplined person" should refrain from relying on those leniencies.

[2a] *Shulḥan Arukh, Oraḥ Ḥayim* 156:1

Some are lenient in forming a partnership with non-Jews today because non-Jews today do not swear by their idols. Even though they mention their idols, their intention is for the Maker of heaven and earth; it is only that they associate the name of Heaven with something else. We do not find this to be a violation of not placing a stumbling block before the blind because they are not enjoined from theological association.

[2b] *Shulḥan Arukh, Yoreh De'ah* 148:12

One may even give the money to priests, as they do not use them for offerings or beautification of their idols but eat and drink from them. There is also the concern of provoking hostility if we separate ourselves from them on their holiday, when we live among them and have dealings with them all year round. Therefore, if someone enters the city and finds them rejoicing on their holiday, they should rejoice with them, in order to avoid provoking hostility, thereby deceiving them (all in *Tur*). Nevertheless, a scrupulous, self-disciplined person should take pains to avoid rejoicing with them if they are able to do so without provoking any hostility (*Beit Yosef* in the name of the Ran). Similarly, if someone today sends a gift to a non-Jew on a day when its receipt will be taken as a sign, one should send it the evening before, if possible; otherwise, one may send it on the holiday itself (*Terumat HaDeshen*, 195).

* * *

Rabbi Eliezer Ashkenazi

Rabbi Eliezer Ashkenazi (1513–1586) was a leading Torah scholar of his generation, who served as a rabbi in Cairo, Italy, and Poland.

The quotation below is taken from Ashkenazi's commentary on the Passover Haggada, discussing the pastiche of biblical quotes beginning with "Pour out Your wrath on the nations that did not know You" (Ps. 79:6). There, he positively views Christians and Muslims as those who do know God, who believe in the Creation of the world and in the

Exodus. They are not to be cursed, and this vengeful paragraph is not to be directed at them. And even those we do curse for having wronged and oppressed us, we curse on national – rather than religious – grounds.

[3] *Sefer [Gedolim] Maasei Hashem* (Venice, 1583), 134d–135a

Some of the non-Jews among whom we exiles take refuge have come to think – God forbid – that we are cursing them. Since we have a clear obligation to pray for their welfare, how can we offer two contradictory prayers to God? Of course, we would never curse the king, under whose protection we live. The verses that we recite testify to this: God should pour out His wrath on the peoples who did not know Him, meaning, they deny the exodus from Egypt because they never got word of the miracles. But all the non-Jews among whom the Jewish nation has been scattered evidently know about the Exodus, believe in it, and understand its significance. The implication of what we say is that He should not pour out His wrath upon those who know His name. We must keep ourselves from sinning to God and never curse those who know His name, only idolaters and those who do not believe in the Creation of the world. Those who destroyed the Temple were pagans; they did not profess the belief that spread to Edom and Ishmael for they had yet to be invented. Scripture thus explained that those non-Jews who destroyed the Temple did not know the Lord, and consumed Jacob and laid waste his habitation. But now that these non-Jews and the Muslims know the Lord and acknowledge the Exodus, we must never curse them based on our religion. If we do curse those who act wickedly toward us and afflict us unjustly, even that curse must not be based on our religion. Instead, it should be like anyone who curses someone who acts against and harms them. Just as a person curses their children or siblings when they act wickedly or unjustly toward them, so do we curse those who act wickedly toward us on an individual basis. But we must never curse an entire nation, even if there are those among them who have acted wickedly against us, because it is not the will of the Omnipresent. We are only to curse individuals who act wickedly toward us and oppress us – no one else. Our holy Torah declares in the name of the first monotheist that it is not God's will, as it says, "Will you really wipe out the innocent with the guilty?" (Gen. 18:23). And the chief prophet said, "One man sins and you fume against the entire congregation?" (Num. 16:22). These verses make clear that we are not permitted to curse, on the basis of religion, nations that acknowledge the Exodus and know God, even if they have not accepted the Torah.

THE SEVENTEENTH-EIGHTEENTH CENTURIES

Rabbi Moses Rivkes

Rabbi Moses Rivkes (1591–1671) served as a rabbi in Vilna, and his *Be'er HaGola* is famous for providing the sources for Karo's rulings in the *Shulḥan Arukh*.

In one comment, he relies on the rulings of the Rema [2] and Rabbi Eliezer Ashkenazi [3] to permit saving the lives of non-Jews, even when halakha forbids rescuing idolaters.

[4] *Be'er HaGola, Ḥoshen Mishpat 425, letter shin*

The Sages said [that one may not save a non-Jew's life] only with regard to the non-Jews of their time, who were true idolaters and did not believe in the Exodus from Egypt nor in the Creation of the world. But the non-Jews among whom we, the scattered Jewish people, take refuge, believe in the Creation of the world, the Exodus, and other fundamental religious beliefs, and their intention is for the Maker of heaven and earth, as halakhic decisors have written and as is cited in Rema's gloss on *Oraḥ Ḥayim* 156. Not only is there no prohibition against rescuing them, but there is even an obligation to pray for their welfare. The author of *Maasei Hashem* elaborated on this in his Haggada on the verse, "Pour out your wrath on the nations that did not know you" (Ps. 79:6). King David prayed to pour it out on the non-Jews who do not believe in the Creation of the world nor the significance of the miracles that God wrought for us in Egypt and during the Giving of the Torah. But the non-Jews in whose midst we live and under whose protection we take refuge believe in all of this, as he wrote. We are vigilant to pray continuously for the welfare of the kingdom and the success of its ministers, and for all the countries and places under their rule. And Maimonides wrote that the law follows R. Yehoshua in chapter *Ḥelek* (Sanhedrin 105a) that even pious non-Jews have a portion in the World to Come.

* * *

Rabbi Moses Hagiz

Rabbi Moses Hagiz (1672–1750) was a leading Torah scholar in Jerusalem and one of the fiercest opponents of Sabbateanism. He wrote various halakhic works, including *Leket HaKemaḥ*, rulings according to the order of *Shulḥan Arukh*; *Elleh HaMitzvot*, about the enumeration of the 613 mitzvot; and the responsa collection *Shtei HaLeḥem*. He also devoted his pen to the realm of Aggada, with compositions on the spiritual uniqueness of the Land of Israel, the acquisition of Torah, and anti-Sabbatean polemics.

In *Elleh HaMitzvot*, Hagiz gives the reason behind mitzva 564, "Do not abhor the Egyptian, because you were a stranger in his land" (Deut. 23:8), as the inculcation of gratitude for those who have treated us well, even if they, like the Egyptians, have also treated us terribly. He enumerates the wonderful things that the surrounding non-Jews have done for the Jewish people, from granting personal freedom to engage in commerce and live in peace, to allowing religious freedom and venerating and defending the Talmud from attack. It is in this context that he characterizes Christians as those who know God.

[5] *Elleh HaMitzvot* (Jerusalem: Horeb, 1964), 316–320

It is blindingly obvious that there is room [to show gratitude] for this lengthy exile. We are slaves, yet in our servitude we have not abandoned our God, and He has placed grace upon us before the noble kings of distant lands. Today, they are the rulers of the lands in which the Jewish people live – may their glory and splendorous piety be exalted! By the grace of God, they are hospitable to us every day, granting us the religious freedom to observe everything that God has commanded us in the laws of His holy Torahs, the Written Torah and the Oral Torah. [...]

Open your eyes as well to the source I wrote you in *Leket HaKemaḥ*, which I published last year on the Talmud, on folios 53 and 54.[5] It is clearly attested not only by the religious leaders of Lutheranism but also by the Church Fathers, who were supporters of the Roman

---

5. The Christian sources are in fact quoted beginning on 54a.

Pope. Anyone well acquainted with them and their books knows it is a true kindness from the Giver of the Torah, who made it graceful and beautiful to all its beholders. Not only do those wise men praise the Sages of the Talmud for being unparalleled in everything pertaining to the law, but they even defend and advocate for us against any enemy or zealot who speaks ill of the aggadic statements and miraculous tales mentioned therein. They vigorously report the truth: there is nothing unholy that opposes the kingdoms or religions of the land in practice, and it ought to be translated into their script and language, Latin, so that the scholars among them can study it. For it is pure and upright, containing no perversity; it is filled with wisdom, knowledge, and fear of the Lord. [The Sages] followed the first sagacious philosophers by concealing profound matters in recondite garb, so that it not accessible to just anyone. [...]

That is why we have the Jewish practice on every Shabbat to recite a blessing for the king and his officers and advisors with a Torah scroll on the platform (*bima*) – because it is Torah. Any fool who believes or says the opposite, that our Torahs instruct us to deceive, steal from, curse, and seek ill for them – God forbid! – is not only wrong but a sinner who spreads sinfulness. They are definitely a descendant of Amalek, who would always persecute the Jewish people and did not recognize the way of God, because "God is righteous in all His ways" (Ps. 145:17). [...]

It is an explicit verse, "Pour out your wrath on the nations that did not know you, on the kingdoms that did not call Your name" (Ps. 79:6). The Sages referred to them by the name *nokhri* because they estranged (*shehitnakker*) themselves from their Creator and did not acknowledge the fundamental religious beliefs. But whoever believes in the existence of God, the Creation of the World, prophecy, and reward and punishment, like Christians today, is called religious, and we have no license to harm them financially, and certainly not to kill them! All of those among whom the Jewish people live today know that there is one God, a single Father for all of us, and they call to Him. The Torah certainly did not command us to seek their ill-being. [...] The seventy bulls sacrificed on Sukkot prove this, as we are commanded to effect good and not evil....

*   *   *

Rabbi Elazar Fleckeles

Rabbi Elazar Fleckeles (1754–1826), chief disciple of Rabbi Ezekiel Landau (author of *Noda BiYehuda*), served as the head of the rabbinical court in Prague. He is author of the responsa collection *Teshuva MeAhava*.

In the preface to *Teshuva MeAhava*, Fleckeles has a brief piece called *Kesut Einayim*, which is intended to refute the claim that certain Jewish sources endorse or encourage hostility toward non-Jews, a claim that had disastrous effects in the real world. He expresses the need to preserve harmonious and cordial relations with all non-Jews, idolaters included. He concludes, "It is clear as day that the nations nowadays who observe the seven mitzvot have a portion in the World to Come and are called pious."[6] He goes into detail about how a Jew may not cause them financial injury at all, nor trick, denigrate, or hate them. It is even an obligation, he says, to pray for and seek their welfare, and to give *tzedaka* to their poor. Fleckeles then specifies the particular obligation toward modern European non-Jews, continuing Rabbi Jacob Emden's positive approach to Christianity. He writes that Christians observe Noahide law and are called "pious" and "those who fulfill His will."[7]

[6] *Kesut Einayim* 10

If these laws were said about idol worshippers who violate His will, it is all the more true regarding those who fulfill His will, i.e., the nations that keep the seven mitzvot and are called pious. Whoever acts righteously will be judged accordingly. All the invectives and epithets, curses and imprecations recorded in the Talmud and other Jewish books are aimed at the ancient nations that did every abomination hated by God, like the Sabeans…, worshippers of idols and abominations who destroyed God's Temple [and] killed the pious of the Most High. It is about them that David said, "Pour out your wrath on the nations that did not know you, on the kingdoms that did not call Your name. For they have consumed Jacob and laid waste his habitation" (Ps. 79:6–7). […]

Praise be God, now all the idolaters are gone, and there is no remnant of the ancients who worshipped Baal, Ekron, and their ilk. Yet, it

---

6. *Kesut Einyaim*, end of §1.
7. *Kesut Einayim*, §10.

is still a mitzva to publicize their shame, because perhaps there are still some who worship the stars in faraway lands. It also prevents the further rise of wicked people in the world who boast of their gods and chase the vanities of the non-Jews so that they themselves become vain, like the followers of Shabbetai Tzvi, who corporealize the Godhead, believe in dreams and talismans, and adopt every form of idolatry in the world, defending the calves of Jeroboam. I have treated this at length elsewhere.

THE NINETEENTH CENTURY

Rabbi Israel Lipschitz

Rabbi Israel Lipschitz (1782–1860) served as the head of the rabbinical court in various German cities. He is best known for *Tiferet Yisrael*, a comprehensive commentary on the Mishna that is divided into two parts: *Yakhin*, which focuses on the mishnaic text itself, and *Bo'az*, which has extended discussions and innovative ideas.

The Mishna in Bava Kamma (4:3) states the law regarding a Jew's animal attacking a non-Jew's and vice versa. In his commentary, Lipschitz dedicates a lengthy passage to the mistreatment of non-Jews. He begins by stating that it is prohibited to steal from or mislead them, and the continuation represents his position that contemporary Christians are monotheists who recognize the divinity of the Torah and observe the Noahide law.

[7] *Tiferet Yisrael*, Bava Kamma 4:3

If [the prohibition to steal and mislead non-Jews] applies to idolaters, who, according to the Sages, considered our money and lives free for the taking…, it is certainly an obligation on us now concerning our brothers among the nations, who acknowledge a single God; honor His Torah, believe in its divinity, and call it Holy Writ; and keep the seven mitzvot as is required by Torah law. They also prevent anyone – as important as they may be – from touching even the smallest hair on our heads, and do not snuff out even our lowliest flame. What is more, they do many kindnesses with our poor, many of whom are sustained by their generosity alone. Given all of this, how could we be ingrates and not say, as Joseph did, "How could I do this great evil and sin to God?" (Gen. 39:9).

* * *

Rabbi Jacob Zvi Mecklenburg

Rabbi Jacob Zvi Mecklenburg (1785–1865) was rabbi of Königsberg, Prussia, and a partner of Malbim (Rabbi Meir Leibush Wisser) in the struggle against the Reform movement. He is known primarily for his Torah commentary *HaKetav VeHaKabbala* and his commentary on the siddur titled *Iyyun Tefilla*, which is often printed together with Rabbi Jacob Lorberbaum's *Derekh HaHayyim*.

In his commentary on the siddur, Mecklenburg has a slightly different version of one blessing recited every morning. In lieu of *shelo asani goy*, he has *shelo asani nokhri*. Both *goy* and *nokhri* are typically translated as "gentile" or "non-Jew," so what is the difference? He claims that *nokhri* refers to the faithless, regardless of nationality. The person can be a Jew or a non-Jew. With that definition, the blessing is patently not about the non-Jews of modern Europe, who believe in God and the eternity of the soul, have laws and morals, and tolerate the minorities among them, including the Jews. He even applies the rabbinic statement to them: "A non-Jew who studies Torah is like the High Priest."[8]

[8] *Siddur Derekh HaHayyim ... im Peirush HaNifla Iyyun Tefilla* (Tel Aviv: Sinai, 1954), 42

Shelo asani nokhri. [...] This is also the meaning of *ben nekhar*, namely, it is a descriptor for whoever rejects the foundation [of monotheism] and denies the existence of God. [...] There is no difference between a Jew and a non-Jew: whoever denies the existence of God is called a *nokhri* or *ben nekhar*. [...] The essential meaning of *nokhri* is one who denies His existence – regardless of place, time, or person. The blessing of "who has not made me a *nokhri*" does not belittle, in any way, the nations among whom we live, because they all acknowledge His existence, and they themselves despise anyone who does not [acknowledge His existence]. They are also not enjoined from theological association. Know that the Jerusalem Talmud says about this blessing, "as it says, 'All the nations are like naught before Him; they are considered nothing

---

8. Bava Kamma 38a.

and void to Him' (Is. 40:17)," and this is cited in Abudarham. Our rabbis have thereby taught us that this blessing was instituted concerning
those ancient, savage nations, likened to beasts of the field. They denied
God and rejected the eternity of the soul. They did not adjudicate theft
because everything was permissible; murder, adultery, bestiality – they
treated none of these as a sin. Even today we hear of the savages who
dwell in the desert, whom everyone considers animals. These are the
peoples whom Scripture says are like naught, nothingness, void to
Him … and the blessing was instituted only with respect to them. Those
nations under whose protection we live, who acknowledge the existence
of God and divine providence, who believe in the eternity of the soul,
who hate theft and injustice and deal decisively with robbery and murder, who seek the well-being of those peoples who reside among them,
without distinguishing Jew from non-Jew – about such nations did the
Rabbis say, "A non-Jew who studies Torah (their seven mitzvot) is like
the High Priest." This *Baraita* appears in *Torat Kohanim* (*Aḥarei Mot*, ch.
13), where they conclude:

> It similarly says, "Open the gates" (Is. 26:2) – it does not
> say, "Let the priests, Levites, and Israelites enter," but "Let
> a righteous nation (*goy*), keeping the faith, enter."
>
> It similarly says, "This is the gate to the Lord" (Ps.
> 118:20) – it does not say, "Priests, Levites, and Israelites
> [shall enter]," but "The righteous shall enter through it."
>
> It similarly says, "Rejoice" (Ps. 33:1) – it does not say
> "Priests, Levites, and Israelites," but "Rejoice, O righteous,
> in the Lord." […]
>
> Thus, even a non-Jew who fulfills the Torah (their seven
> mitzvot) is like the High Priest.

See also *Tosafot*, Avoda Zara 3. From the discussion of their mitzvot in
Sanhedrin 59, it is plain that "they are considered nothing and void to
Him" is not said about people like these. The Jerusalem Talmud therefore teaches that our blessing was instituted only regarding those nations
that deny the existence of God and the like.

* * *

Rabbi Elijah Guttmacher

Rabbi Elijah Guttmacher (1796–1874), a student of Rabbi Akiva Eiger, served as the rabbi of Grodzisk in Saxony and was a halakhic decisor and kabbalist. He was one of the forerunners of Zionism and promoted the idea of a natural path to the ultimate redemption.

Guttmacher argues that one must pray for peace between countries and for their prosperity. He instructs the reader to have this in mind when reciting the ten verses of the *malkhuyot* section of the Musaf *Amida* on Rosh HaShana, and when reciting the *Barekh Aleinu* blessing of the weekday *Amida* throughout the year. Just as we pray for Jews in need in mercy, so should we pray for upstanding non-Jews. He even attests that during the *Yizkor* prayer, his community would include the names of non-Jews.[9] In the quotation below, Guttmacher explicitly differentiates between Jeremiah's call to pray for the welfare of the nations, because it is in our own best interests, and the contemporary obligation to love the nations of the world and pray for their welfare, even when there is no immediate benefit for us.

[9] *Yeriot Shlomo*, vol. 3, 996–997[10]

When Jeremiah concludes, "for through its welfare shall you have welfare" (Jer. 29:7), the implication is that one should pray only for the nations in whose midst you reside. But this was said only about the nations of antiquity, who were cruel and did excessive harm to the Jewish people, which is what led to the letter that he sent. [...] But when you suffer among the non-Jews, remember the rule formulated by the wise [Solomon], "Like water face to face" (Prov. 27:19): If you beseech God on their behalf and you love them, then the love shall be returned to you.... The statement was only about the ancient, savage nations, but

---

9. Meir Hildesheimer, "The Chosen People and Citizens of the State: Jews and the Nations in the Thought of Rabbi Elijah Guttmacher" [in Hebrew], in *The Scepter Shall Not Depart from Judah: Leadership, Rabbinate and Community in Jewish History, Studies Presented to Professor Simon Schwarzfuchs* [in Hebrew], ed. Joseph R. Hacker and Yaron Harel (Jerusalem: Bialik Institute, 2011), 374.

10. Cited in Meir Hildesheimer, "Exile and Redemption in the Thought of Rabbi Elijah Guttmacher" [in Hebrew], in *A Hundred Years of Religious Zionism* [in Hebrew], ed. Avi Sagi and Dov Schwartz (Ramat-Gan: BIU Press, 2003), 80.

today there is much greater cause to beseech God on their behalf, even when it produces no benefit [for us].

* * *

Rabbi Zvi Hirsch Chajes

Rabbi Zvi Hirsch Chajes (1805–1855) was an important rabbinic scholar in Galicia whose most popular work is the introduction to rabbinic literature known as *Mevo HaTalmud*.

Following Rabbi Jacob Emden, Chajes stresses the religious superiority of Christianity to polytheism. Christians affirm fundamental tenets of theology, so they are considered the pious of the nations of the world who have a portion in the next world, and they have the status of the *ger toshav* who accepts the seven Noahide mitzvot. All this he writes in *Kuntres Tiferet Yisrael*, a series of rebuttals to the libelous claims of the Damascus Affair of 1840. In *Kuntres Aharon*, Chajes responds to a critic by doubling down on his position: even according to Ritva's (Rabbi Yom Tov of Seville) opinion that a Jew must die rather than convert to Islam, that does not prove that Islam fails to fulfill Noahide law and strips its adherents of the status of *ger toshav*.

[10a] *Kuntres Tiferet Yisrael*, in *Kol Sifrei Maharatz Hayyot*, vol. 1 (Jerusalem: Divrei Hakhamim, 1958), 489–490

If we look at [the Jews'] righteous conduct toward idolaters who offered incense to Baal and did not believe in the existence of God nor His unity, nor in divine providence or divine recompense, it should certainly be so toward the Christians, who believe in the heavenly origin of the Torah, the existence of God, recompense in the World to Come, and other fundamental principles of faith. There is no doubt that they have the halakhic status of *ger toshav*, and those who observe the seven mitzvot because they were commanded them by God through Moses are like the pious of the nations of the world who have a portion in the World to Come, as the halakha states...that the pious of the nations of the world have a portion in the World to Come. And the Christians observe the seven mitzvot and believe that the Mosaic Torah was given from God to Moses, and they believe in the existence of God. Although they theologically associate something else in their worship, Rema (*Oraḥ Ḥayim* 156) cites the Ran and Rabbeinu Yeruham in the name of *Tosafot* (Bekhorot 2b) that non-Jews are not enjoined from theological association. [...]

We also say (Avoda Zara 3a): Even a non-Jew who learns Torah about the seven mitzvot is said to be "more precious than pearls" (Prov. 3:15), and the seven mitzvot constitute the entirety of rational law, which both the Christians and Muslims adjudicate wherever their jurisdiction extends. They also police the observance of forbidden sexual relations, murder, courts of judgment, blasphemy, and theft, and they are extremely exacting in their punishment of transgressors. Even [consuming] a limb from a live animal is alluded to by the apostle Paul, who warned them not to eat from what has been strangled. Muslims also are not idolaters (*Yoreh De'ah* 124), and they are exacting about the seven mitzvot. They are also prohibited from eating pork, blood, and an unslaughtered animal, and what is not slaughtered while facing the *qibla* [the Kaaba in the sacred Mosque in Mecca] – see *Yoreh De'ah* 14:7; Quran *Sura* 2, "The Cow," and *Sura* 4, "The Table." And anyone who observes the seven mitzvot because it is commanded in the Torah by God through Moses is considered a *ger toshav*. See also what Maimonides wrote in chapter 12 of *Hilkhot Melakhim* (ed. Venice), and *Kuzari*, IV:23, who wrote: "The Hagarites introduce and pave the way for the expected Messiah, who is the fruition. They will all become his fruit when they acknowledge him, and the tree will revert to being one. Then they will revere the root that they had formerly disparaged."

[10b] *Kuntres Achron*, in *Kol Sifrei Maharatz Ḥayyot*, vol. 2 (Jerusalem: Divrei Ḥakhamim, 1958), 1036

What Your Honor has written in the name of the Ritva regarding the Muslims who believe in the Creator's unity, that "be killed and do not transgress" nevertheless applies.... [...] There is no proof from Ritva's words, because he is specifically dealing with a Jew who is obligated to believe in the Torah's eternity.... [...] But a Noahide who observes their mitzvot from tradition and believes in the Creator's unity is not called a heretic for believing in Islam, and they can definitely be considered a *ger toshav* if they observe the seven mitzvot based on a continuous tradition, even if they have not accepted Noahide law anew....

But one can also consider these monotheists from a different angle. Even though they observe their seven mitzvot as a tradition from their forefathers, I already quoted Maimonides above from *Hilkhot Melakhim* 10:6, that a Noahide is not allowed to invent a religion. Even though this new religion includes their seven mitzvot, they also have new ones, like the Christians' consumption of bread and wine on Easter and the Muslims' prohibition against eating pork and drinking wine. Since these are permitted to Noahides, they are only obligated in this by dint of their new religious law. And since the invention of religion is prohibited for Noahides even if it does not uproot Noahide law, this would be a reason why Christians and Muslims would not have the status of *ger toshav*.

* * *

Rabbi Samson Raphael Hirsch

Rabbi Samson Raphael Hirsch (1808–1888) was a prominent rabbinic figure in Germany. He founded the *Torah im Derekh Eretz* philosophy, served as rabbi of the Adass Jeschurun synagogue in Frankfurt-am-Main, and was the leading Neo-Orthodox opponent of the Reform movement. He was a prolific writer, and his well-studied works include a commentary on the Torah, a commentary on the siddur, and a series of works expositing the philosophy of Judaism: *The Nineteen Letters*, *Horeb*, and writings on Jewish education. His responsa and talmudic novellae have been collected and published in *Shemesh Marpe*.

In *Horeb*, Hirsch waxes poetic about the state of his non-Jewish contemporaries. Evidently, he views Christians and Muslims as believers in God and in the veracity of the Revelation at Sinai, and as keepers of Noahide law. He therefore applies to them the designation of *ger toshav*.

[11] *Horeb: A Philosophy of Jewish Laws and Observances*, trans. Dayan Dr. I. Grunfeld (New York: Soncino Press, 1962), Chapter 77, pp. 379–380[11]

The Jewish people can rejoice today in the midst of the peoples among whom they mostly live. Behold how the holy light God placed among you at Sinai has spread far and wide and has already scared away a great part of humanity from the delusion and the abomination of idol worship. Rejoice that in Europe, in America, and in part of Asia and Africa non-Jewish peoples also have become illumined by the revelation of the one God given to you and have adopted a doctrine which teaches them to perform the seven duties which, according to your doctrine, are binding on all men: idol worship, blasphemy, theft, murder, forbidden sexual relations, [consuming] a limb from a live animal, and courts of justice (Sanhedrin 56b). Rejoice in this. According to your law, whoever expressly accepts these duties in the presence of three persons as having been enjoined upon all men by God in His revelation to Moses, such a person has the status of *ger toshav*. Toward such a person you are not only to practice all the obligations of justice – as indeed [you must] also toward an idolater – but "you are also commanded to sustain them." You must esteem them and love them as a genuine person, since they perform all the duties God requires from all people. And your love and esteem toward them can suffer no detraction from the fact that they do not also perform the duties of Judaism, since these they have not been commanded, and they are incumbent only on the congregation of Jacob.... But in respect to the laws of marriage, etc., the *ger toshav* is no exception; you may not intermarry with them..., and for the same reason their wine is also prohibited....

* * *

Rabbi Israel Moses Hazan

Hazan (1808–1862) served as a member of the high court in Jerusalem beginning in 1842 and served as Chief Rabbi of Rome and Chief Rabbi

---

11. With minor adjustments for style and consistency.

of Corfu. Notable works include his responsa *Kerakh shel Romi, Nahala LeYisrael, Kedushat Yom Tov,* and *Iyyei HaYam.*

In *Kerakh shel Romi,* Hazan writes that there is no problem imitating non-Jews in matters of aesthetics or music, because these belong to the human spirit. The fact that non-Jews use them in religious rituals does not mean that they cannot beautify or adorn our own houses of worship. To the contrary, we *should* harness the products of our human talents in our own service of God.

In this context, he relates to Rabbi Moses Maimonides's claim in his responsa that he annulled the public repetition of the *Amida* because Jews would converse during that time and the Muslims would scorn them for their dismissive attitude toward prayer. In a responsum of his own, Radbaz (Rabbi David ibn Zimra) rejected this reasoning because of Islam's negative attitude toward Judaism: "They consider our prayers heresy and our Torah a substitute in which we added and took away, and much more like this. Since we are nothing in their eyes regardless, we have made no difference, so we should fulfill our halakhic obligation." Hazan draws a distinction between taking away a rabbinic institution and adding beauty to the synagogue. He further observes that Radbaz was speaking about Muslims, and his characterization would not apply to Christians, who do not reject our faith and do validate our beliefs and Torah: "We are like two saplings nurtured from the same well." This aligns well with Rabbi Jacob Emden's opinion.

[12] *Kerakh shel Romi* 1

[O]ne can deduce from Radbaz's own words that if we register as important to the non-Jews among whom we take refuge, it would be appropriate to annul that rabbinic institution [of repeating the *Amida* prayer] in the face of their scorn. As he wrote: "We have made no difference, so we should fulfill our halakhic obligation" – the unambiguous implication being that had we made a difference, we would not fulfill our halakhic obligation. Radbaz was speaking about the scorn of the Muslims, who truly do not value our belief and Torah and denigrate it. [...] Whatever the case, Radbaz was speaking only about Muslims, who neither know nor grasp the foundational principles of religion, nor do they see any value in us, who have come under their rule, enslaved unto death.

When we had our own sovereignty and grandeur they were still Arabs of the desert, comparable to beasts of the field. This is not the case with Christians, who are very wise and continuously search for the truth, and through their comprehensive inquiry and profound wisdom have found that we are blameless in remaining steadfast in the observance of our divine Torah. Furthermore, they genuinely recognize the value of our holy Torah and the wisdom of our talmudic Sages. Both we and they are like two saplings nurtured from the same cistern. They would never scorn our Torah or prayer rite as such; that would be sacrilegious for Christian scholars of such eminent stature. If there be any scorn, it concerns only our wretched behavior in all our places of worship, especially in our houses of prayer. Some of their greatest scholars have written treatises praising our worship and tradition, and to this day some of the most enlightened of our generation strive to improve our future, writing good and consolatory things about us. Even those of them who oppose us have never spoken ill of our worship or prayers per se. It is only that they have seen a few anti-gentile sentiments in our books, and that our Torah kept us apart from them and their worship and allowed us to hate them. Based on this, they thought that we are under a religious obligation to corrupt society or the like. But their error has already been exposed thousands of times by Jewish and even Christian scholars, and it all stems from their minimal grasp of history. It was the ancient non-Jews who corrupted society with their idolatrous practices, in which they spilled the blood of their sons and daughters, committed adultery, and idolized every ungodly abomination. It was about them that the Torah imposed the extreme measure of rooting them out. These non-Jews are the opposite: they contribute to civilization and believe in the Creator, divine providence over the individual, and many such beliefs – I need not elaborate because it is well known and I have nothing to add. The bottom line is that there is a massive difference between Muslims and Christians in this regard, because Christians have never considered our prayers and worship as heretical or shameful, as the Radbaz wrote of the Muslims. To the contrary, they praise and extol our liturgy and our unification of Him. Since they regard us with respect, even the Radbaz would concede that it is appropriate to improve our houses of worship and especially our synagogues, so that they not scorn us, saying, "a glorious Torah in an ugly vessel." They know the value of the Torah, the mitzvot, and prayer, which have been translated into their local languages.

* * *

Rabbi Jehiel Heller

Known as "the prodigy of Kaidanov" as a child, Rabbi Jehiel Heller (1814–1861) was a preeminent Lithuanian rabbi. He held a few rabbinical posts and composed the responsa collection *Ammudei Or*.

In 1852, he published an article on the topic of "respect for non-Jews in our time" in his book *Shnei Perakim*. It was published in St. Petersburg in Hebrew with an accompanying German translation at the behest of the Russian government. It dealt with the obligation to show honor to the czar and respect to non-Jews. This piece is the most detailed and important one in the entire volume.[12] Heller claims that although Maimonides rules that we do not accept a *ger toshav* when the Jubilee cycle is not observed, that limitation is only on individuals. An entire nation can be granted the status of *ger toshav* even in the absence of Jubilee observance. Accordingly, contemporary Christian nations, whose religion rests on the principles of Noahide law, have the status of *ger toshav* and the pious of the nations of the world. Exceptionally, he sings the praise of the Christian nations, from their fulfillment of the seven Noahide mitzvot to their other good qualities reflected in their polities and laws.

[13a] *Shnei Perakim*, 50–51

The principle of accepting a *ger toshav* applies only to an individual non-Jew who decides to separate from the non-Jewish nations and must accept upon themselves the seven mitzvot in front of three knowledgeable Jews. We are not permitted to accept such a person in this way, namely, for observing the seven mitzvot alone, except when the Jubilee

---

12. For a discussion of the volume, see Azriel Shohat, "On the Book *Shnei Perakim*" [in Hebrew], *Sinai* 102 (1988): 63–71 (esp. 68–70), and Eliezer HaKohen Katzman, "On the Figure of R. Y. Heller, Author of *Ammudei Or*" [in Hebrew], *Yeshurun* 4 (1999): 655–662.

is observed. The Raavad (ad loc.) elaborates on the reasoning, because we have an obligation to sustain such a *ger toshav* who comes to dwell among us…. None of this applies to an entire nation that demonstrates exceptional piety before the Creator and accepts the mitzvot established by the Omnipresent for all humanity. A nation like this definitely has the status of *ger toshav* in every respect necessary for what the Torah considers the degree of the pious nations of the world, for this world and the next one.

[13b] *Shnei Perakim, 55–58*

Now…let us return to the nature of the Christian nations among whom we take refuge. I say: not only do they fulfill all the conditions for a *ger toshav* required by the Torah, but they exhibit many additional good and meritorious qualities before our heavenly Father. Let us specify briefly how all the particulars of the seven laws are fulfilled meticulously and eagerly.

1. Regarding idolatry, since they accept the yoke of His kingdom as they are commanded and shun idol worship, we have no complaint against them whatsoever.

2. Regarding the six incestual relations enumerated above, they have ardently accepted them and even added a few more that Jews may not marry. They assuredly receive reward for them, as Maimonides wrote (*Hilkhot Melakhim* 10:5): "A Noahide who wishes to perform one of the other mitzvot of the Torah in order to receive reward is not to be prevented from performing it according to halakha. If he brings a fire-offering in the Lord's Temple, when it is reestablished, it is accepted."

3. Regarding murder, one need not explain the severity with which they treat it and the lengths they go to prevent it – it is common knowledge.

4. Regarding blasphemy, they also treat this severely like any criminal law, and they have added many other restrictions that befit God's honor. The punishment for stealing some-

thing consecrated to their or someone else's house of prayer pales in comparison to that for stealing from another person. The full fury of the law is brought down on them. They have many similar just laws set down for God's glory and to place His dread upon them. Regarding theft, they have accepted it with all its laws, as everyone knows.

5. Regarding courts of judgment, one can clearly see that not a single detail is missing from what they were commanded. They have appointed judges and officers who investigate a legal matter to discover the truth. They have legislated about every matter laws that suit a proper society, and they expend great, noble, laudable effort on the pursuit of true justice. Judgment is not dispensed summarily and blindly. Everything is written down faithfully, and every weighty or difficulty matter is brought by the local judges to those greater than they, who will issue a ruling in accord with the truth. Who would deny them their due praise? Their lofty and great reward from the Creator shall be commensurate with the immensity of their efforts.

6. Regarding [consumption of] a limb from a live animal, we have never seen anyone violate this by severing a limb from a live animal and eating it.

We have thus far demonstrated their perfect observance, down to the last detail, of the seven mitzvot they have been commanded. If we were to detail all their merits and righteous attributes, we would run out of space. They include: compassion and sympathy for each and every person no matter who they are; compassionate care of the downtrodden and sick with the support of their mighty government; their astounding expenditure on the many hospitals in every state; their intensive attending to all the needs and treatments of patients, to the point that the highest minister will visit a peasant patient, and every minister and officer on the king's staff, when reviewing their unit, makes it a priority to visit the hospital to seek their welfare and see to their needs…. Here you have it, a full accounting of how these nations have attained the degree of the pious of the nations of the world according to Torah law, and are called *ger toshav* in talmudic parlance.

[13c] *Shnei Perakim, 67*

In [the Sages'] time, when the nations were generally murderous, they prohibited anyone from being alone with them or accompanying them on the road. In our time, all of these rules have changed (see *Ḥavvot Ya'ir*); it is our well-known practice to relate to them with love and friendship and to consider them like any upstanding Jew for purposes of seclusion.

Rabbi Elijah Benamozegh: The Role of World Religions in Realizing the Torah's Universalist Vision

Assaf Malach

Rabbi Elijah Benamozegh (1823–1900) was born in Livorno, Italy to a family of Moroccan origin. He served for nearly half a century as rabbi of his hometown, where he also ran a renowned publishing house. From a young age he studied Kabbala and the sciences, and he was known for his deep knowledge of both. Much of his literary legacy bears directly on the subject of this volume.

Em LaMikra, a Hebrew commentary on the Torah, was published in 1862 and 1863. A running theme is the Bible's attitude toward and treatment of other nations and religions, especially the Egyptians.

In 1867, Benamozegh published *Morale Juive et Morale Chrétienne*. In this French volume, Benamozegh deals extensively with the indebtedness of Christian principles to Judaism and their interrelationship. He perceptively notes that the most direct sources of Christianity's universalism are Jewish. He spends considerable time establishing the advantages of Jewish morality with its national-political character over the universalism of the Christian ethic that stands aloof from this-worldly concerns. Other compositions by Benamozegh lay bare the kabbalistic sources from which, so he claims, the Christians siphoned their fundamental doctrines.

Benamozegh's magnum opus, *Israel et L'Humanité*, centers on the relationship between the Jewish people and the rest of humanity, and on their respective roles in the divine plan. A draft spanned 1,900 large pages in French, but it did not see publication in the author's lifetime. It finally went to press in 1914, but in a shorter format that ran to approximately 1,000 pages. It had been edited and adapted by Aimé Pallière, a student of Benamozegh with a unique story: he was a Christian who wanted to convert of Judaism, but Benamozegh persuaded him not to convert and to instead disseminate the seven Noahide laws among his fellow coreligionists.[1]

The thought of Benamozegh has three key components. First is the idea that the Jewish people are a "kingdom of priests" (Ex. 19:6) who are on a mission to religiously reform the entire world by bringing it to observe the seven Noahide mitzvot. Second, the major religions (Christianity and Islam) are primary instruments for disseminating the Torah's message, and they will continue to play a starring role in spreading universal religion in the future. He even reveals that he would personally become emotional and swell with pride when he would hear a priest reading from Psalms [5b]. At the same time, he incisively criticizes the grave errors of Christianity and Islam in their selectiveness and misuse of the Torah's words. Only the correction of these errors will enable

---

1. There is a significant disparity between *Morale Juive et Morale Chrétienne* and *Israel et L'Humanité* in orientation and tone. The former dwells on the advantage of Jewish morality, whereas the latter emphasizes the universal religion contained within the Torah. This has generated speculation about Benamozegh's exact opinions; see, e.g., Jacob Fleischmann, *The Problem of Christianity in Modern Jewish Thought, 1770–1929* [in Hebrew] (Jerusalem: Magnes Press, 1964), 129–130. Some have tried to argue that this is not a true discrepancy between Benamozegh and Benamozegh, but between Benamozegh and Pallière. However, a comparison of the original manuscript with Pallière's 1914 edition reveals few significant differences; see *Clémence Boulouque, Another Modernity: Elijah Benamozegh's Jewish Universalism* (Stanford: Stanford University Press, 2020).

them to spread the universal religion. Third, Benamozegh intricately elaborates a theory of Noahide law, and in so doing lays emphasis on a shared spiritual and moral foundation, and on the importance of religious diversity arising from distinct ethnicities and nations.

At very beginning of *Israel et L'Humanité*, Benamozegh announces that the book will show that the telos of Judaism is to create a universal religion for all humanity, and to reconcile the national and universal sides of the Torah [1a–1b]. The ancient Israelites isolated themselves from the peoples of their time precisely to fortify themselves for this long-term goal of establishing a universal religion [1c]. Note that the Jewish God is the Creator, the God of all, and not some local God; His message is a universal one for all humankind. In order for the divine word to be implemented, the Jewish people needed to become a kingdom of priests devoted entirely to the religious ideal [1d]. This is the reason behind the Torah's national-ethnic character – "Mosaic Law" – to be distinguished from its universal aspect – "Noahide Law."

In this connection, Benamozegh posits that non-Jews practiced a kind of monotheism before the giving of the Torah, that ancient religions incorporated belief in one supreme God above their minor deities [2a, 2d]. The divine wisdom in the Torah can be traced to the mysteries of the Kabbala, which parallel some of the esoteric doctrines of ancient religious civilizations: Egypt, Greece, Persia, and India [2b–2c]. He also establishes the importance of Noahism, the universal religion embedded within the Torah that is part of its core message [3a]. It forms the religious and moral basis for all of human civilization [3b], which is why the Torah requires all the nations of the world to observe it, and why it is more rational and intuitive than the Mosaic Law [3c, 3e]. This begs the question raised throughout this volume: Does Noahism exhaust non-Jewish religion, or is it the shared substrate from which each culture nurtures its own spirituality and relationship with God? Benamozegh forcefully argues for the latter, because the Infinite cannot be reductively accessed by a single religious modality. The very nature of God necessarily creates space for many religions [4a]. Nevertheless, he insists on the singularity of Judaism, the most developed form of divine service, from which the other religions must learn and thereby perfect their own faiths [4b]. Benamozegh spills much ink on the place of Christianity and Islam in history, declaring both of them, though more so Christianity, worthy of admiration [5b]. They have spread Jewish beliefs among the nations, bringing the entire world closer to the epoch of universal religion, and faithfully realized the Torah's mission [5a]. Christianity is particularly singled out for its immense contribution to promoting moral values among many peoples, these values having been taken directly from Judaism [5c–5d]. This does not, by any stretch, mean that these world religions are free from fault. The Christians, says Benamozegh, reject the Torah's system and fail to understand the necessary duality of Noahism *and* Mosaism, which consecrates Jews as the priests of the world [6a–6b]. Ancient Christianity was too extreme: either everyone had to follow Mosaic Law, or no one – not even the Jews – could observe it. Yet the world needs a priestly nation in parallel to its universal religion. He identifies the root cause of Christianity's problem: to cling to a pure, abstract religiosity and morality that could encompass all of humanity, it divested itself of all ethnic, national, and social obligations that might weigh it down. It failed, paradoxically giving rise to terrible religious violence [6c–6e]. In Benamozegh's eyes, Islam has the opposite problem because it assumes the obligations that Christianity put aside while throwing away Judaism's spiritual and metaphysical side [7].[2]

SOURCES[3]

Reconciling the National and Universal Sides of the Torah

[1a] *Israel and Humanity,* 43–44
But is Judaism in fact a universal religion? If Judaism had been only a purely national religion, it could not have given birth to two religions with truly universal aspirations. [...]

---

2. For a more extensive treatment of these issues, see *Musar Yehuda Le'ummat Musar Notzer* (next footnote); Gitit Holzman, "Universalism and Nationality in Judaism, and the Relationship between Jews and Non-Jews in the Thought of Rabbi Eliyahu Benamozegh" [in Hebrew], *Pe'amim* 74 (1998): 104–130; Alessandro Guetta, "The Relationship between Kabbala and Christianity in the Thought of Elijah Benamozegh" [in Hebrew], *Pe'amim* 74 (1998): 97–103.
3. *Israel et L'Humanité* has been translated into English as *Israel and Humanity*, ed. and

We were inquiring just now if Judaism is a universal religion, and we answered affirmatively. But here in fact is the way the question should have been posed: *Does Judaism contain* a universal religion? If we formulate the problem in this way, we can find the explanation of the greatest religious phenomenon of antiquity, the key to the disputes of the first centuries of the Christian era, the solution to the crisis which confronts the various faiths at this moment, and, so to say, the last religious hope of humankind. And it is because we understand it thus that we have answered without hesitation that Judaism *is* a universal religion. [...] [I]t indeed contains at its heart, as the flower conceals the fruit, the religion intended for the entire human race, of which the Mosaic Law, which seems on the surface so incompatible with that high destiny, is but the husk or outer cover.

[1b] *Israel and Humanity*, 58

Two great lessons will emerge, we hope, from our labor. On the one hand, we shall demonstrate, contrary to the allegations of the rationalist critic, that Judaism, far from being a purely ethnic religion, has a distinctively universalist character, and that it has not ceased to concern itself with humankind and its destinies. On the other hand, we shall show that the ideal which Hebraism has evolved of man and social organization not only has never been surpassed, but has not even been approached, except from a distance; and that it is in accepting this ideal, in reforming its Christianity on this model, that humankind, without disavowing its dearest principles, will be able to have a reasonable faith in God

---

trans. Maxwell Luria (New York: Paulist Press, 1995). This translation is used here, with some modifications for style and consistency.

Morale Juive et Morale Chrétienne was initially translated into Hebrew as *BiShvilei Musar*, trans. Simon Marcus (Jerusalem: Mossad HaRav Kook, 1966), and was more recently translated again into Hebrew as *Musar Yehudi Le'ummat Musar Notzeri*, trans. Eliyahu Rahamim Zayyani (Haifa: Yeshivat Or ViYeshua, 2007). The citations are translated from this latter edition. Although an English translation was published in 1873 as *Jewish and Christian Ethics with a View on Mahomedism*, it is outdated in some respects and occasionally paraphrastic.

Note that the sources here, unlike those in the other chapters of this volume, are divided by topic. Each section focuses on a theme or aspect of Benamozegh's thought and collects relevant sources from his various works.

and in His Revelation. We shall show that in Judaism, universality as ends and particularism as means have always coexisted .... [...] As we believe firmly that only orthodox Judaism can answer the religious needs of humankind, it is to *it* that we address ourselves, to learn if, even as it incontestably favors the yearnings of universal religion, it also possesses the necessary means to realize them.

[1c] *Israel and Humanity, 45*
If one examines closely that Mosaic code which seems to raise an impassable barrier between Israel and humankind, one soon discovers the reason for those peculiar laws .... The idiosyncratic religion of the Jews was a means of protecting and of realizing the authentic *universal* religion, or Noahism, as the rabbis called it. In this fact lies the explanation of all that otherwise remains incomprehensible in the doctrines, laws, and history of the Jewish people.

[1d] *Israel and Humanity, 53–54*
For Judaism, the world is like a great family, where the father lives in immediate contact with his children, who are the different peoples of the earth. Among these children there is a firstborn, who, in conformity with ancient institutions, was the priest of the family, charged with executing the father's orders and with replacing him in his absence. It was this firstborn who administered the sacred things, who officiated, instructed, consecrated. In recognition of these services, he received a double portion of the paternal heritage and the consecration, or laying of hands, a kind of religious investiture, which the father sometimes granted to one of his sons .... Such is the Jewish conception of the world. In heaven a single God, father of all men alike; on earth a family of peoples, among whom Israel is the "firstborn," charged with teaching and administering the true religion of humankind, of which he is priest. This "true religion" is the Law of Noah: It is the one which the human race will embrace in the days of the Messiah, and which Israel's mission is to preserve and propagate meanwhile.

[1e] *Israel and Humanity*, 144

Thus, the Land of Israel and the nation of Israel are simply the two specific instruments providentially chosen to attain a universal end. The fortunes of this country and its peculiar people are bound up with those of all humankind.

Ancient Monotheistic Beliefs and Universal Religion

[2a] *Israel and Humanity*, 103–104

After the introduction of polytheism, the knowledge of the true God did not disappear entirely among the non-Jews. The Bible explicitly acknowledges this. [...] Let us now, however, examine the evidence of the knowledge of God *outside* of Israel, according to the biblical accounts. [...] What we see is paganism and Hebraism each taking a step toward the other, in order to find a meeting-ground in a conception which we shall find to be that of the larger part of the gentile world: a supreme God *together with* subordinate gods at His feet. The difference between Jewish belief and that of the pagans lies in this: Israel saw in these subordinate gods only so many divine *attributes*, whereas the pagans lavished their worship on precisely these diverse forms, which they hypostasized and perceived as divinities. Much later, we can observe a difference of the same order between Christianity and the Jewish Kabbalah.... Thus, for example, the Christian doctrine of the Trinity transformed into distinct persons what were for the Kabbalists divine attributes. Jewish monotheism was known to the pagans in the form of a *pan-monotheism*, for the conception of a supreme God together with deified subordinate forces is nothing other than that.

[2b] *Em LaMikra*, Numbers 3:45

The soul of the Torah is the Kabbala, which accords with the ideas current in a certain place and time. It alone can silence the critic who says that the laws of our Torah are taken from Egyptian law and custom. The truth is that they *are* similar in many ways and cannot be dissociated as some have tried to do. This is not because Moses learned from heretics, but because the divine wisdom he possessed was known to our ancient ancestors and aligns in some respect with what the preeminent priests of Egypt knew and had received from tradition. Not only them, but also the priests of India, Persia, and Greece, who have laws and beliefs that rival the Egyptians. Mark what the kabbalists say: Of all the nations, Egypt most closely approaches holiness.

[2c] *Em LaMikra*, Genesis 23:6

Let us point out a precious similarity, which certainly can be no coincidence. In India, the greatest of the divine triad is called *Brahm*. Moreover, in the same way that Abram's (אברם) name was changed to Abraham (אברהם), so *Brahm* (ברם) became *Brahma* (ברמה) with the addition of a letter *heh* at the end.... [...] We know for certain that in Indian belief, *Brahm* or *Brahma* is the Creator.... You will be amazed if you know that according to Kabbala, Abraham is identified with Ḥesed, the Attribute of Mercy by which the world was created.

[2d] *Em LaMikra*, Genesis 24:50

[T]hree times we find the name of the Lord mentioned by non-Jews. [...] Evidently, the supernal power and sublime dominion over all human, natural, and divine potencies is attributed to this glorious name. I think this is the case because they conceived of the God of Israel as the supreme God, and even if they worshipped other gods, they still believed in Him as the most supreme of all.

[2d] *Israel and Humanity*, 228

The first intellectual act to which the first man was called seems to have been a revelation from the Creator: [...] God blessed them and God said to them, "Be fertile and increase, fill the earth and master it" (Gen. 1:27–28). Moreover, the revelation is Adamic, it is addressed to the primal parents of humankind, for it is humankind itself which is destined to populate the whole earth. There exists an entire group of *aggadot* whose dominant idea, expressed in various ways, is that Adam ought to have been what Israel later became. It is to him, the Rabbis add, that the Law had to be given. The obligation imposed upon him in the earthly paradise consisted of the observance of all the positive and negative precepts of the Torah. It seems indeed that all distinction between Israel and humankind is here being obliterated in order to show more distinctly that the divine revelation belongs to all the children of Adam and not only to the sons of Abraham.

The Essence of Noahism

[3a] *Israel and Humanity*, 241

This local, ethnic quality of Mosaism and its nearly total absence of organized proselytism are ample proof that the religion of Israel is not destined to become the universal religion. Yet Israel insists on declaring that certain general principles are obligatory for every human creature, a code of laws which cannot be evaded with impunity, whose observance is required by divine justice. Can we doubt that Israel believes itself in possession of a religion which is universal in a way that Mosaism is not, a religion whose basic substance appears even in its Scriptures? Can there be any doubt that here indeed is that other aspect of the Law, which addresses all men and epochs?

[3b] *Israel and Humanity*, 242

"We must distinguish between the Canaanite peoples and others, between the obligatory wars and those which are optional." In these latter [instances], surrender is all that Israel has the right to exact of the vanquished. Even if their religion is the most crass kind of polytheism, it must be respected, and its adherents placed under no obligation of any sort. As for the obligatory wars – that is, those which Israel was commanded by God to wage against the Canaanites – this people, so proud of its Mosaic Law, imbued with its own grandeur, was in fact satisfied with very little, with what modern civilization indeed would not hesitate to demand of a barbarous tribe: the fulfillment of the Noahide Law, the minimal code of religion and morality which any society requires in order to survive.

[3c] *Israel and Humanity*, 260

This Noahide, or universal, code to which all humankind is subject must, in the nature of things, be more rational than the Mosaic code, more accessible to intellectual perception. Rationality is, in fact, its principal characteristic, even its principal component. The most cursory study of the subject will amply demonstrate this.

[3d] *Israel and Humanity, 265*

The second Noahide precept forbids polytheism and requires the non-Jew, like the Jew, to acknowledge only one God. Let us hasten to add, however, that the Noahide religion is far more permissive in this matter than Judaism itself. Whereas Israel must observe the oneness of God with uncompromising rigor, without any trace of reference to other divine beings, at least in worship, the non-Jew is thought not to sin if in his religion he relates other divinities to the authentic God, provided that he acknowledge and worship only a single supreme God.

[3e] *Israel and Humanity, 279–280*

As regards ethics: It is certain that when Scripture speaks of human behavior, it addresses humankind in general, and that its precepts embrace all humanity. And this is so not only in the Prophetic books and in the books of the Writings, such as Proverbs, but even in the Torah, which also affirms that the moral life is indispensable to the dignity of all men without distinction, as the Sages acutely observed in connection with the immoralities of the pagans. Moses says, "For all those abhorrent things were done by the people who were in the Land before you, and the Land became defiled" (Lev. 18:27), suggesting that ethical laws are universal, applying to non-Jews as well as Jews. […] This universal moral standard is invoked not only in the pagan's relation to God but also in his relation to Israel, and in a general way in the relations of all men with one another. […] Perhaps this uniformity of humankind's moral code explains why the Mosaic Law is so substantially dominated by national, political precepts rather than ethical ones. Moral values are perhaps assumed to be generally known, whether by a natural instinct of humankind or through a tradition common to all peoples. In human culture, as a rule, the most fundamental beliefs tend to be taken for granted and not formally spelled out.

[3f] *Israel and Humanity*, 310

Let us note carefully the two conditions declared to be essential for the prayer of non-Jews to be heard by God. First, their worship must be in harmony with that of the Israelites, for it is said, "Thus all the peoples of the earth will know Your name and revere You, as does Your people Israel" (II Chr. 6:33). Then they must acknowledge the priestly mission of the Jews, for the text adds, "And they will recognize that Your name is attached to this House that I have built" (ibid.). The first of these conditions presupposes the existence of a code for the non-Jews, not altogether identical to that of Israel (for in that case there would be no grounds for distinguishing non-Jew from Jew) but yet linked to it in a way which corresponds exactly to the character of the Noahide code. The second condition is precisely that which Maimonides, following the Talmud, prescribes for Noahide religion if it is to be considered legitimate: that it be regarded not only as a kind of moral philosophy, or even a natural religion, but as the original Revelation, given to the entire human race, whose custody has been confided to Israel.

The Importance of Religious Diversity

[4a] *Israel and Humanity*, 300–301

According to the rabbis, the universalism implicit in the giving of the Mosaic law can be seen not only in the plurality of languages used by God but also in the very content of Revelation. At the same time that it addresses each people in its own tongue, the law makes itself accessible to every individual by adapting itself to the particular quality of his mind. Religious truth thus has many voices in order to speak to various levels of intelligence. Every human, like every people, has a natural disposition to receive truth in one way rather than another, to contemplate it from a particular perspective. So it is, as we have said, with the very idea of God. These diverse conceptions of God are hypostatized by the various peoples into their own particular divinities, but when joined together in a higher synthesis, they become, with respect to human worship and human understanding as a whole, the authentic God. This is how the unity of humankind is the necessary condition – and, subjectively, the agent or instrument – of the oneness of God. The many-sidedness of the divine Law (if we may describe it as such), its multiplicity of voices, is but the result of this principle extended to all of religion. Just as each people takes from the idea of God that which it is capable of apprehending, so does each people take from religion that which best suits its temper and mentality. For some, it is metaphysics, with the exalted symbols and rites which come from it: these are the people whom Jesus called "children of light." For others, [it is] anthropomorphism, with its imagery of sacred animals, its allegories and incarnations. Some peoples are drawn to profound speculations and mysteries, others to superstitions and barbaric cults. We notice every day that if two related ideas are presented simultaneously to several minds, these minds will not perceive the same relationships between the ideas. [...] In fact, we find Catholic philosophers acknowledging the justness of this principle, even in the religious order: faith in a spiritual truth [writes Mariano] presupposes differences, even asserts and engenders them. Out of diversity, unity acquires strength, solidity, truth. A unity with that is indistinct, indifferent, or inert, is manifest evidence that faith, spirit, and truth are faint or diseased.

Such are the rational or metaphysical grounds of the multiplicity of the revelation at Sinai.

[4b] *Israel and Humanity*, 314

We may observe, however, that the number stops at seven, which still endorses the principle of plurality and variety of religions. Judaism recognizes that the worship of God must take diverse forms adapted to the particular genius of each people and the character of its environment, but without compromising the all-embracing oneness, whose guardian and model is Israel.

[4c] *Israel and Humanity*, 249

The Mosaic Law accepts as legitimate the presence in the Land of Israel of foreigners who do not adhere to the Mosaic religion. Such a "proselyte of the gate" or resident stranger (*ger toshav*), fellow citizen though not coreligionist, is to be distinguished from the "proselyte of the law" (*ger tzedek*), who has completely converted to Judaism. Not only are proselytes of the gate exempt from the dietary prohibitions in the Law, but Israelites, who cannot eat the flesh of an animal which has not been ritually slaughtered, are urged to give it to them rather than sell it to an ordinary stranger (Deut. 14:21). This statute is valuable to us for two reasons: the charitable motive which inspires it and its clear recognition of a legitimate though non-Mosaic category of religion.

Christianity as Disseminator of The Universal Religion Found in Judaism

[5a] *Israel and Humanity*, 45

It was that very faith in the universal religion which the Jews believed was contained in its essence in their ancient doctrine, and whose sway they must one day establish, which gave birth to Christian preaching. It is this which gave the disciples of Jesus their conviction that they were the instruments of a universal mission, and the courage to pursue its fulfillment to the ends of the earth. [...] [N]ever were there differences between them with respect to the universal aspiration they shared: the obligation to evangelize the nations and lead them to the worship of true God.

[5b] *Israel and Humanity*, 50–51

No impartial and reasonable man can fail to recognize and appreciate, as is appropriate, the exalted worth of these two great religions, more especially of Christianity. There is no Jew worthy of the name who does not rejoice in the great transformation wrought by them in a world formerly defiled. We cannot listen to the noblest and most precious names in Judaism, the echoes of its holy books, the recollection of its great events, its hymns and prophecies, in the mouths of so many millions of former pagans of all races, joined together to worship the God of Israel in churches and mosques, without feeling imbued with a legitimate pride of gratitude and love toward the God who effected such great miracles. As for ourself, we have never had the experience of hearing the Psalms of David on the lips of a priest without feeling such sensations. The reading of certain passages of the Gospels has never left us unresponsive. [...] We can abandon ourself all the more freely to these agreeable impressions because we are aware of returning, in them, to a realm which is in fact our own, of enjoying our own possession and being thus all the more Jewish as we do justice to Christianity.

[5c] *Musar Yehudi Le'ummat Musar Notzeri, 61–62*

Ultimately, this religion [Christianity] took a great stride for morality and humanity, by smashing the altars still smoking with the blood of innocents, by eliminating the dens in which fornication was elevated to the level of religious obligation, by declaring the common heritage of all humanity and the universal brotherhood of all human beings, by draining the swamp of egoism, arrogance, brute force, and wealth that have sullied the faces of the poor and wretched, the subjugated and enslaved. These good deeds and many more deserve recognizion from the generation and appreciation from all humanity, and deserve recognition from all humankind. The imprint of Hebraism is discernible in these acts, and it looks on with joy and appreciation. Hebraism esteems these devoted children who left her bosom filled with her spirit, inflamed with the same passion that led the Pharisees who "crossed sea and land to make a single convert" (Matt. 23:15). The Christians have not ushered in the messianic era and perhaps may have even pushed it off. Nevertheless, they have paved the way for the Messiah's arrival and spread the word about his kingdom. The Jewish people do appreciate this, even though the Church has disgraced them. Though they still bleed from the wounds it inflicted, that has not stopped them from continuing to proclaim this.

[5d] *Musar Yehudi Le'ummat Musar Notzeri, 110*

Whatever the foundations of Christian morality, and whatever our opinion of their solidity, there is no doubt that a majestic edifice has been built upon them, and that countless generations have found refuge under its roof. So much suffering, so many wounds have found an almost heavenly cure there. It has spread so much good to the entire world and everywhere inculcated the courage to do what is right and the fear to desist from what is wrong. Thousands of great men have bent the knee at its sight. Let us join them and stand in awe at the initiative of a handful of Jews, pay respect to this branch taken from the august tree of Israel that was grafted onto non-Jewish stock. Its indebtedness to Judaism is clear; one can see the spirit of the Patriarchs, prophets, and Torah scholars in it, so that we can invoke what our forefather Isaac said, "The voice is Jacob's, but the hands are Esau's" (Gen. 27:22).

The Errors of Christianity: Failure To Understand the Necessary Duality of Mosaic and Noahide Law and the Doctrine of Supersessionism

[6a] *Musar Yehudi Le'ummat Musar Notzeri*, 62

These descriptions of Christianity, with its true and legitimate achievements, became a springboard for more extravagant pretensions. Without any justification, fairness, or logic, Christianity proclaimed its morality superior to Hebraic morality. Drunk on its own praise, it liberated itself from the old ways of thinking.

[6b] *Musar Yehudi Le'ummat Musar Notzeri*, 69

My argument is that in the Roman period, like in all the epochs that followed, neither Christianity nor Christian morality had anything to offer man's natural feelings. Christianity knew only how to obstruct the natural development of such feelings, which generated confusion whenever it needed to take a position on a person's obligation to their country. Christianity preached the great principle of universal brotherhood, which it had drawn from Judaism, without recognizing what Judaism knew – that this principle had to be circumscribed by another principle: national brotherhood.

[6c] *Musar Yehudi Le'ummat Musar Notzeri*, 70–71

One way or another, universalist apathy or a universalist empire always entails the negation and effacement of national diversity. Why? Because of something Christianity utterly lacks: a social or political dimension. This results from either its extreme and exclusivist morality, or its pan-nationalist aspirations ever on the cusp of realization. Christianity's social morality was not accompanied by social justice. Beside the altar it knew not how to keep a throne: either the throne was completely consumed by the altar, or it faded in its shadow.

[6d] *Musar Yehudi Le'ummat Musar Notzeri*, 72

With the best of intentions, Christianity believed that it could do no better than seat itself on the throne and grip the gavel. [...] Christianity believed that dogma could be a substitute for political institutions, ritual for national duties, ethics for social obligations. [...] The spirit controlled and manipulated as if it were a body, and belief ringed by punishments, torture, and the gallows, translate directly into violence, injustice, and tyranny, pressed into the service of a religion that is all about charity. And precisely because it spoke only of charity, with nary a word about justice; and precisely because it preached only love, but never respect; and precisely because it single-mindedly devoted itself to the cult of most sublime perfection, scorning any inferior achievement [...] Christianity was doomed to be violent.

[6e] *Musar Yehudi Le'ummat Musar Notzeri*, 162–163

On two scores Christian morality does not hold a candle to that of Judaism: country and society. When Jesus preached love for all human beings, and Christianity successfully painted itself as the sole face of human morality, this was at the cost of a love no less sacred for country and society. [...] Christianity recognizes only one country: the world, or, better yet, heaven. It recognizes only one society: spiritual society. One's country, with its rights and needs, with the limits it sometimes imposes on universal charity – in the manner that one right sometimes impinges on another; the civil society that is truly human, in that it encompasses bodies *and* souls, with its rights and claims, the relations it weaves between its members and the rules and laws that regulate them – Christianity ignores all of this. Does Christianity recognize the political foe? No. Does it recognize social justice? Also no. One can confidently posit that without the possibility of a political enemy, there can be no country, and without social rivalries there can be no society and no social justice.

[6f] *Musar Yehudi Le'ummat Musar Notzeri*, 64–65

With what did Christianity replace the God of the Hebrews...? It attributed perfectibility to the Creator Himself, or at least to His external word. Christianity taught that the word of God itself can be perfected gradually, that it can adapt to circumstances, ways of life, and even human failings! Christianity projects onto God the flexibility of Paul, who presents as a Jew to Jews and as a non-Jew to non-Jews. It facilitates the base concessions of the Jesuits to Chinese idolaters. It makes God in its image, like the gods of Homer, instead of making man in God's image, as Moses teaches. Christianity not only thumbs its nose at common sense and logic, which do not ascribe more than one will to God, but it also empties revelation of meaning, undermining its own foundations and undercutting its strongest basis. [...] A revelation that proceeds ploddingly, in step with man's capacities, and does not in its very first utterance pronounce the last word, taking the risk of being misunderstood or unappreciated, whittles the eternal truth down to a size that is palatable to hearts and minds. Such a revelation should be immediately suspect to anyone with even a modicum of discernment, and it produces no benefit whatsoever because it does not tell people anything they cannot come up with on their own.

Islam: Devotion to the National and Political

[7] *Musar Yehudi Le'ummat Musar Notzeri*, 250–251
If Jesus adopted the more spiritual, profound, and religious side of Hebraism... It is my contention that Muhammad recognized the tangible side of Hebraism accessible to everyone, the side that the Jews brought with them everywhere: exoteric monotheism. He therefore transformed that into the be-all and end-all, the ultimate paradigm for his religion. If Jesus drew from the moral, profound, and spiritual side of Hebraism..., Muhammad took for himself the opposite, its social and aristocratic side.... If Christianity brings the principles and rules of life in the next world into the heart of this-worldly life, if it effaces this world and subsumes it under the next..., Muhammad does the exact opposite: he fashions and regulates the World to Come according to the model of this world. He transfers its pleasures and pains, passions and caprices – the delights of the flesh – to the next world, to the point that the Resurrection of the Dead becomes nothing more than a return to and continuation of life on earth. In a word, Islam adopted the social

and aristocratic side of Judaism, whereas Christianity preferred to cling to the religious, metaphysical side.

Rabbi Abraham Isaac HaKohen Kook: "Divine Religions" and the Central Role of the Jewish People

Sarel Rosenblatt

Rabbi Abraham Isaac HaKohen Kook (1865–1935) was one of the greatest rabbis, leaders, and thinkers that the Jewish people were privileged to have in recent times. He was the first Ashkenazic Chief Rabbi of what would soon become the State of Israel, and he laid the halakhic, theological, and philosophical foundations for a Judaism wrestling with modernity, especially in view of the Jewish people returning to their land. In his wide-ranging thought, Kook sought to formulate a Jewish position on many major issues, one of which was how to think about and relate to other religions.

Kook's thoughts go in many directions in his writings, and quite frequently his positions on a single issue seem contradictory. He said about himself that he harbored dueling intellectual tendencies which found expression in his compositions. These contradictions, however, push and pull one another dialectically to limn a more complete, harmonious picture of the divine wisdom. The same is true of Kook's thinking on the role of other religions, and the legitimacy of them and their founders. It displays two trends, one inviting and the other keeping at bay. This chapter explores both, seeking to understand how they can coexist and what practical implications they carry.

MONOTHEISTIC RELIGIONS AS "DIVINE RELIGIONS"

The first full treatment of this issue appears in Kook's early treatise *LiNevukhei HaDor* (*For the Perplexed of the Generation*). "What religion is called divine?" he asks [1]. He is not satisfied with answering whether a particular religion meets the halakhic definition of idolatry. He wants to know whether it can be considered a "divine religion." In this, he follows in the footsteps of Rabbi Joseph Albo, who wrote in the fifteenth century: "It is possible for there to be two divine laws simultaneously for separate nations, and…each one's adherents can attain human flourishing."[1]

The classic halakhic discourse on non-Jewish religion centers on limiting social contact with idolaters. This sets up a binary assessment of religious non-Jews: either they are idolaters with whom Jews should minimize contact, or they are not and Jews can be indifferent about their particular religious beliefs and practices.[2] Like Albo, Kook expands this uninspiring model to add the possibility of viewing non-Jewish religious identity positively. He applies two rabbinic dicta to pious non-Jews: "A non-Jew who studies Torah is like a High Priest," and "The holy spirit rests on someone according to their deeds, be they man or woman, slave or maidservant, non-Jew or Jew" [2].[3] In their original contexts, though, these statements carry quite different meanings. The first, from the Talmud, refers to a non-Jew learning Torah, not their own holy books. The second, from the Midrash, is a great equalizer that speaks about the power of one's actions – not the fulfillment of religious duties specifically. Kook works these ancient statements into his stance on non-Jews who profess monotheism but observe their own religious

---

1. *Sefer HaIkkarim* 1:25. See further the chapter dedicated to Albo earlier in this volume.
2. There are also additional halakhic institutions intended to prevent intermarriage with non-Jews, irrespective of their religion.
3. Respectively, Bava Kamma 38a and *Tanna DeVei Eliyahu*, ch. 10.

precepts. What is the theological foundation for his positive appraisal of monotheistic religions? Kook writes that this comes from a place of strength: belief in the divinity of the Torah is the foundation of intellectual freedom and spiritual liberty, and we ought to hoist this up high for everyone to see. The flag of tolerance flies high precisely because it sits on the peaks of belief.[4]

The Torah's view, according to Kook, is that the faithful have a "binding obligation…to abide by and preserve" their religion, and "every enlightened person" therefore should recognize that they are "engaging in divine service appropriate for them." Furthermore, their religious piety helps advance "the most exalted and universal moral goal" [1]. In other words, it is in the interests of the Jewish believer for non-Jewish monotheists to keep the faith.

Kook is aware that the "common folk" are intolerant of all other religions. He diagnoses this view as beneficial only for "the narrow-minded" Jews, who need to put other religions down in order to boost theirs up. "But this has no truth to it," Kook tells his readers. Also, this apologetic tactic is likely to backfire. Continuously feeding scorn for other religions can ferment into a generalized anti-religious sentiment that is unforgiving to Judaism, too. For this reason, Kook feels the need to "instill the value of other faiths according to the Torah" [2]. This is not merely a more effective tool but a position that interlocks with Kook's idea of divine unity: this is the foundation of tolerance; it proceeds not from a carefree attitude to faith but from wisdom and unwavering belief that God controls everything, and that He always treats every nation and individual with kindness, for they are all His handiwork. (*LiNevukhei HaDor*, ch. 52) [3]

Of course, individuals are undeniably different, and peoples, nations, and cultures are plainly distinct. Kook treats this as a triviality: it is only natural that every culture has its own religion with a unique path to the same universal end:

> The pathways to morality and means of acquiring good
> character, which are rooted in fear of Heaven, differ by

---

4. *LiNevukhei HaDor*, ch. 52, p. 256.

nation based on historical circumstance, race, land, and material and spiritual experiences. What impresses the splendor of the divine light and the glory of Heaven upon one nation does not upon another. (*LiNevukhei HaDor*, 14:1) [2]

The religious ideal is universal, but the paths to it are particular to each nation and culture.

If the existence of non-Jewish religions is justified, one must consider the character of their founders and leaders. In terms of the cardinal tenets of Judaism, Kook is of the opinion that "the principles of belief contain no opposition to other religions" and that other religions may be the recipients of divine guidance or even prophecy:

> [Perhaps] they have been privy to an efflux of knowledge, prophecy, or the holy spirit, or some other befitting divine assistance has been rendered to a number of nations through their leaders and pious individuals.[5]

Theologically speaking, Moses's unparalleled prophecy and the sanctity of the Torah given at Sinai do not gainsay the possibility that deeply spiritual and pious gentiles were illumined by a ray of divine enlightenment that inspired them to establish their religions. These religious founders apply their closeness to God and the spark of prophecy to the flock they know intimately, which endows the resulting religion, in its practices and laws, with "religious value worthy of admiration." Although this religious service has no connection to the Jewish people, "we can view them as drawing closer to God's light" [2]. Rabbi Nathaniel b. Rabbi Fayyumi proposed a similar approach to non-Jewish religions eight centuries earlier in Yemen: "But it is possible for Him to give additional commands to whomever He wishes, and to send whom He wishes to whomever He wishes, since all the worlds are His possession and creation."[6] Kook's

---

5. *LiNevukhei HaDor*, ch. 52, p. 255.
6. See page 49.

contribution is that these divine agents can receive a type of prophecy and even have "perceptible miracles" wrought for them.[7] In Nathaniel's theology, the divinely appointed messenger is the recipient of some degree of revelation by which he reveals a heavenly book for his people. In lieu of this, Kook speaks of "an efflux of knowledge" or "some other befitting divine assistance," allowing for a wider range of media to establish the legitimacy of a religion. The founder need not come down from the proverbial mountain with a book in hand.

Furthermore, Kook discerns echoes of divine wisdom within the human being, even in the absence of a directed burst of sapiential energy from above. He praises "the human spirit" and "individual talent" for their ability to generate moral insight and to craft laws similar to the "rational mitzvot" of the Torah. That is what it means for humans to be created in the divine image. "The foundation of the Torah is pure humanity," Kook declares.[8]

This allows us to better grasp Kook's halakhic agreement with Rabbi Menahem Meiri of medieval Provence that we define the *ger toshav* (resident alien) of halakha on the basis of ethical behavior and not religious belief. In a letter from 1904 he writes:

The halakha accords with Meiri, for all the peoples that are bound by proper interpersonal laws already have the status of *gerim toshavim* in all our obligations toward them.[9]

Whereas Meiri distinguishes between the planes of beliefs and behavior, Kook sees religious and spiritual value in the latter itself.

---

7. See further *LiNevukhei HaDor*, ch. 52.
8. *LiNevukhei HaDor*, ch. 34, p. 174.
9. *Iggerot HaRe'iya* 1:89, p. 99. However, in order to permit the sale of land in the Land of Israel to non-Jews for the Sabbatical year, Kook did not rely on this halakhic position alone. See *Mishpat Kohen* 61 (written in 1909), and cf. 58 (written a few years prior). For an elaboration of Meiri's opinion, see the chapter dedicated to his thought in this volume.

JUDAISM'S UNIQUENESS AND ITS RELATIONSHIP TO OTHER RELIGIONS

Baked into Kook's legitimation, appreciation, and favorable view of other religions is an essentially dialogical, and by extension critical, posture. By dialogical I mean that the Jewish people are supposed to feel for and respond to the broader spiritual and cultural currents swirling around them in order to learn from them and respond by broadcasting the Torah's wisdom to the world. This dialogue is carried out with a critical eye because the Jews have a universal obligation to identify what among the nations of the world requires refinement and supplementation. As a thinker at home in the traditions of Kabbalah and Hasidism, Kook translates the Lurianic mythos of the breaking of the vessels and dispersal of the divine sparks into spiritual and cultural terminology as well. In his account, the diverse fragments of human expression, including its religions, are meant to be complementary, fitting together like a vast puzzle that reveals the divine spirit in its fullness. Since the Jewish people bear the message of divine unity, there must be an inherent connection between it and these scattered sparks of the divine. This has a practical ramification: "That is why we cannot afford to ignore any stirring when we come to investigate the spiritual power of the Congregation of Israel" [4]. Their belief in God's unity requires Jews to keep a finger on the spiritual pulse of humanity, tracking it as it courses through other religions and cultures. At the same time, for every religion to reach its full flowering and achievement, and for all religions to form the beautiful mosaic of the divine, the Jewish people have an obligation to fulfill their universalist mission: ensuring the religious and moral progress of the nations of the world. According to Kook, the Jewish people are suited for this charge for two reasons. First, the nation was born through divine revelation to patriarchs, so that its very purpose has always been to create divine unity in this world. Second, the prophecy of Moses and heavenly Torah are a loom that weaves together this dazzling array of spirituality into a holistic and harmonious fabric of existence [7]. Two areas of activity will facilitate this religious progress. The first is an educational campaign to teach Torah to non-Jews. When the world shifts from exile to redemption, the walls of the study hall will fall away, so to speak, and Torah will surge outward beyond the domain of the Jewish people. Kook compares the exilic condition to the darkness of night, in the face of which people retreat into the safety of their homes. In the Diaspora, Jews withdraw into their shells to strengthen their own identity. When the redemption comes and Jews are held high, a period of "great love" begins and the Torah lights up the globe. In service of this mission, teachers of Torah must delve into its reasoning and determine how to translate them "according to the superficial conception of the non-Jews" [5]. Furthermore, in the messianic era, the primary purpose of Torah study and mitzva performance will be "for all of humanity" [6].

The second endeavor is the establishment of a spiritual center for the religions of the world and for all of humanity, "a hub of peace and love" and a "unifying center of divine knowledge in the world" [1–2]. Organizing the nations around a center for ethics and religion helmed by the Jewish people will bring about "the ultimate perfection of the human race" in societal, moral, and religious terms.

One can now understand why Kook does not consider correct theology and moral behavior sufficient criteria to fully legitimize other religions. There must also be recognition of the Jewish people's spiritual uniqueness and a rejection of any supersessionist theory [7–8]. To put it differently, Kook connects the legitimacy of other religions to their internalization of the same holistic worldview and their willingness to participate in a network that seeks to build bridges between faiths, especially with the Jewish people and the Torah [1]. All of this is intended to induce religious cross-pollination and manifest the full spirit of God in this world.

A CHANGE OF MIND?

In the years after 1904, when Kook takes up residence in Jaffa, his stance toward other religions, and Christianity in particular, takes a dramatically negative turn. Camaraderie is replaced by criticism, integration by isolation. As the years go on, Kook increasingly hardens his stance on Christianity, as indicated by the scope and tone of his criticism.[10]

---

10. The disparity between Kook's earlier and later writings is evident in the number and language of anti-Christian passages. It is not only that he critiques Christianity more

These later arguments against Christianity and other religions are unique in the genre of Jewish polemics. Kook does not take up the cudgels against the usual targets: supersessionism, anti-Semitism, problematic theology (in the simple sense of idolatry), or questionable historical narrative. Instead, Kook is perturbed by the real-world consequences of these beliefs, especially the Christian conception of humanity's state and the connection between God and humanity. Judaism requires that people take responsibility for theology, as this forms part of the cosmic *teshuva*, an elevation of the entire world as it returns to God's arms. Kook's analysis of Christian belief finds that it conveys the exact opposite: abrogation of the mitzvot and the doctrine of original sin define spirituality as disconnected from the physical and political realms, and they express despair at the ability to reform and sanctify them [9].

The questions beg themselves. What caused this drastic change in Kook's thought? Why did he focus on these specific issues?

In a letter from 1908, Kook writes that this change is deliberate, and he explains it [10]. At the peak of the Second Aliya, Kook is bearing witness to "the hope of the Jewish people and its revival being realized under the cover of gradualness, in the land of the living." Simultaneously, he evaluates this as a period of vulnerability, because the Jewish people are "still curled up, like a fetus in its mother's womb." Kook wants to protect the gestating nation so that it makes it to term. But many Jews

---

strongly and warns about its dangers repeatedly, but the language is elevated to the level of metaphysics and grows much harsher. In an example from the first *kovetz* of *Shemona Kevatzim* (*Kovetz* 1:239), he refers to the abrogation of the physical mitzvot in Christianity and explains why the "true" divine teaching must include both beliefs and acts. Beginning in the fifth and sixth *kevatzim* (many cited in *Orot HaEmuna*, edited by Rabbi Moshe Gurevits in Kook's lifetime, and many used by Rabbi Zvi Yehuda Kook when he edited *Yisrael UTeḥiyyato*), Kook uses terms like "corrupting venom," "Amalek" (*Kovetz* 6:208), and "positive spiritual pollution" (*Kovetz* 6:209). In the first *kovetz* (*Kovetz* 1:267), Kook criticizes other religions – Christianity among them – and says that they should be dealt with by increasing spiritual light and finding the holy sparks within them. Later, in the fifth *kovetz* (*Kovetz* 5:57), he writes that nothing should be accepted directly from Christianity – to be contrasted with all other religions – and that one should not partner with its devotees on anything, owing to the deviousness and "poison" contained within Christianity's positive elements. Only by refusing to accept anything from that religion will it ultimately be reformed.

have absorbed the widespread notion that church and state ought to be separate, "two systems in contradiction, opposing each other." He traces this idea to other religions, particularly Christianity and Islam, and the basic cultural assumptions regnant in contemporary Europe.[11]

In the face of contemporary trends, Kook declares, "It proves nearly impossible now to demarcate the special form of that stellar defense, the light of Israel against those would diminish it." He had gone to great lengths to defend other religions, and he even considers his record on this as "stellar." But now he senses that his audience needs to hear a different message that accentuates the distinctiveness of the Jewish people and transforms the line separating Judaism from other religions into a trench [11]. He wants to merge religion with national identity in order to forge a Zionist ethos that will take Judaism as the basis for national revival in the Jewish homeland.

Still, we must probe the matter further. Why did Kook at the turn of the century think that "the perplexed of the generation" would be persuaded to strengthen their religiosity and take ownership of their heritage through the defense of other religions and the revelation of their commonality, and only a few years later we find him convinced that the opposite argument will have the same effect?

In a number of writings from the first decade of the twentieth century, Kook writes that a "new heresy," unlike anything that has ever threatened people of faith, is swiftly taking root.[12] Joseph Avivi has convincingly demonstrated that Kook is referring to the philosophy of Friedrich Nietzsche and apparently also to the literary activity of Micah Joseph Berdyczewski, who translated Nietzsche's ideas into Hebrew.[13] This modern wave of thought alters the trajectory of Kook's line of thinking. Interestingly, Avivi observes an affinity between Kook's new argumentation and Nietzsche's own criticism of Christianity:

---

11. On Kook's attitude toward Islam more specifically, see Eliyahu Galil, "Islamic Belief Is Better than Christian: Islam in Rabbi Abraham Isaac HaKohen Kook's Thought" [in Hebrew], *Asif 6* (2019): 645–655.

12. *Eder HaYekar*, 32–34.

13. Joseph Avivi, *Kabbalah of A. I. Kook* [in Hebrew] (Jerusalem: Ben-Zvi Institute, 2018), chs. 29–31.

> Nietzsche hated Christianity because it detests and dis-
> tances itself from life. Berdyczewski followed his lead and
> opposed the book and halakha, which restrict life and the
> passions. Nietzsche and Berdyczewski both urged man to
> seek out the natural life, in all its roiling and storminess....
> Rabbi Kook agrees that one should seek out life, but he
> asserts that true living flows from the divine emanation.[14]

Nietzsche criticized Christianity and wrote somewhat wistfully about the Judaism of the Old Testament while decrying the "slave morality" that began developing in the Second Temple era. Kook identifies two antithetical responses to Nietzsche among Jews. On the one hand are secular Zionists, who voice a similar critique of the talmudic-halakhic tradition. On the other hand are halakhic scholars who reject Nietzsche and also disassociate themselves from the Zionist movement, which they deem a symbol of human strength, grit, and initiative that refuses to be restrained by ancient traditions. Kook responds to both sides by finding the grain of truth in the "new heresy" and turning the Nietzschean criticism against other religions. Only Judaism most forcefully and fully expresses the power of life and human greatness. If you nod your head at Nietzsche, Kook says, you are saying yes to Judaism. To make this bold claim requires positing a sharp distinction between Judaism and other religions. Kook spent much time trying to paper over the cracks dividing Jews from the nations of the world, but now the ascendancy of the "new heresy" and the fragile state of national rebirth in the Land of Israel compel him to call attention to the fault lines underneath.[15]

The fact that Kook himself points to these two factors precipitating his near-reversal is incredibly helpful for determining the extent to which we can term this a change of mind. Based on the foregoing,

---

14. Ibid., 625.
15. Yehudah Mirsky argues in his *Rav Kook: Mystic in a Time of Revolution* (New Haven: Yale University Press, 2014) that World War I and its great bloodletting fed directly into Kook's change in attitude toward Christianity, and comparisons between his writings before and after the Great War do support this contention. Still, as Avivi has demonstrated, one can detect this shift in approach to other religions in the years before the outbreak of war.

Kook's new tack should not be taken as a rejection of his earlier, reasoned theological-philosophical approach. Unearthing connections and underscoring disconnections both have a time and place. One must judiciously decide which approach is most appropriate in present circumstances, and occasionally take stock and reassess. Kook takes political and cultural readings, considers educational and other effects, and assesses the progress of national revival. Only then does he use these inputs to determine the correct option. At different junctures, he reaches opposite conclusions.

It is noteworthy that even during his more isolationist period, Kook stresses the importance of preserving "natural moral fellowship" [12] with the targets of his attack. All human beings, Christians included, ought to be treated properly, because "the light of humanity's divine image" can cut through all darkness.

Additionally, in a letter penned in 1908, Kook says that the purpose of the Jews is not to destroy Christianity or Islam but to rectify them completely. Following a comment of the Vilna Gaon, Kook argues that Christianity is not to be hated in toto, but only for its negative elements. Jacob, progenitor of the Jewish people, remarks to his brother Esau, a traditional rabbinic symbol of Christianity, "I have seen you like one sees the countenance of God" (Gen. 33:10); therefore, "the fraternal love between Esau and Jacob, between Isaac and Ishmael, transcends all of those troubles."[16]

CONCLUSION AND CONTEMPORARY IMPLICATIONS

In considering the issue of non-Jewish religiosity and religions, Rabbi Kook situates himself within the tradition that does not only grant them legitimacy, but considers them a blessing. He rejects the exclusivist view of one "true religion" that does not allow for any other religious expression, because his idea of the truth is modular. The seven Noahide laws are not the ceiling for non-Jewish religious aspirations but the floor. Furthermore, Kook's idea that the divine wisdom is revealed multitudinously, of which even the religious resolutions of the human intellect

---

16. *Iggerot HaRe'iya* 1:112.

form a part, implies that one can accept the yoke of Heaven and grow outside of Judaism. By the same token, the founders of other monotheistic religions could have had genuine miracles worked for them.

What sets Kook's thought apart from those of predecessors in this tradition is his attempt to bring order, even centralization, to the variety of non-Jewish religions. In his holistic and organic worldview, Kook yearns for a universal bond that aligns peoples and religions in concentric circles, with the Jewish people settled in the Land of Israel at its heart. The Jews have the obligation to steward global progress more generally and to reform every religion more specifically. The obverse also is true: the major religions must recognize the importance of the Jewish people or at least repudiate their own replacement theologies. Only this configuration best expresses human comprehension of God's unity and the human fellowship that derives from there. One can understand, then, why the Jewish people have a unique obligation to keep abreast of what is happening in the world, and why the failure of a religion to conform to Kook's vision, like a puzzle piece bent out of shape, elicits an acerbic response. The complete realization of God's unity in this world is at stake.

Kook also writes a good amount about difference – on the gaps between Judaism and other faiths – and he does not hold his tongue. He explains his motivations as answering the needs of the time, to disentangle Jewish identity from European culture, with its nascent heresy and the pernicious effects of certain religious ideas on Jewish self-identity. It presented a bane to all Jewish observance and sounded a potential death knell for the fledgling Yishuv.

If the analysis presented in this chapter is correct, Kook's thought instructs us to look honestly, unflinchingly at the world today. We should examine the cultural currents sweeping through the world and try to objectively assess the state of the Jewish people. We must then come to a decision: do we pursue more bridge building, advocate for time apart, or pursue a little of both? While this is a crucial topic that deserves separate treatment, I would like to say a few words about it here.

First, both Islam and Christianity have undergone significant changes in the past century, some positive and some negative. For example, since Vatican II in the 1960s, Christianity has been intensively engaged in internal reform to root out the causes of anti-Semitism, bloodshed, and suppression of human rights. It has even explicitly retracted its belief that Israel's election by God was revoked.

Second, the secular culture of the West is a far cry from what it was in the early twentieth century, when Kook wrestled with it. Postmodern deconstruction, materialism, unbridled capitalism, individualism, and abandonment of tradition alarm leaders from all religions. Social media generates polarizing and divisive discourse. Religious extremism continues to ignore all the good that Western human rights have brought to the world, and it has brought about a great loss of life. As for modern Jewish life in Israel, the revival of the Jewish people in their land is no longer at risk, but we need to be concerned about the loss of identity – particularly in the Diaspora – and of the grand vision of being a light to the nations, ministering to the world as a holy people. I think that one can make the case that today, even the holy Rabbi Kook would agree that we should bring the Torah out into the world pleasantly and offer our critiques of cultures and religions constructively, by extending hands in friendship to all those seeking to call in the name of the Lord.

SOURCES

[1] *LiNevukhei HaDor 8*
In this chapter, Rabbi Kook lays the framework for thinking about other religions. He seeks to distinguish between faiths worthy of the title "divine religion" and others that remain mired in idolatry. Over the course of the chapter, in a section not cited here, he explains why we ought to learn to appreciate even those religions that have little in common with Judaism.

Our understanding of religions requires clarification. What religion can be termed divine, a binding obligation on all its adherents because they are members of a people or peoples whose ancestors agreed to abide by and preserve it? And what religion can be said to be an error, so that no one in their right mind should be obligated to uphold it? [...]

The religion that enables the lofty development intended for humankind, as described above, ought to be the entire truth. Any idolatrous religion, then, cannot lead to this; only knowledge of God's unity can cause humanity to orient itself around a single center of spirituality, and ultimately around a central place and idea, a hub of peace and love.

There is no hope that idolatry in its error can yield this perfection, leaving only Judaism and its offshoots.

One should not look unfavorably upon these offshoots as they are. The founders might have been divinely inspired to try to improve a designated part of humanity in a suitable manner. From this angle, perceptible miracles to strengthen belief might have been made available for this end goal, because it concerns the perfection of humanity, whom God has been looking after from the inception of existence until its end. Error was introduced into this because it was impossible to endow them with the natural inclination to ultimate perfection, so that there would be a sole center of spirituality in the world. Obviously, no nation in the world aside from the Jewish one is superior in an absolute sense due to its spiritual attainments in morality and divine religion. Therefore, only in this respect will they be partially negated; they will need to recognize that the single center must exist in this world, and that counsel and guidance in moral behavior ought to be taken from the original source, in its immaculate purity. [...] The entrenched belief in the books of Christianity and Islam, that, Heaven forfend, the stature of the Jewish people has been voided, must itself be voided, so that humanity can fulfill its eternal aim and goal. The enlightening and refining moral content of every religion, though, deserves respect, and every enlightened person ought to know that those who practice them out of tradition are engaging in divine service appropriate for them. In the end, every moral refinement holds the promise of achieving the most exalted and universal moral goal.

Whatever their divine inspiration – be it accompanied by a vision of the imaginative faculty or only by some other potency and energetic spirit, so long as it realizes the ultimate perfection of the human race, it should be upheld by those who have banded together on account of their history or some other cause.

[2] *LiNevukhei HaDor* 14:1
This chapter is a direct continuation of the previous source. It elaborates on the proper attitude to adopt toward other religions, and specifically addresses those voices that categorically reject all other religions.

There are others who believe it impossible to genuinely believe in the truth of the Torah unless one also believes that all other faiths are worthless, and that those who adhere to them gain nothing from them. But this has no truth to it. Indeed, there are certain ideas circulating among the Jewish nation that lead many common folk to think this way, and this thinking also has, at times, reinforced Jewish belief among the narrow-minded, who cannot fathom the Torah's sublimity and sanctity unless they hold other faiths to be erroneous and useless. This ill-conceived line of thinking, however, has many negative repercussions. The scorn for other faiths deeply ingrained in the masses is also responsible for the wicked and godless treating the pure belief of the Jews in the same way. They claim that they are identical: this is religion and that is religion. Therefore, to save our youngsters from corrosive influences such as these, we must instill the value of other faiths according to the Torah.

We need to divide all the religions of the world into three categories, except for Judaism, which even secular scholars of religion say is the matron of religions. The worst of the lot are idolatrous faiths that do not even entertain the idea of a single creator. Better than those are faiths that have not been scoured of the taint of idolatry. Still better than those are faiths that are free from all idolatry, yet they still take a different path from our Torah's. [...]

Even within the darkness of idolatry one can find pure-hearted individuals who want to reprove and thereby improve their people. Realizing that the true and pure light of the divine surpasses their power, they guide them accordingly through good conduct and customs to a greater future perfection. About such individuals it says in *Tanna DeVei Eliyahu,* "I call heaven and earth as witnesses, that the holy spirit rests on someone according to their deeds, be they man or woman, slave or maidservant, gentile or Jew." It is possible to find uniquely spiritually- adept individuals who receive divine assistance in establishing moral practices and customs, for they will ultimately bring their practitioners to recognize the truth and divine light. Since these moral practices guide them, each according to their own path and spiritual stature, to gradually ascend from their spiritual level to a higher one, until they reach the level of truth where the light of Israel enables them to truly perceive God's glory, they have a religious value worthy of admiration. In spite of their distance, we can view them as drawing closer to God's light and internalize that they are doing the right thing by upholding the tradition of their ancestors and the customs established by their elders, because these spiritual adepts were visionaries, sometimes of enormous breadth, and made it their life's work to better the moral and physical state of their people. [...] Those religions founded on the Torah and the Prophets are certainly noble, for their adherents are close to God's light and to knowing His glory. This is the case even though they lack the fundamental principle, revealed only to select individuals, that the full realization of God's will in this world must be completed by the Jewish people. In the same way that He first acted to make His glory and greatness known through the nation He chose, so too the grand finale of God's glory filling the world will occur via the light of the Jewish people. [...]

[...] Every nation ought to heed the counsel of its accepted and confirmed leaders, for they generally were God-fearing and planned to improve their internal welfare. The highest degree of prophecy, which includes knowledge of God and His beneficence for all generations, is the unique heritage of Israel, so that they can constitute an unfailing and unifying center of divine knowledge in the world. Lower levels of inspiration to justice and goodness are not fit to be centralized for all humankind and befit whatever nation has such inspiration; therefore, they can be found within every nation and culture. As such, those religious practices instituted by the greats and the most pious of the nations of the world ought to be recognized as their divine service, and we should not denigrate them at all, for "the Lord is close to all who call Him, to all who call Him genuinely" (Ps. 145:18), and "all hearts seek out the Lord" (I Chr. 28:9).

Every single Jew must avoid developing an affinity for any religious mores or practices of other religions, and one ought to think of the vigilance involved in maintaining this distance like the modesty that keeps a man away from someone else's wife. It is not the product of jealousy or envy, God forbid, but of the purity of the soul and sanctity in character and deed.

[...] The pathways to morality and means of acquiring good character, which are rooted in fear of Heaven, differ by nation, based on historical circumstance, race, land, and material and spiritual experiences.

What impresses the splendor of the divine light and the glory of Heaven upon one nation does not upon another.

[3] *LiNevukhei HaDor 39:1*
Here, Rabbi Kook develops his historiosophical theory, according to which human culture constitutes a never-ending process of trial and error. From this standpoint, one can better appreciate and even justify those cultures caught in the orbit of idolatry: they were doing the best they could considering where humanity stood at the time.

The same is true regarding idolaters – every nation has its particular spiritual stature. This is the foundation of tolerance; it proceeds not from a carefree attitude to faith but from wisdom and unwavering belief that God controls everything, and that He has always treated every people and individual with kindness, for they are all His handiwork. Souls first need to be elevated through ethical behavior and right thinking, and then the power of universal harmony will appear. Peace on the individual level between members of the nation and its factions will easily spread to all, and visions of peace will be actualized, until all of God's people once again become God's familiars, knowledgeable in the Torah and fulfilling it out of love.... Then, all peoples will recognize our glory and will say about us, "the holy people, the Lord's redeemed" (Is. 62:12). [...] This notion of respect for the human collective and divine love for every human being will not be diminished; in fact, the light of the holy fire will only be increased through safeguarding the exceptional sanctity of God's people.

[4] *Shemona Kevatzim, Kovetz 1:26*
In this quotation, Rabbi Kook clarifies the concept of "the Congregation of Israel," a sobriquet of the sefira *known as* Malkhut *that is associated with the Jewish people, as a congregating force that brings together diverse streams of human spirituality. This understanding has a practical ramification.*

All the diverse spiritual currents of human existence have a root in the Congregation of Israel, given that it is – in the mystical sense known specially by those souls aspiring to transcend to pure bliss – the center of our humanity. That is why we cannot afford to ignore any stirring when we come to investigate the spiritual power of the Congregation of Israel, the "Bride (*kalla*)" that is "crowned (*kelila*) by all colors."

[5] *Ein Aya, Berakhot* 1:1

This is the opening piece of Rabbi Kook's commentary on the aggadic material in Tractate Berakhot. He views the first mishna of the Oral Torah as a symbol of the Jews' tendency to wall themselves off during their exile. He imaginatively conceives of the period of redemption as a time when Jews will go out into the world and teach Torah to non-Jews.

"From when does one recite the *Shema* at night? From the time the priests enter to eat their priestly tithe." The recitation (*keriat*) of the *Shema* at night and in the morning gesture toward the two types of declaration (*keria*) of God's name that are incumbent upon the Jewish people. We must accept the yoke of Heaven on ourselves, and through our declaration of God's unity act so that ultimately all the world's inhabitants will recognize and know that the Lord, the God of Israel, is King, and His dominion extends over all.

In exile, which is comparable to night, our primary activity concerns ourselves alone, so that we can withstand the waves that wash over us, in the name of God. Therefore, faith (*emuna*) pertains to the night: Whoever did not say *Emet VeEmuna* (True and Faithful) at night did not fulfill their obligation. For us it is enough to have faith and accept the truth from our forefathers who saw God's light and glory with their own eyes.

But at the time of redemption, when the horn of Israel will be lifted, it will consequently be the time for the action of the recitation of the morning *Shema* – *Ahava Rabba* (Great Love) – so that all peoples will say that the light of Israel shall be a light for the world. At that time, therefore, the reasons of the Torah will be revealed; "there shall not be light of *yekarot* and *kippaon*" (Zech. 14:6) anymore – these are the reasons of the Torah that are precious (*yekarim*) in this world and insignificant (*kefuyim*) in the next. For in order to draw close those who are distant, words of truth (*emet*) must be perfectly clarified and the matter translated according to the superficial conception of the non-Jews. That is why *Emet VeYatziv* (True and Firm) of the morning is translated into Aramaic.

The Jewish people are God's priests in this world. In handling their own internal affairs, which do not involve outsiders, they are like priests. Not so when they teach Torah or even when they offer sacrifices, because then they do have a relationship with outsiders, acting on their behalf. Whether they are their own agents or agents of God, they are agents regardless. When they enter to eat the priestly tithe, they enter a world exclusive to priests, and they may not partner with non-priests at all, because non-priests have no portion of this food and must be kept separate. Similarly, the time for reciting the general *Shema* at night causes the Jewish people to dwell alone, in order for them to protect their spiritual attainments, the everlasting life that God has placed within them. This explains the conceptual connection between the recitation of the *Shema* at night and the time when the priests enter to eat the priestly tithe.

[6] *Ein Aya, Berakhot* 1:171
Rabbi Kook adds to what he said in the previous source and marks the messianic era as a period when the Jewish people will be focused primarily on bringing perfection to the entire world and less preoccupied with their own national, particularistic concerns.

"Ben Zoma said to the Sages, But does one mention the Exodus from Egypt in the days of the Messiah, etc. [Redemption from] the subjugation of the kingdoms will be primary and the Exodus from Egypt secondary." The Jewish people merited freedom, i.e., their own perfection, through the Exodus, but the universal perfection of humankind will only occur in the days of the Messiah. It will specifically be preceded by [the Jews'] dispersion, for the name of the Lord will thereby begin to be known in the world. But knowledge of God will not be complete, nor can it be complete, until the horn of Israel is uplifted. Since universal human perfection will be achieved through us during the messianic period, when we will truly be uplifted as a kingdom of priests, [redemption from] the subjugation of the kingdoms will become the main goal, and the particularistic perfection of our nation practically secondary. We will have already achieved national perfection by that point; we won't need to focus our efforts on it, nor will we have need of its intermediate goals. Our main activity will be striving for universal perfection. Given that universal perfection is made possible only through Jewish observance of the Torah and the mitzvot, the purpose of our actions will be primarily for all of humanity, and only secondarily to achieve the individual perfection of every Jew, an ongoing process since the Exodus from Egypt. Our own perfection will be achieved of its own accord by the light of God.

[7] *Kevatzim MiKetav Yad Kadsho*, vol. 2, *Pinkas HaDappim* 1:11

Here Rabbi Kook ranks Islamic belief in God above that of Christianity, yet he explains why it is Judaism specifically that brings about a fuller revelation of God's unity in the world.

Islamic belief is better than Christian belief in its stronger propensity to purify the concept of God's unity. Nevertheless, even it cannot reveal the fullness of holistic being, in which the sum of all life's endeavors, aspirations, and discoveries depend alone on the recognition of the absolute good and the desire to reveal its dominance. This can only be made manifest by a nation whose very nationhood was originally constituted by the revelation of God's unity, so that all its existence is ingrained in it. Indeed, Islam will be among the first to recognize the special stature of the Jewish people. Within the individual personality, the divine unity yearns to be revealed by a faith such as this that rallies around it. But caught in the whirlwind of national living and an all-out battle for existence, it lacks the strength to rise up. For this the light of the Jewish people stands ready.

[8] *Shemona Kevatzim, Kovetz* 1:32

In this short paragraph, Rabbi Kook articulates his primary critique of Christianity and Islam.

In those faiths inclined towards the foundations of the Torah, such as Christianity and Islam, the poison lies not in their different theology in itself but in the resulting ruination of the practical mitzvot and the quashing of the nation's hope for its complete revival.

[9] *Orot HaTeshuva* 12:10

Throughout his writings, Rabbi Kook speaks at length of teshuva as more than an individual act of repentance; it is a global, even cosmic, movement or return. For him, Christian belief stands in contradiction to this conception of teshuva, *arousing his opposition.*

Teshuva is the innovation of being alive. It is impossible for it not to alter the character of one's entire life as life goes on. [...] The rest of the consolatory verses provoke the strengthening of *teshuva* and spell out its worth. But to wallow in this consolation and let go of life's sacred callings to the point that one becomes mired in sin and says "I am saved," is the deadly path of idolatry's indulgence. [...] This approach abandons truth and judgment to follow one's heart; it is heresy, which leads to murder for every reason and lust for every pleasure. Even so, it feigns self-righteousness and offers consolation for it all, though it has no legs to stand on, being one big lie. [...] The fruit of these ideas and the conduct of those raised in this culture testify to its inner spiritual essence. It has no power except from the sparks of holiness stolen from the living store of the Jewish people, which it ejects slowly until it has completely shaken them off.... Then when that spark of holiness wholly absorbed by the nations is deemed useless, it serves to awaken and arouse the heart of many peoples, to transform them with a pure language, for them all to call in the name of the Lord, with the spirit of the Lord – a spirit of counsel and might, a spirit of knowledge and fear of God. Not an ungodly spirit, a spirit of stupidity and weakness, a spirit of foolishness and moral abandon, which bolsters false personas out of indulgence, deriding and jeering at every leader of integrity. This "grace of the nations" is a wellspring of cruelty and despicable acts.

[10] *Iggerot HaRe'iya* 1:164

In a letter from 1908, Rabbi Kook writes to his student Moshe Seidel about the proper pedagogy to adopt in light of cultural changes occurring in Europe. He indicates a shift in his own approach. He writes that it is not the time to take the side of other religions but to withdraw and etch lines in the sand.

We see with our own eyes that the time has come when the light of God shines for us. The hope of the Jewish people and its revival is being realized under the cover of gradualness, in the land of the living. The great spirit, in which life eternally resides, is still curled up, like a fetus in its mother's womb. [...] [...] Our independent culture, which has nothing in common with any other people, and our national revival in the Holy Land, destined to be a place of panoramic vision, belong to a unified, veridical dream. Only by mistake are they construed as two systems in contradiction, opposing each other. [...] The practical strength to found and plant, to build and ready everything for a powerful people to live on its land as it once did, shall be aroused in God's progeny, who will learn to return to Him lovingly and fully conscious, out of fruitfulness and zest for life. Songs of life, full of divine energy, have been created, and fields of a new and shining culture fructify – mantled with purity they give forth their song. The old is renewed and the new is sanctified, and together they burn like flaming beacons over Zion. And Zion's beauty begins to attract the best of her builders and the masters of architecture, agriculture, industry, and commerce. Eventually, they too will be misted by the dew of everlasting life, waters of purification will be sprinkled upon them, and they will recognize their own resilience and joy by being the ones to build walls and ramparts for the Jewish people in the most cherished land. The spirit of religion has been beaten down and crushed, a banality in Christian Europe and Muslim Asia. It fares no better in the latter, nor could it have. It could not coexist with the societal upheaval.... [...].

Because justice looms so large and assumes so many forms, it proves nearly impossible now to demarcate the special form of that stellar defense, the light of Israel against those who would diminish it. The times require dealing with big ideas: let the vigorous ones soar like a flare, and the details will fall into place variously, according to the size of the spirit and the intensity of its reception in the heart of every thinker.

[11] *Orot Yisrael* 5:9
In this passage, Rabbi Kook seeks to sharpen the fundamental difference between Jews and non-Jews.

When one considers the human being and all other animals, one can draw up a list of all their similarities. Despite them all, however, one observes that the point of difference that makes man superior to beast actually encompasses everything that makes the human being what he or she is. A person cannot nor wishes to give it up for all the money in the world, and will willingly endure great suffering if it means not losing the uniqueness of the human being.

The difference between Judaism and all other religions – even those inspired by it – is the same. Numerous similar phenomena appear across them. But how could there not be similarities? Even if they were not taken wholesale from Judaism, the human spirit has a universality to it in many respects. Individuals, and certainly groups and nations, differ, but this commonality continues to express itself. Regarding the religions that emerged after the giving of the Torah and the appearance of the Jewish people on the world stage, and certainly those that drew their strength specifically from Judaism, similarities were inevitable. But these similarities, in all their abundant detail, do not erase the substantive point that differentiates them. The entire spiritual essence is tucked into that point of difference, which imbues the points of similarity, down to their very details, with a unique spirit. The similarity becomes an external resemblance, whereas the interior could not be more different. The Jewish people cannot nor do they wish to give up that spiritual point for all the equivalence in particulars; they will always endure their fate as a nation that dwells alone and is not counted among the nations.

[12] *Shemona Kevatzim, Kovetz 6:209*
This is one of many passages in which Rabbi Kook witheringly attacks both other religions and European culture. Here he stresses that this incisive critique should not diminish the feelings of fellowship that one should feel toward members of these groups.

None of this limits the intellectual vision and natural moral fellowship for any people or individual, in any place, at any time, among any nation or land, within this general spiritual pollution. The light of humanity's divine image shines through to extend hope to all, and the intellectual luminosity of natural virtue glows even beyond this. […] Together, supernal wisdom and inferior wisdom speak as one, illuminating the world with the light of life, the light of peace, and blessings of all worlds.

Rabbi Yehuda Léon Ashkenazi (Manitou): The "Equation of Fraternity" and Interfaith Dialogue as Rectification of the Primeval Murder

Sarel Rosenblatt

Rabbi Yehuda Léon Ashkenazi (1922–1996), known by the moniker Manitou,[1] was born and raised in the Muslim milieu of Algiers, and in adulthood he lived in Christian France. A descendant of illustrious kabbalists and communal rabbis, Manitou was well-versed in Kabbala and rabbinic literature, but he also attended the University of Paris and the University of Algiers and took classes with leading intellectuals.[2]

---

1. In a Native American language it means "great spirit." The nickname was given to Ashkenazi when he was in the Jewish Scouts in France.

2. For a personal and intellectual biography, and on the founding of L'école de Pensée Juive de Paris, see Yossef Charvit, "Identity and History – The Cultural Heritage of Rabbi Yehouda Léon Askénazi (Manitou)" [in Hebrew], *Pe'amim* 91 (2002): 105–110;

Beginning in the 1950s, Manitou became an outstanding rabbinic figure among Francophone Jewry.

During World War II, when he was a young man, Manitou served in the French Army, and he was an eyewitness to the destruction of French Jewry during the Holocaust. His experiences greatly influenced his critical stance toward French philosophy and Western thought in general, and also toward Christian theology, which he considered an integral component of the West's philosophical and cultural traditions. The collapse of the traditional Jewish *kehilla* and its institutions in the wake of the two wars precipitated a severe identity crisis among French Jewry. Together with André Neher and Emmanuel Levinas, colleagues at L'école de Pensée Juive de Paris, Manitou picked up the gauntlet to rehabilitate the Jewish community and reinforce its identity.

One of the core methodologies of Manitou's thought is engaging in critical comparative analysis of Judaism and other religious and philosophical systems. Manitou knew his Quran and New Testament,[3] and he acquired great familiarity with Christian and Muslim thought. He also studied Eastern religions. Over his lifetime, he participated in scores of interfaith dialogues with leaders of various religions. After learning his ideas, one walks away wondering if it is impossible to understand the uniqueness of Judaism and its contribution to the world without broad and deep knowledge of the manifold spiritual and intellectual strands that form the great weave of human culture.

Manitou develops this comparative approach out of two opposite yet complementary movements. In order to strengthen the communal identity of French Jewry as they try to put their broken lives back together in the postwar era, he focuses on the uniqueness and superiority of the Torah. To discover what the Torah injects into the larger

---

and Gabrielle Ben Shmuel, "The Historiosophical Thought and Kabbalistic Elements in the Biblical Exegesis of Rav Yehuda Léon Askenazi (Manitou)" [in Hebrew] (PhD diss., Bar-Ilan University, 2009), 12–32.

3. Manitou even had a Jewish interpretation of Christian Scripture that he sought to teach Christians. See *Midrash BeSod HaHafakhim: Zehut Musarit Ivrit*, trans. Itai Ashkenazi (Jerusalem: Beit Morasha, 2009), 147–161. His son-in-law, Israel Pivco, told me that Manitou claimed to possess an old Spanish tradition, passed down from father to son, of the correct Jewish reading of the New Testament.

conversation of civilizations, however, requires going out into the world to encounter what is out there. Without this advance and retreat, Jewish identity is incomplete and the Jewish people cannot fulfill their destiny. Although Manitou's writings are filled with particular insights into and criticisms of other religious worldviews that are worthy of examination, this chapter takes a step back to answer a more basic question: What was Manitou's position on the very existence of other religions?

UNIFICATION OF THE DIVINE ATTRIBUTES AND THE EQUATION OF FRATERNITY

The form of Manitou's philosophical project is characterized by the push outwards and pull inwards described above, but what gives internal structure to his entire thought is his conception of divine unity, what he calls "the unification of the divine attributes." He views it as the mission of the Jewish people, using their prophetic tradition, to form connections between all the nations of the world and to mend any tears in existing relationships. This worldview celebrates – on the most fundamental level – the sheer diversity of our teeming globe. When referring to the variety of qualities or ideas, Manitou uses the term "unification of the divine attributes," and when referring to human diversity, he speaks of "the equation of fraternity."

The human world is a vibrant one, and the many types that populate it who invest their energies toward different ends are all expressing the same thing: the complete revelation of God in the world. The ultimate goal for them all is to productively interlock and synchronize according to the parameters of divine morality. The more they move in unison, the more space there is for God in their lives, and the world's holiness correspondingly increases.[4] According to Manitou, the Tower of Babel was humanity's attempt to realize this vision of unity – an attempt that failed. The aspiration to *unity* was replaced by *uniformity*, a violent ideology that erases identities and monochromatizes the rainbow. In response, God spread out humanity across the world, which gave rise

---

4. *Sod Midrash HaToledot*, vol. 1, 69–70. References to volumes 1–4 are from the edition published by the Manitou Institute in 2012.

to the world civilizations we know. Every people and nation express one genuine facet of the multifaceted divinity. Like a mirror shattered into seventy pieces, each one is a sliver of the original, perfect image of the divine [1].

Manitou says that there are two possible reactions to this state of affairs. The first is polytheistic, and he detects its reverberations in post-modern thought. It accepts multiplicity as an immutable fact and denies the possibility of uniting disparate powers. Either they all keep to their own domain, or it's everyone against everyone. The second reaction is to want to bring everyone together. The universalist impulse strives to generate unity across lines of identity so that everyone can work as one. But universalism can devolve into imperialism, whereby a single nation or religion wants to impose its orders on everyone else and issue them all a uniform identity. Instead of a unity of equality the result is a uniformity of inequality. Manitou conceives of Jewish monotheism as more than belief in one deity and no others, but also a belief that there is an inherent (if dialectical) connection that binds the discrete human endeavors in the world.

For Manitou, the roadmap to successfully reuniting the world lies in biblical stories, the oral tradition of halakha and Aggada, and Kabbala. The sefirotic tree symbolizes this harmonious unity visually; it depicts the interrelationships between all the *sefirot* as they all maintain their static positions. On this metaphysical map that can be roughly divided into three columns, Manitou identifies the Jewish people with the middle line of sefirot that seeks to connect those sefirot to the right and left of it. In this sense, whenever Jews encounter a new mode of human existence, they attempt to discover two things: what truth and justice it holds, and what its legitimate boundaries ought to be. If it is overstepping them, it is suppressing other vital energies and creating a mode of existence liable to be immoral. The unity Manitou envisions is intended to bring together people as much as ideologies. He gets right to the bottom of it:

> One can speak endlessly about being moral, about values, but at the end of the day the Creator's demand of me is much simpler: how I can let others live in my world, and

how they can let me live in theirs. Without reciprocity there is no solution to this moral problem, to the equation of fraternity. (*Sod Midrash HaToledot*, vol. 3, p. 151) [2]

The paradigmatic example of this is the story of Cain and Abel. The two brothers had their own qualities and characteristics that assigned them individual destinies. Cain was a man of the earth and possessed creativity and practical arts; Abel was a man of the spirit and was gifted in pedagogy. The former sought to dominate the latter and silence him, and he finally quieted him forever. This tale about the first murder exposes the root of violence, a desire to silence the other. Ultimately, it recounts the failure of the equation of fraternity. What is that equation exactly? It is Manitou's encapsulation of an interpersonal relationship based on mutual respect, in which each person makes room for the other in spite of their essential difference. One of the major problems that plagues human society is how people relate to one another, what Manitou calls "the ruler-ruled problem." Here is Judaism's approach:

> Let us both be subjects.[5] This is the Torah's position. Each one recognizes that the other is above them, and then no one is inferior. This requires reciprocity. Each one considers the other a subject, and so long as this recognition is mutual, then there is no subject. This is the challenge we have faced since the time of Cain and Abel. (*Sod Midrash HaToledot*, vol. 3, p. 167)

Morality demands that a person not only recognize the other and allow them to flourish but also develop a relationship in which they can live side by side in mutual respect. Manitou turns the story of Cain and Abel into a template for relationships between families, tribes, peoples, and religions. The semantic field of "family" is essential for all of these.[6]

---

5. As opposed to objects.
6. See also Yossef Charvit, "From Monologues to Possible Dialogue: Judaism's Attitude toward Christianity Accroding to the Philosophy of R. Yéhouda Léon Askénazi

According to Manitou, the essence of the seven Noahide mitzvot is this moral demand. The purpose of Judaism is therefore:

> to recover the primordial unity of humankind, in which there is a place for every nation, contingent on the acceptance of a few basic rules of behavior flowing from moral – rather than theological or spiritual – considerations. (*Sod Midrash HaToledot,* vol. 1, p. 196, n. 561)

Manitou's original reading of this biblical episode lays the blame for the terrible outcome at the feet of Abel, too, because he failed to educate Cain. Manitou identifies the Jewish people with the figure of Abel, placing on our shoulders the ongoing responsibility for the state of the world and humanity:

> "Brother" and "peace." [...] With these words Hebraism begins. The Hebrew searched and ultimately found the solution to the equation of fraternity, a solution that became an essential, integral part of our way of life, which we are to bequeath to the entire world. (*Sod Midrash HaToledot,* vol. 8, p. 115) [3][7]

Throughout his life, Manitou suffered harassment: from Muslims as a young man in Algeria, and from Christian anti-Semites as an adult in France. All the same, he writes that the Jewish people have an obligation to build bridges with other religions to restore the fraternity lost:

> People talk a lot today about the universalist side of the Jewish people and of the Torah, but they forget that everything begins with a simple pair of words: "brother" and "peace."

(Manitou)," in *Interaction between Judaism and Christianity in History, Religion, Art and Literature,* ed. Marcel Poorthuis, Joshua Schwartz, and Joseph Turner (Leiden: Brill, 2009), 319.

7. For more on the failure of the Jewish people to complete the messianic mission of repairing the world, see *Midrash BeSod HaHafakhim: Zehut Musarit Ivrit,* trans. Itai Ashkenazi (Jerusalem: Beit Morasha, 2009), 187–188.

Our task is difficult because we mainly run up against the side of Esau, the camp of "whoever is strongest prevails." This is not only the case with Christianity, which has experienced massive secularization, but also Islam. They are no less violent. I lived among them and know what I am talking about. Nevertheless, we have never lost hope for a better world. We have searched and are still searching for our brothers everywhere, out in the field. (ibid.) [3]

Even though the Jewish people have been the victims of violence from every quarter over their storied history, and knowing full well that the task is a colossal one, Manitou declares that the Jewish people must rectify the inequality of human relations and that their tradition uniquely equips them to do so. He looks to the biblical Joseph, "the *tzaddik*," as his guiding light, because he was able to stare reality in the face while holding onto his dreams.[8] Likewise, the unbrotherly treatment Manitou was personally subjected to, and the long suffering of our people, do not shake his grip from the flag of fraternity. He views Christians and Muslims, and all of humankind, as brothers and sisters for whom we are searching in order to repair our relationships and bring back the primordial unity, divine and human, that has disappeared.

THE KABBALISTIC FOUNDATION OF INTERFAITH RELATIONS

The methodology of comparative analysis explains Jewish concepts by contrasting them with those from other religions. Most of the time, Manitou is interested in demonstrating that the Jewish approach is the most comprehensive, and that others lead to real negative consequences like oppression, enmity, and violence. Manitou's readers might come away thinking that he rejects the legitimacy of other religions or degrades their beliefs. I would like to present an alternative reading of Manitou that revolves around what he considers the goal of comparative criticism and the role of the Jewish people. To fully grasp what I mean, we need to enter the world of Manitou's Kabbala.

---

8. *Sod Midrash HaToledot*, vol. 8 (Jerusalem: Manitou Institute, 2020), 114.

The Godhead is revealed in this world through many channels. The world and its contents are composed of the *sefirot* and divine emanations. In kabbalistic theosophy, the paramount question is not whether a person believes in God but the manner in which they apprehend Him. To which of the divine names and attributes do they relate? In Manitou's eyes, a scientific, philosophical, or existential conception of God, one that is utterly devoid of theology, still reflects a sliver of the divine that is manifest in this world. In a sense, the biblical narrative from Adam to Moses is about the gradual historical unfolding of human recognition of God. In the beginning, He is known as *Elokim*, a name that represents the attribute of judgment and the unyielding laws of nature. Only Jacob begins to discover the Tetragrammaton more, which represents the attribute of mercy that can break the laws of nature and establish a more expansive consciousness of human nature and the world. This four-letter name corresponds to the *sefira* known as *Tiferet*, whose position in the middle of the sefirotic tree connects it to the various divine potencies, and therefore more fully reveals the Godhead to the world. Even Abraham and Isaac were only privy to partial knowledge of God. Abraham represents the attribute of lovingkindness and Isaac the attribute of judgment, but the two are only merged in Jacob, who represents *Tiferet*.[9]

Manitou's oeuvre therefore contains endless parallels between philosophical and religious ideas and the various names of God and the *sefirot*. Paradigmatically, Christianity is construed as an extreme manifestation of the attribute of lovingkindness[10] and Islam of the attribute of judgment,[11] and the modern, secular worldview is interpreted as an expression of the name *Elokim* as revealed through the cold, hard laws of nature.[12] The Jewish people, associated with *Tiferet*, are supposed to study the map of humanity under the light of Torah and morality and decide where and how to strategically emplace the bridges.

9. For a discussion of Manitou's exegetical use of Kabbala, see *Sod Midrash HaToledot*, vol. 1, p. 24.
10. *Sod Midrash HaToledot*, vol. 2, p. 47; vol. 1, p. 68; and many more.
11. Ibid.
12. *Sod Midrash HaToledot*, vol. 2, pp. 211–219. See also *Shaarei Dim'a* (Bet El: Sifriyat Ḥava, 2016), vol. 1, pp. 29–36.

This brief explanation of Manitou's use of Kabbala affirms that he does not reject other religions. In the same way the name *Elokim* is not rendered superfluous or illegitimate by a fuller revelation of the Tetragrammaton, the attribute of lovingkindness and the attribute of judgment remain integral parts of the divine configuration. For example, Manitou writes about Christians:

> At their spiritual level, they are correct when they say that faith is a merit and that one can be redeemed through faith. [...] Therefore, to a certain extent, one can say that they are kind of similar to the state Abraham was in, since they are at the beginning of the road, and this is a tremendous merit. (*Sod Midrash HaToledot*, vol. 2, pp. 47–48)

Elsewhere, even more forcefully:

> If the Jews are Israel, then who are the Christians? [...] The reality of two Israels in competition with one another in their aspiration for universal peace is clearly a conflictual one, which neither Christians nor Jews can allow to exist. [...] We are confronting an issue of brothers seeking fraternity, just as the left hand and right hand are not congruent but can grasp one another. We will not limit ourselves with noting the questions that trouble us but rather together – Christians and Jews – we are to proceed and rediscover the roots of our traditions and identify the principle that separates us and simultaneously links us: the mystery that is Israel.[13]

From a kabbalistic point of view, Manitou imagines the relationship between Judaism and other religions as the one that exists between the limbs of a single body. There is therefore a desire and a responsibility to successfully synchronize them.

---

13. Charvit, "From Monologues to Possible Dialogue," p. 330, with minor stylistic adjustments.

This is no less true, in Manitou's view, of Judaism and Islam:

> Ishmael returns to the house of his father Abram through Islam, which only became the national "religion" of the Arab-Ishmaelite nation much later, thousands of years after Abraham. Ishmael thus repented before the God of Abraham. (*Sod Midrash HaToledot*, vol. 1, p. 307)

The very reception of Islam by the Arab nation constitutes progress, a penitential return to the Abrahamic tradition.[14]

For Manitou, legitimation of other belief systems is only the first step toward the ultimate goal: the unification of the various divine attributes by joining them and placing them in balance, which leads to their calibration and rectification. He tried to achieve this through the critical analyses performed in his lectures, but another avenue was meeting face-to-face with representatives of other religions for dialogue and debate. Manitou was after a highly specific kind of dialogue, and grasping it will give us a deeper look into Manitou's theory of the relationship between Judaism other religions.

DIALOGUE AS "GENUINE DEBATE" AND THE ROLE OF THE JEWISH PEOPLE

In 1953, at the conclusion of the Finaly Affair,[15] Manitou was sent by the Jewish community in France to speak at the annual convention of Christian theologians in Lyons. Here is his description of that episode:

---

14. Interestingly, Manitou thought that the return of the Jewish people to the Land of Israel would improve relations with Christianity while greatly harming relations with Islam. See *Sod Midrash HaToledot*, vol. 1, pp. 297–310.

15. The Finaly brothers were two young boys whose parents were murdered in Auschwitz and who were hidden by Catholics in Grenoble, France. After the war, their relatives came to collect them, but the Church refused to give them up, claiming that they had been baptized and were therefore Christian. After a drawn-out legal saga that concluded with rulings in the family's favor and additional attempts by the Church to hide them away, the children were returned in 1953 and moved to Israel.

We were at the end of the Finaly Affair so I had to explicitly address it. I began: "For two thousand years, you have claimed that you need to explain to us who the true Israel is, who we Jews who reject your words are, what our historical destiny is, and so on and so forth. I, insignificant as I may be, stand before you today and ask you: Hasn't the time come for us, the Jewish people, to explain to you who you are, and what you truly believe?" A hush came over the room; they were speechless. I have to tell you that they received my harsh words with great courage, and over the course of an hour I explained to them how we Jews view Christianity and understand their beliefs. Apparently this was their first time hearing it, certainly in public. It was then that I initiated a dialogue with important Christian theologians that continues to this day. (*Sod Midrash HaToledot*, vol. 7, p. 271, n. 714)

In this passage are the two foundations of Manitou's interfaith dialogue: reciprocity and "genuine debate."

Dialogue, like the equation of fraternity, requires a person to relate to the other as a subject. Typically, the practical implication of recognizing someone else means accepting them as they are. In the dialogue espoused by Manitou, by contrast, it means listening to what the other has to say. What grants the interlocutor subjecthood is genuinely listening to "their voice" and giving them the floor to say what they truly feel and believe. Within this framing, Manitou characterizes all the Jewish-Christian disputations throughout history as unidirectional and one-sided. The Jew's role has always been to listen or defend himself, never to air his own opinions about Christianity. To achieve reciprocity, the dialogue must meet two conditions. First, "we must first solve the problem of anti-Jewish hatred, because it stymies all progress."[16] So long as another religion seethes with loathing for Judaism, or at the very least seeks to replace or subjugate it, no real dialogue is possible. Furthermore, to grant recognition to the Jewish people includes conceding

---

16. *Sod Midrash HaToledot*, vol. 3, p. 170.

that it is the successor of the biblical Israelites who were chosen by God and never replaced, and therefore can lay the biblical claim to the land. Second, the other religion must give up missionizing activities. If there is premeditation to effect a conversion, the dialogue is fundamentally flawed. There can be no basic respect, no confidence, no listening. It is no parley but war.[17]

The hope that the Jewish people will fulfill their destiny by disseminating the equation of fraternity through encounter and dialogue is at the heart of Manitou's thought, specifically in light of his theological and philosophical criticism of other religions. To understand why this is so, we must explore his definition of "genuine debate."

Genuine debate has two opposing elements. Each side, out of its own belief, adopts a critical perspective of the other's worldview, in order to clarify for them the moral truth that derives from their philosophical or theological views.[18] At the same time, awareness of the essential

---

17. Karma Ben-Johanan writes: "Ashkenazi [=Manitou] believes that 'sincere dialogue with Christians' can become possible only when Christianity turns into a kind of Judaism in exile; in other words, when it is not interfaith dialogue but dialogue between Jews and Jews" (*A Pottage of Lentils: Mutual Perceptions of Christians and Jews in the Age of Reconciliation* [in Hebrew] [Tel Aviv: Tel Aviv University, 2020], 264). I understand Manitou differently. Dialogue does not require accepting the position of the other but being prepared to sincerely listen to them. Manitou says precisely this in one place: "It is not the Jewish and Christian Bibles that oppose one another but rather the Talmudist and the Evangelist, who turn their backs on one another and never communicate. If this dialogue were to begin someday, it would be on the day the Christians recognize and respect the Jews as people worthy of love, and especially the day the Christians recognize the honor of Judaism, whose seal is truth" (Charvit, "From Monologues to Possible Dialogue," p. 332, with minor modifications). Lacking from Ben-Johanan's account is the language of "the unification of the attributes" (or "the equation of fraternity") that grounds Manitou's thinking about other religions, and which features prominently in Yossef Charvit's article, "From Monologues to Possible Dialogue." Perhaps this is because these ideas are absent from the two lectures that Ben-Johanan cites numerous times in her book: a lecture delivered in 1961 on which Rabbi Shlomo Aviner's *The Believer and the Philosopher* [in Hebrew] (Jerusalem: Sifriyat Hava, 2013) is based, and a lecture from 1979 translated into a Hebrew article titled "Greek Myth and Jewish Midrash" [in Hebrew] (reproduced in *Midrash BeSod HaHafakhim*, 147–161).

18. According to Manitou, the Gospels were contemporaneous with rabbinic Midrash, so they are to be understood using midrashic instead of mythic exegesis. This

difference between sides is continuously maintained, so that no one switches teams. One side has the obligation to listen while the other has the obligation not to erase the identity or uniqueness of the other.

An example will clarify matters. Manitou feels strongly that Judaism ought to explain to Christianity why its conception of grace – expressed as the principle of free grace or in turning the other cheek – is excessive and liable to result in destructive consequences in the opposite direction. Similarly, Islam needs to be made to understand why its idea of judgment, intended to make a person submit before God, impinges on a person's inherent potential as a being made in the image of God. A few Eastern religions should be shown how redemption from suffering ought to be achieved through working on interpersonal relationships and not by striving for nirvana or self-liberation from human ambition. Judaism has no designs to convert everyone, but it does aspire to identify what quality each and every nation and religion brings to the world, in order to refine, tweak, and reform them. Manitou comes to this from his grand vision of "unification of the divine attributes," the idea being that each one of these qualities will be perfected by being receptive to the other qualities and communicating with them.

Reciprocity, which Manitou deems of prime importance for dialogue, does not translate into an equivalence of roles, nor does it conceive of the human being as a *tabula rasa*. Reciprocity is the respect every person feels toward the established difference of the other, and this is conveyed through penetrating dialogue – not by avoiding it. For Manitou, to be a "Hebrew" is to bear the prophetic tradition passed down from Adam to the Jewish people, which comprises foundational ideas about morality and sanctity governing how a person relates to the self, the other, and God. The Hebrew shoulders the responsibility to transmit these ideas to the world not to produce clones, but to close the earth-spanning, diverse circle of humanity.

Many years after Manitou first went out into the world looking for his brothers, participating in dozens of meetings and conventions with leaders across the spectrum of religions, he noted his great disappointment upon realizing that he was the target of repeated attempts

---

interpretation ought to be presented to Christians.

"to convert him."[19] Even so, he stayed optimistic, especially regarding Christianity.

His opinion on dialogue with Christians can be found in his commentary on the Jacob-Esau story cycle, which, according to traditional rabbinic interpretation, symbolizes the relationship between Judaism and Christianity. In the Torah, Esau invites Jacob to join him at Mount Seir, but he is rebuffed. Manitou explains that Jacob senses that Esau still has it out for him; in the words of Rabbi Shimon bar Yoḥai: "It is a rule that Esau hates Jacob."[20] Nevertheless, Jacob promises that one day he will meet him in Seir. The prophet Obadiah foresaw this eventual reunion: "Saviors shall ascend Mount Zion to judge the mount of Esau, and the kingdom shall be the Lord's" (Ob. 1:21). Jacob and Esau are supposed to finally gather for a meeting guided by respect and reciprocity:

> On the day the vision of the prophets will be realized as global peace, the day when Christian and Jew can finally talk straight, we Jews will have to tell the Christians how much we have waited for this reunion and how much we have loved them from afar. They have come a long way to extricate themselves from their heathendom, and they have now begun to deal with our family's affairs.[21]

The Catholic Church's attitude toward Judaism has transformed dramatically in the past sixty years.[22] In 1965, Vatican II produced *Nostra Aetate* (In Our Time), which fundamentally changed the negative Christian attitude toward Jews, and in 2015, the Vatican condemned any mission to the Jews. In 1993, Ashkenazic Chief Rabbi of Israel Meir Lau met with Pope John Paul II, and that same year diplomatic relations between the Vatican and Israel were established. Manitou had this to say: "All of these cannot leave a believer unmoved. ...This is divine providence at work. Let us

---

19. *Sod Midrash HaToledot*, vol. 7 (Jerusalem: Manitou Institute, 2019), p. 271.

20. *Sifrei Num.* 69.

21. *Midrash BeSod HaHafakhim*, p. 153.

22. For a detailed account of the changes in the Catholic Church's attitude toward the Jews see Ben-Johanan, *A Pottage of Lentils*, 21–165.

help it succeed with humility and prayer."[23] He writes in a similar vein: "This is the first time in two thousand years that the Catholic Church recognizes that the Jews are Israel. [...] Mutual recognition brings the rivalry between identities to an end."[24] All these developments kindled Manitou's hope that measurable progress had been made and that the conditions were ripe for beginning a genuine dialogue with Christianity.

Although Manitou is ready for dialogue with Christianity, he acknowledges that some Jews are still traumatized by our treatment at the hands of Christians:

> Only today has the possibility for genuine debates materialized. I have become convinced that it is possible, by which I mean productive, only with Sephardic *hakhamim*. Ashkenazic rabbis are not yet ready for this. I have come to comprehend that they are not yet free of this fear. They lived under *Edom* in dreadful conditions and feared standing up to Christian theologians and speaking candidly about their dogmas. Such a fear does not exist among the Sephardic *hakhamim*, who had a completely different experience among Muslims. Thus, they can stand opposite Christian theologians and speak to them openly. (*Sod Midrash HaToledot*, vol. 7, p. 271)

Manitou claims that Sephardim are more open to interfaith dialogue than Ashkenazim, a reasonable outcome of their respective experiences under Islam and Christianity.[25] Regardless of their historical veracity, Manitou's point gets across: Ashkenazic Jewry should overcome their fear of Christianity without forgetting the trauma that induced it, and set their sights on deep dialogue with Christianity and other religions. We should be constantly reevaluating the Church's attitude toward the

---

23. Charvit, "From Monologues to Possible Dialogue," p. 333, with minor stylistic adjustments.
24. Ibid., p. 332.
25. For the influence of Islam on Jewish thought in Arab lands, see *Sod Midrash HaToledot*, vol. 1, p. 195, n. 560.

Jews and Judaism to see if the conditions have matured for renewal of relations and dialogue.

The Abraham Accords signed in 2020 between Israel, on one side, and the United Arab Emirates, Bahrain, Sudan, and Morocco, on the other, should also be taken to signal a new age in the history of Judaism and Islam. Let us think and act in the spirit of Manitou's words: "This is divine providence at work. Let us help it succeed with humility and prayer."

CONCLUDING THOUGHTS

Lately, Manitou's thought has been liberated from the confines of French and has sailed into broader Jewish discourse on a Hebrew raft. His students have been publishing his lessons in elucidated books, and there are still more to come. And they are meeting a deep need among the learned. In them, the reader encounters an illustrious Jewish thinker who consolidates fundamental concepts and beliefs by constant contrast with the major philosophical schools in Western culture and the religious tenets of other religions. This is methodologically groundbreaking. In the same way Manitou's teachings strengthened Jewish identity as old barriers crumbled or were hurdled under conditions of increasing global interconnectivity, so they continue today. In this chapter, I have attempted to expose the basic conceptual structures of Manitou's thought. I have argued that his contrastive methodology has a more profound purpose than fortifying the belief of the perplexed. He wants to reinstate Judaism as a major player in interfaith discourse and on the international stage, thereby realizing its original mission of repairing a fractured world and unifying the divine attributes.

This chapter has shown how the equation of fraternity is necessary for the "genuine debate" Manitou so desires, and how it calls each of us to nurture healthy, fearless, and sincere relationships with other religions. It yearns for the day when every Jew will remember that "everything begins with a simple pair of words: 'brother' and 'peace'" [3].

In July 1990, Manitou was invited to be the Jewish representative for the establishment of the Temple de l'Universel in Paris. Other religions represented included Hinduism, Buddhism, Zoroastrianism, Christianity, and Islam. Manitou composed a special prayer for the occasion, with which it is fitting to end this chapter:

> Our Father, Existence of all existence, Creator of the universe, Master of the world, Builder of our homes on the land in which Your Presence was revealed in the past:
>
> Your children have built this Universal Temple in fulfillment of the commandment, "Let them make Me a sanctuary, so that I may dwell among them" (Ex. 25:8). Heaven and earth are filled with Your voice, yet from the beginning, the echo of Your glory has distanced itself to accord time and purpose to existence. Return! May Your absence cease! May it be Your will that our unity augment Your truth, as the prophet Isaiah declared: "For My house shall be called a house of prayer for all peoples" (Is. 56:7).[26]

SOURCES

[1] *Sod Midrash HaToledot*, vol. 1, p. 46 – Humanity as a broken mirror and a flower bouquet

The kabbalists say that humanity is like a mirror that was shattered into seventy pieces during the Generation of the Dispersion. Trying to see using this or that fragment of the mirror yields a distorted image. One cannot deny that there is an image, but it is partial at best. That is what happened with the seventy nations in the Generation of the Dispersion – another failure.

The result was that every people and nation assumed one of the seventy parts of Adam's original identity. Since then, there have been seventy different modalities or facets so that humankind becomes "each one according to his tongue" (Gen. 10:5), and each and every one is *sui generis*. Every nation develops and cultivates certain values that accord with the partial identity they have inherited from the primordial splintering of

---

26. Charvit, "From Monologues to Possible Dialogue," 320, with minor stylistic adjustments.

original man's unity. Whenever a nation identifies an opportunity and has the wherewithal, it tries to force its "cultural model," its cultural identity, on the other nations. The Sages term these endeavors "empires" (*malkhuyot*). The avowed ideal of every empire's founders is to rebuild the human universal, the same one that was shattered into seventy pieces. At the outset, all attempts are sincere and genuine, but they are doomed to fail because all too quickly every empire turns imperialist and suffocates other identities. The history of empires is a history of the persistent failure to realize this dream of humanity, to reconstitute the primeval unity and live in peace. [...]

The goal of Jewish messianism is to unite humanity in such a way that every tribe of humanity, every nation maintains its special role, and the Jewish people – "a kingdom (*mamlekhet*) of priests and holy nation" (Ex. 19:6) – are what unifies them all.

Humanity is like a floral bouquet. Every flower has a role to play in the arrangement, and the absence of one type renders it incomplete. The bouquet of empires is uniform, with room for only one kind of flower, whereas that of Jewish messianism is multicolored, composed of seventy flowers of all types that together make a genuine bouquet. The task of the Jewish people is to be the unifying factor that binds them all together and refashions them into a real bouquet.

It was therefore important to emphasize that the enterprise of empires was very similar in its imagined, utopian goals to the Creator's messianic enterprise through engenderment, from Adam to the true "son of man" symbolized by the Messiah. Over the course of history, too many Jews fell victim to the enterprise of the empires and were persuaded to help put together the "bouquet" of some empire. The flower they thought they were contributing rather quickly found itself outside the arrangement. [...] Abraham and Nimrod set out on their paths from the same existential diagnosis of the world's condition. It is impossible to leave as is, because it is dissatisfying. Nimrod channels his rebellion, his dissatisfaction, toward the Creator.

Abraham's rebellion against the state of the world brings him into the service of the Creator's enterprise. He decides to serve God in order to rectify the situation. At that point, Abraham became Nimrod's nemesis, and so Nimrod now has two enemies: the Creator and

His people Israel, who follow Abraham's path. And this has continued down through history. The two prominent ideologies of the twentieth century, which viewed themselves as founding thousand-year empires, were the atheist-materialist Nazi ideology and the Marxist-Stalinist ideology, both of which had a deep-seated hatred of the Jews and everything they stand for.

[2] *Sod Midrash HaToledot*, vol. 3, p. 151 – The equation of fraternity

The criterion of morality is a key to understanding the biblical narrative from the fourth chapter of Genesis onward. I usually begin my indepth study of this book from this chapter because it presents the first moral dilemma in history through the story of Cain and Abel. And it is a problem we are supposed to solve over the course of history. I know that many lay the emphasis on Adam's sin, but this is a mistake, because on the level of the collective this sin was rectified by King David. The entire history of the world is a rectification of Cain's sin, and this problem ought to preoccupy us collectively throughout history, in the course of the "engenderment" – the rectification of fraternal relations between people. [...] Cain's challenge is to allow Abel to educate him. Cain's fraternity is being tested. They are supposed to solve the equation of fraternity *together*. Cain fails, as does Abel. If they had solved it at the get-go, the rectification would have been effected by them; the child born from the mixing of the line of Cain and that of Abel would have been the perfect "son of man," for whom, one could say, the world was created. Since Cain could not manage to be the consummate human being, the entire history of the world is a rectification specifically of his sin.

"'You shall love your fellow like yourself' (Lev. 19:18) – this is a great principle of the Torah."[27] It begins with Cain and Abel. One can speak endlessly about being moral, about values, but at the end of the day the Creator's demand of me is much simpler: how I can let others live in my world, and how they can let me live in theirs. Without reciprocity there is no solution to this moral problem, to the equation of fraternity.

---

27. Y. Nedarim 9:4.

[3] *Sod Midrash HaToledot*, vol. 8, 114–115 – "Brother" and "Peace"

The Torah does not speak of any mystical-magical act to reach the messianic era. It does speak of human activity, what humanity needs to do to bring this world to its true state. The key is first and foremost morality. The Torah's ethic is not "whoever is strongest prevails."[28] Nor is it the naïve morality of Christianity, of turning the other cheek. Its morality is founded on the realization that I am a creation, my fellow is a creation, and both of us are creations of the same Creator. It is with this frame of mind that I approach the issues of this world. […]

If we grasp this point, we can also understand the importance of the equation of fraternity and unequivocal demand for reciprocity. If we waive this demand, we end up, in effect, with Christian morality. Scripture addresses the equation of fraternity when it uses the word "brother." We saw this when we learned about the significance of the encounter between Jacob and the shepherds. Additionally, when Jacob sends Joseph to Shekhem, he tells him, "'Go check the welfare (*shelom*) of your brothers and the welfare of the flocks and bring me back word.' So he sent him from the valley of Hebron" (Gen. 37:14). This verse contains the words "brother" and "peace" (*shalom*). They appeared earlier in the dialogue between Jacob and the brothers, and this is no coincidence. With these words Hebraism begins. The Hebrew searched and ultimately found the solution to the equation of fraternity, a solution that became an essential, integral part of our way of life, which we are to bequeath to the entire world.

People talk a lot today about the universalist side of the Jewish people and of the Torah, but they forget that everything begins with a simple pair of words: "brother" and "peace." Our task is difficult because we mainly run up against the side of Esau, the camp of "whoever is strongest prevails." This is not only the case with Christianity, which has experienced massive secularization, but also Islam. They are no less violent. I lived among them and know what I am talking about. Nevertheless, we have never lost hope for a better world. We have searched and are still searching for our brothers everywhere, out in the field.

---

28. Bava Batra 34b.

Rabbi Jonathan Sacks's
Approach to Other Religions

*Johnny Solomon**

R*abbi Lord Jonathan Sacks (1948–2020) was one of the most important Jewish thinkers of our time. In his dozens of books and numerous lectures, Rabbi Sacks – who served as the Chief Rabbi of Great Britain for over two decades – dealt, among other things, with the question of Judaism's relationship to other religions. We therefore briefly review his important views on the matters discussed in this book.*

"One of the most striking facts about the Hebrew Bible is that though it focuses almost exclusively on the history of Israel, it does not begin with it."[1] With this introduction, Rabbi Jonathan Sacks draws the conclusion that

---

* Rabbi Johnny Solomon received semikha from Rabbi Sacks, and he has taught numerous courses on Rabbi Sacks' thought for LSJS, Herzog College, and Melton. He is the Chief Learning Officer (CLO) of WebYeshiva and he provides online spiritual coaching and halakhic consultation services as #theVirtualRabbi.

1. Rabbi Lord Jonathan Sacks *Crisis and Covenant* (Manchester University Press, 1992), 249.

from Abraham onward, the Hebrew Bible begins to tell a story about one family, and eventually one nation, who will become an example to all humanity of what it is to live under the sovereignty of God. "Through you," says God repeatedly to the Patriarchs, "shall all the families of the earth be blessed...." Judaism is the particular case that exemplifies the universal rule that the world exists under the sovereignty of God, and that every person is the image of God.[2]

The fact that the biblical story narrows in scope as it proceeds from Creation to the election of Abraham, then, does not indicate that the Torah is only interested in the Israelites. Just the opposite: it demonstrates that ultimately the story of the Jews is the story of all humankind.

But if this was the case, a crucial question remained: what was to be the relationship between "Abraham and his family,"[3] who were "set apart from other peoples" (Lev. 20:26) – meaning that they were to become a people "marked by their *non*-universality"[4] – with the rest of civilization?

In response, Rabbi Sacks focuses on the foundational principle emphasized in the beginning of the Bible: every human being is created in the image of God. From here we learn that God's image is present "in the one whose faith is not mine and whose relationship with God is different from mine."[5]

Rabbi Sacks' reading may seem obvious to some readers. Yet various Jewish thinkers have disagreed, arguing that while every person can develop a unique relationship with God, the fact that Jews have a particularly unique relationship with God and have been "set apart from other peoples" means that the Bible tells the story of the evolution of God's relationship with humanity. On this reading, Jews are not just different than other people. They are innately better.

2. Rabbi Lord Jonathan Sacks, *Radical Then, Radical Now* (Harper Collins 2001), 87.
3. *Crisis and Covenant*, 250.
4. Ibid.
5. Rabbi Lord Jonathan Sacks, *Not in God's Name* (John Murray Press, 2015), 205.

Yet this is precisely what Rabbi Sacks seeks to reject. He does so by focusing on the story of the Tower of Babel, which, as he notes, immediately precedes the story of Avraham:

> The story of Babel, set as it is immediately prior to the choice of Abraham, is crucial to an understanding of Judaism. In it, mankind is depicted as "one people with one language".... But humanity sets itself the project of ousting God.... The divine response is to divide humanity into a multiplicity of languages, peoples, and cultures. To be sure there is the promise, implicit in Genesis, explicit in the prophets, that one day mankind will be restored to its original harmony. But *not yet*: not until a metaphysical "end of days." In the meantime and for all historical time, human civilization is irreducibly plural.[6]

For most readers, the existence of a multiplicity of languages – the outcome of the story of Babel – provides little more than an answer to the question as to why different people in different countries speak different languages. But for Rabbi Sacks, this idea is fundamental. It helps explain a profound idea that was to feature in his most substantive books dealing with the relationship between Judaism and other faiths:

> Implicit in Judaism is a deep analogy between faith and language. A language is spoken by a people; there is no such thing as a private language or a universal language. We are born into a linguistic community; we do not choose to be born to English- as against French-speaking parents, and yet that fact has the greatest significance in shaping our sensibilities. By speaking any natural language we are participants in the history of a civilization: its nuances of meaning and association were shaped by the past and yet persist into the present. And to speak a language is to internalize its rules of grammar and semantics; without these

---

6. *Crisis and Covenant*, 249–250.

rules we cannot express ourselves articulately. Applying these ideas to Judaism: faith is neither private nor universal. It is a phenomenon, in the first instance, of a particular people. Just as we can be born in a linguistic community so we can be born into a faith community and its obligations.[7]

What this means, according to Rabbi Sacks, is that "faith...is neither universal nor subjective but, like language, a phenomenon of communities and their rules, traditions, and histories."[8]

The implications of this idea are nothing short of monumental. As Rabbi Sacks went on to delineate in his 2002 book, *The Dignity of Difference*, arguably the most profound exposition ever written by a Jew about Jewish attitudes toward the rest of the humanity:

> The radical transcendence of God in the Hebrew Bible means nothing more or less than that *there is a difference between God and religion*. God is universal, religions are particular. Religion is the translation of God into a particular language and thus into the life of a group, a nation, a community of faith. In the course of history, God has spoken to mankind in many languages: through Judaism to Jews, Christianity to Christians, Islam to Muslims.[9] Only such a God is truly transcendental – greater not only than the natural universe but also than the spiritual universe articulated in any single faith, any specific language of human sensibility.

---

7. *Crisis and Covenant*, 252–253.
8. *Crisis and Covenant*, 268.
9. It should be noted that a number of leading rabbis objected to some of the statements found in this paragraph and elsewhere in *The Dignity of Difference*, making the claim that they were heretical. While Rabbi Sacks disagreed with their conclusions, and even published a supplementary booklet of Torah sources to support his approach, political pressure forced him to reissue a revised edition of *The Dignity of Difference* where statements such as "God has spoken to mankind in many languages: through Judaism to Jews, Christianity to Christians, Islam to Muslims" were replaced by, "As Jews we believe that God has made a covenant with a singular people, but that does not exclude the possibility of other peoples, cultures and faiths finding their own relationship with God within the shared frame of the Noachide Law."

How could a sacred text convey such an idea? It would declare that *God is God of all humanity, but no single faith is or should be the faith of all humanity.* Only such a narrative would lead us to see the presence of God in people of other faiths. Only such a worldview could reconcile the particularity of cultures with the universality of the human condition. This means that religious truth is not universal. What it does *not* mean is that it is relative.

There is a difference, all too often ignored, between absoluteness and universality. I have an absolute obligation to my child, but it is not a universal one. Indeed it is precisely this non-universality, this particularity, that constitutes parenthood – the ability to feel a bond with *this* child, not to all children indiscriminately. That is what makes love, love: not a generalized affection for persons of such-and-such a type, but a particular attachment to this person in his or her uniqueness....

God as we encounter Him in the Bible is not a philosophical or scientific concept: the first cause, the prime mover, initiator of the Big Bang. He is a parent, sometimes male ("Have we not all one father?"), sometimes female ("Like one whom his mother comforts, so will I comfort you"), but always bearing the love that a parent feels for a child he/she has brought into being. The God of the Hebrew Bible is not a Platonist, loving the abstract form of humanity. He is a particularist, loving each of his children for what they are: Isaac *and* Ishmael, Jacob *and* Esau, Israel *and* the nations, choosing one for a particular destiny, to be sure, but blessing the others, each in their own way. The God of Abraham teaches humanity a more complex truth than simple oppositions – particular/universal, individual/ state, tribe/humanity – would allow. We are particular *and* universal, the same *and* different, human being as such, *but also* members of this family, that community, this history, that heritage. Our particularity is our window on to universality, just as our language is the only way we have of understanding the world we share with speakers of other languages. God no more wants all faiths and cultures to be the same than a loving parents wants his or her children to be the same. That is the conceptual link between love, creation and difference. We serve God, author of diversity, by respecting diversity.

This concept of "universalizing particularity" – which acknowledges the notion of chosenness without channeling it for the sake of establishing or affirming a social or spiritual hierarchy – is central to the worldview of Rabbi Sacks.[10] "There is one God," Rabbi Sacks notes, even as "there are many faiths. That tells us that God is bigger than religion."[11] Based on the premise that "religions are like languages,"[12] Rabbi Sacks explains that

the existence of English does not refute, replace, or supersede the existence of French, Italian, or Urdu. Each language preserves a unique set of sensibilities. There are things you can say in one that you cannot translate, without loss, into others. That is why we are enlarged by their multiplicity and would be impoverished if one disappeared. Nonetheless, they describe the same reality, as religions reach out to the one God. They do not, should not, threaten one another. To believe otherwise is to mistake religion for God.[13]

This means that in order for Jews to relate to people of other faiths, it is essential for them to distinguish between God and religion:

Though God is our God, he is also the God of all, accessible to all: the God who blesses Ishmael, who tells the children

---

10. For more on his approach to this issue and how Rabbi Sacks reached this conclusion, see "Interview with Chief Rabbi Lord Jonathan Sacks" in *Universalizing Particularity*, 122–123.
11. Rabbi Lord Jonathan Sacks, *Celebrating Life* (Bloomsbury USA, 2019), 155.
12. Ibid.
13. Ibid.

of Jacob not to hate the descendants of Esau, who listens to the prayers of strangers and whose messengers appear as strangers. Only a faith that recognizes both types of covenant – the universal and the particular – is capable of understanding that God's image may be present in the one whose faith is not mine and whose relationship with God is different from mine.[14]

Unfortunately, as Rabbi Sacks explains, too many Jews latch onto only one of these two dimensions. Yet those who focus exclusively on universalism diminish their timeless bond with their coreligionists. And those who place excessive emphasis on particularism diminishes their respect for, and identification with, those of other faiths. "The split between particularism and universalism," as he puts it, "is nothing less than a breakdown of traditional identity at the very time that the Jewish future, and the world, need Jews to be both."[15]

Nor did Rabbi Sacks direct this message of "universalizing particularity" to Jews alone. Many of his books were written primarily with non-Jewish readers in mind. He believed that people of all faiths should celebrate their unique faith commitments while acknowledging that "God is bigger than religion."

Indeed, as Rabbi Sacks developed this idea – which he was later to call the concept of "The Dignity of Difference" – he delivered classes on the subject to a broad range of Sikh, Muslim, and Hindu students. Through those interactions, he "noticed how Sikh, Muslim, and Hindu students were walking an inch taller after these study sessions…They said to themselves: we always knew we were different, but we always thought that was a bad thing." Rabbi Sacks concluded: "I suddenly realized that the concept works. So I had the concept ready to hand before the events of 9/11."[16]

His closing remark underscores an important point. Much of the thinking underpinning *The Dignity of Difference* had already been

---

14. *Not in God's Name*, 205.
15. Rabbi Lord Jonathan Sacks, *Future Tense* (Schocken Books, 2009), 118.
16. Rabbi Lord Jonathan Sacks, *Universalizing Particularity* (Brill, 2013), 123.

developed and expressed prior to 2001. But it was only following the Al-Qaeda terrorist attacks that the danger presented by those who regard their religion as the sole pathway to God and salvation became starkly apparent. As he was to later write, "One belief, more than any other is responsible for the slaughter of individuals on the altars of the great historical ideas. It is the belief that those who do not share my faith – or my race or my ideology – do not share my humanity."[17]

Despite the temptations of religious fundamentalism, as he proceeded to explain in his 2015 book *Not in God's Name*, he insisted we have the capacity to avoid interfaith and intergroup violence. The Bible urges us to recall that

> something transcends our differences. That something is God, and He has set His image on each of us. That is why every life is sacred and each life is like a universe. The unity of God asks us to respect the stranger, the outsider, the alien, because even though he or she is not in our image – their ethnicity, faith or culture are not ours – nonetheless they are in God's image.[18]

Ultimately, then, Rabbi Sacks believed that "the multiplicity of faiths is not a tragedy but the gift of God, who is closer to us than we are to ourselves and yet lives in lives quite different from ours."[19] And "since mankind in its diversity cannot be reduced to a single image, so God cannot be reduced to a single faith or language. God exists in difference and thus chooses as His witness a people dedicated to difference."[20] Accordingly, "the great challenge to religions in a global age is whether, at last, they can make space for one another, recognizing God's image in someone who is not in my image, God's voice when it speaks in someone else's language."[21]

---

17. *The Dignity of Difference* (Bloomsbury Publishing Plc, 2002), 45.

18. *Not in God's Name*, 194–195.

19. *Celebrating Life*, 158.

20. *Radical Then, Radical Now*, 72.

21. *Celebrating Life*, ibid.

Religiosity as an Innate Quest for God

Yakov Nagen

We have seen above that Noahide law does not exhaust non-Jewish divine service, and that Jewish thinkers and halakhists over the centuries have, to varying degrees, expressed approval of non-Jewish religiosity and religions. Insofar as these consist of more than the seven Noahide laws, what is the source of their contents and legitimacy? I submit that they are expressions of an innate human drive – possessed by every member of our species – to search out and touch the divine. These religious gestures sprout from below instead of being delivered from above.

HUMAN RELIGIOUS INSTINCT

A straightforward reading of verses in the Written Torah and of dicta in the Oral Torah legitimates and approves of natural expressions of worship. The first ritual act in the Torah is the sharing of one's bounty with God. Cain and Abel, farmer and shepherd, offer the fruit of their labors to God not because of some command, but because they feel internally impelled to do so.[1]

A few generations later, after the waters of the great Flood have receded, Noah constructs an altar on which he offers animal sacrifices. Nowhere does God order him to put animals saved by the ark on the pyre, yet the burnt flesh is described as pleasing to God.[2] *Pirkei DeRabbi Eliezer* lays bare Noah's thought process:

> Noah reasoned to himself: The Holy One rescued me from the floodwaters and then brought me out of that prison. Am I not obligated to bring sacrifices and fire-offerings before Him?
>
> Noah immediately brought of the pure animal species.... He built up the original altar on which Cain and Abel had brought their fire-offerings.[3]

Noah's response to God's kindnesses is emotional and spontaneous. The natural instinct to convey thanks to God exhibited by Cain and Abel finds continued expression here.

Prayer also began as a human initiative. "Another son was also born to Seth, and he called his name Enosh. It was then that the name of the Lord began to be invoked" (Gen. 4:26). The simple understanding is that this positive development originated in a human outpouring of emotion. "It was then…began to be invoked" sounds almost as if it happened on its own, the result of human intuition. Amid the new trials that every day brought, people began to verbally seek out God – not because He demanded it, but because it is human nature.[4] The entire religious gesture of prayer began here as a kind of grassroots movement. It was not orchestrated from above but sprang up from below in the lifetime of Enosh.

---

1. Gen. 4:3–4.
2. Gen. 8:20–21.
3. *Pirkei DeRabbi Eliezer* 23.
4. See Rashbam ad loc.

Rabbinic *aggadot* offer examples of paths of divine worship that were first beaten by a single sincere and religiously intrepid figure, which then became boulevards heavily trafficked by the faithful. The Talmud teaches that Abraham was the first to call God "Master," and Leah was a religious pathbreaker in showing gratitude to God.[5] To enter a mode of consciousness in which we envision ourselves standing before God as a servant before the Master of all creation is only possible because Abraham imagined it first. We have our foremother to thank for being able to approach God while mentally framing the encounter with gratitude for the blessings of our lives.

UNIVERSAL RELIGIOSITY

Even after the giving of the Torah to the Jewish people at Mount Sinai, homegrown service of God – from the Old World all the way to the New – has retained its importance. One indication of a positive outlook appears in a late biblical verse:

> For from the rising of the sun to its setting My name is great among the nations, and in every place incense and pure grain offering are offered to My name – for My name is great among the nations, said the Lord of Hosts. (Mal. 1:11)

The entire world, from Occident to Orient, recognizes the greatness of God's name and makes offerings to Him. Indeed, the Talmud expounds this verse concerning peoples who have never heard of the Jewish God or the Jewish people:

> Rabbi Abba bar Yitzḥak said in the name of Rav Ḥisda, and some say Rav Yehuda in the name of Rav:
> From Tyre to Carthage they recognize the Jewish people and their Father in Heaven. But west of Tyre and east of Carthage, they recognize neither the Jewish people nor their Father in Heaven.

---

5. Berakhot 7b.

> Rav Shimi bar Ḥiyya raised an objection to Rav:
> "For from the rising of the sun to its setting My name is great among the nations, and in every place incense and pure grain offering are offered to My name!"
> He said to him, "Shimi, can it be you? They call Him the God of gods."[6]

The verse seems to challenge Rav because it states explicitly that God's name is great everywhere, which logically includes the area extending from the eastern to the western Mediterranean shore. Rav responds that they recognize a supreme deity that sits above the rest of the pantheon, even if they do not know the specific name of that God or of the people whom He has chosen.

Non-Jewish religiosity wells up from below and meets approval on high. But that does not mean that every religious act is welcomed by God. Cain's offering was ignored while Abel's was lapped up. But it is this human gesturing toward the heavens that constitutes the basis of non-Jewish religiosity.

PARTNERING WITH THE DIVINE

One of Judaism's novel ideas is that human beings are not just passive creatures who receive and respond to God's revelation. Instead, we are active partners with God, with whom we shape reality. This partnership was forged at the beginning of time. After God created the animals, the first human being was the one to assign them names; he was granted the divine ability showcased on previous days of Creation to find the right names that encapsulate their essence. Astonishingly, God is portrayed as watching every word that emerged from Adam's lips for the ingenious names this mere mortal would choose: "And the Lord God formed from the earth every beast of the field and every fowl of the sky, and He brought them to the man to see what he would call it; and whatever the man called each living creature, that was its name." (Gen. 2:19)

---

6. Menaḥot 110a.

Man invents the name, God rubber stamps it, and the name determines the reality. This is quite different from the parallel account in the Quran, where man's unique stature is reflected by God teaching him the names He has already given them.[7] In Judaism, naming is a human endeavor.[8]

The divine image that inheres in the human being is also what enables the human-divine partnership in the Torah. The Jewish people endow the Written Torah with its meaning through the Oral Torah, as the Sages expressed rather sharply:

> Rava said: How foolish are the rest of the people who stand up for a Torah scroll but do not stand up for a great man, because in the Torah scroll "forty" is written, and the Rabbis came along and subtracted one.[9]

The Torah says that forty lashes are to be administered to a transgressor, yet the Jewish people, through their greatest sages, have the power to reduce this to thirty-nine. God gave them the Torah, and they determine its meaning. Rabbi Abraham Isaac HaKohen Kook explains the joint endeavor between God and man that is the Oral Torah in poetic terms:

> With the Oral Torah, we have moved downward to life. […] We feel that the unique character of the national spirit, bound like a flame to a coal in the light of the true Torah, is what lends the Oral Torah its unique form.[10]

God leaves room for humanity, who are made in His image, to join Him in forming and influencing the world. He awaits, as it were, the spiritual searchlights of humankind.

---

7. *Sura 2, Al-Baqara* ("The Cow"), v. 30.
8. For a lengthier treatment of this theme, see the earlier chapter in this volume, "World Religions as Fulfilling Biblical Prophecy."
9. Makkot 22b.
10. *Shemona Kevatzim, Kovetz* 2:57.

There is a deeper dimension to man's shared enterprise with God. As Franz Rosenzweig put it, love cannot be commanded.[11] But when humankind is also reaching for its Creator, as poignantly depicted in Michelangelo's "Creation of Adam," commitment to that love can emerge.

A VIEW FROM ABOVE

To this point, the discussion has centered on the individual human instinct to grope for God, whose outlets God finds pleasing. Can organized monotheistic religions also be understood in this way, as part of the story of humanity searching for the Being in whose image it was made?

To conceive of organized religion in this way necessitates a change in perspective. An individual experiences the ups and downs of life and tries to make sense of what God wants from him or her. The search of one individual does not negate or infringe on anyone else's. When it comes to entire religions, however, which include totalizing visions of the world and specify practices and rituals that embody and realize them, it is harder to see the other as legitimate expressions of human yearning for the divine. It proves difficult to look past the faith ingrained in us since childhood and which we take to be the true path to God.

To escape this inherent limitation, we must try to look at humanity from a God's-eye view. This is how Rabbi Nahman of Breslov explains the verse, "The Lord's eyes are toward (*el*) the righteous" (Ps. 34:16):

> The righteous person sees, because they have the eyes of the Lord, as it says, "The Lord's eyes [belong] to (*el*) the righteous." The righteous person possesses the eyes of the Lord, and the eyes of the Lord roam over the entire earth.[12]

By learning to adopt God's perspective, a person's field of view expands cosmically, taking in all of creation.

---

11. Franz Rosenzweig, *The Star of Redemption*, trans. Barbara E. Galli (Madison: University of Wisconsin Press, 2005), 190.
12. *Likkutei Moharan*, 1:98.

The refusal to let bonds of family, nationality, or ethnicity become a prison for the mind and the soul is what transformed the prophet Jonah. When God first revealed Himself, Jonah refused to agree to set out for Nineveh and goad its citizens to repent. He was concerned solely about what was good for the Jews, his own people, and this would not be in their best interests. Rashi explains:

> Why did Jonah not want to go to Nineveh? He said, non-Jews are quick to repent. If I tell them to, they will repent. I would then be passing judgment on the Jewish people, since they do not heed the words of the prophets.[13]

By the end of his physical and spiritual journey, Jonah learned to show mercy to everything, like the Creator whose mercy extends to all His creations:

> And the Lord said, "You took pity on the *kikkayon*, for which you did not toil and which you did not grow, which appeared overnight and perished overnight. Should I not take pity on Nineveh the great city, in which there are many more than one hundred twenty thousand people who do not know their right hand from their left, and many beasts?" (Jonah 4:10–11)

If Jonah could grieve over a plant, he surely could empathize with the human beings of Nineveh, who shared his divine image, even if it would put his Jewish brethren to shame. Jonah needed to transcend exclusive sympathies for his own people to hold all of humanity in his heart.

THE VALUE OF RELIGIOUS PLURALISM

The worship of God's creatures, and not just of the Jews, wins His appreciation. The aforementioned verse in Malachi establishes this:

---

13. Rashi on Jonah 1:3.

> For from the rising of the sun to its setting My name is great
> among the nations, and in every place incense and pure
> grain offering are offered to My name – for My name is
> great among the nations, said the Lord of Hosts. (Mal. 1:11)

People ignorant of the one God are nonetheless considered to be direct-
ing their worship to Him. In the prophet's time, the nations surrounding
the Israelites were not monotheists; their religious beliefs were warped
and their practices misguided. Even so, God – speaking through Malachi – calls their offerings "pure." They find favor in His eyes.

If religious activity across the globe is dear to God, we ought to
reenvision the relationship of Judaism to God and other religions. Many
prophecies, like the following, express this hope: "for them all to call in
the name of the Lord, to serve Him shoulder to shoulder" (Zeph. 3:9).
The prophets saw in the Temple a place to which peoples of the world
would stream, and Jews still pray daily that all inhabitants of the world
will recognize God, until "on that day the Lord shall be one and His
name one" (Zech. 14:3). The imagery of all humankind serving God
"from the rising of the sun to its setting," conveys that we all live under
the same sun, created by the same God.

John Hick, one of the greatest philosophers of religion of the
twentieth century, likened the relevant transformation in consciousness
to the Copernican Revolution. Before Copernicus, everyone thought
that we are the literal center of the universe; afterward, everyone came
to realize that we are not special, as we along with the rest of the solar
system are held in orbit around the sun. The same is true of religion. We
grow up with the conviction that our religion is the only true one and
that everything in the world revolves around our unique connection to
God. Now we must revise our model of the spiritual universe and place
God where He truly lies: at the center. Different religions– including
our own – revolves around Him, all of them trying in their own way to
capture, harness, and reflect the light He emits.

This paradigm shift, it must be noted, does not erase distinct
identities. John Lennon's "Imagine" asks us to conceive of a world in
which there are no countries and no religion, in which "the whole world
will live as one." With all identity-defining boundaries fractured, one

all-embracing identity can wash over humanity. The new consciousness I am advocating catalyzes connections across humanity *amid* its rich diversity.

While it is no simple feat to transcend the human perspective and access the divine one, so that we can come to view other monotheistic religions in Malachi's sense of "pure," the model presented above is a powerful basis for unity across religious lines and can effect real change.

First, it can revise our theological assumptions and frames. We tend to think that other religions – even monotheistic ones – worship some other deity. To take a recent example, at the height of the coronavirus pandemic in 2021, there was a radio interview with a Muslim nurse named Maher Ibrahim, who made the Israeli news for reciting the *Shema* with a Jewish patient in extremis. Israeli society was so moved by this story that Ibrahim was invited to light a torch on Independence Day. At the end of the interview, the host said, "May God bless you," and then awkwardly added, "and may Allah bless you too." Undoubtedly, the interviewer was being considerate in thinking about Ibrahim's faith, but in a way he missed the entire point of the story: it was out of a sense of unity and *shared* faith that the nurse had acted. If I can internalize the fact that the God of my belief, the God whom I love, the God to whom I pray, is the same God others believe in, love, and pray to, then God's unity is made manifest in the world. Then, God shall be one.

Second, this paradigm enables the formation of bonds that cut to the very core of our identity. It is not merely that we preach the same values or act with the same decency and civility, but that we actually worship the very same God.

Accordingly, one of the benefits of this mode of thinking and interacting is that it is in touch with reality. The world is not, in fact, moving toward a singularity of identity. By recognizing the profound links that hold us in the great chain of humanity even as we express our distinct identity, we prevent the kind of utopian fantasy that is ungrounded and cannot but crash. Realism is about more than practicality in that it promises results in the real world. It also possesses important spiritual value, because it underscores God's connection to reality and understands history as a divine orchestration that reveals the will of God.

DEALING WITH DIFFERENCE

Even if religions have a great deal in common, they undeniably differ in major ways. In some respects, this plurality is legitimate, even desirable. As medieval and modern Jewish authorities have observed, the many nations of the world have organically developed modes of worship that are uniquely suited to them. This diversity is a blessing: part of the beauty of the full revelation of God is the broad spectrum of color, the rich hues, the contrast. A uniform religious world is a monochromatic one that suppresses the fullest expression of God's splendor.

In other respects, these differences are deeply problematic. They generate great controversy and lead not to the full flowering of revelation, but to its suppression. Dogmas held tenaciously can be incorrect and can wreak terrible damage. Therefore, certain differences are to be celebrated and others are to be criticized. We must come together in spite of our differences, but we must also establish healthy boundaries and define the parameters of legitimate religious expression and belief. Interfaith interaction must be grounded in the recognition that the seven Noahide laws establish a baseline of universal human responsibility that is not up for dispute.

I believe that interfaith encounters themselves can correct aberrations that have crept into certain religions. In *Not in God's Name*, Rabbi Lord Jonathan Sacks decried the misuse and perversion of religious beliefs. Exposure to other belief systems can throw the world into a new light and set off a chain reaction that reaches the deepest recesses of religious identity and faith. By interacting with members of other religions, one comes to the realization that there are others who also worship the same God, and it is only that they revere and worship Him differently. By inspiring mutual respect, this can soften hardline, exclusivist tenets and lead to the natural extinction of phenomena like missionary activity and violent jihad. Do not misunderstand me: I am not advocating for increased connection as merely a means to the end of changing the other. It is intended to be a main artery connecting the many religious neighborhoods of humanity and to facilitate profound interconnection. Rabbi Zvi Yehuda HaKohen Kook would often say that to emulate the biblical Aaron, who tradition says loved other people and brought them closer to Torah, one must begin with unconditional, boundless love, and the closeness will automatically follow. The ability to form lasting, deep connections without compromising on the truth, to treat one other like family without sacrificing our uniqueness – that itself is a spiritual value. "A dispute for the sake of Heaven will endure in the end" because it does not pretend that everyone agrees on everything and because both sides still manage to find a way to get along. The key is not to let disagreement engender disharmony, not to let a separation of minds lead to a parting of ways, but to love in spite of everything and to drink from the same bottomless well of peace.

INTERFAITH DIALOGUE AS REDEMPTIVE

In the 1960s, two foundational articles on interfaith dialogue were published in the wake of the emergent change in Christianity's attitude toward Judaism. In an article titled "No Religion is an Island," Rabbi Abraham Joshua Heschel argued that religions need one another to deal effectively with the challenge of materialism and the erosion of identity. He concluded the piece as follows:

> It is…to help one another; to share insight and learning, to cooperate in academic ventures on the highest scholarly level, and what is even more important to search in the wilderness for well-springs of devotion, for treasures of stillness, for the power of love and care for man. What is urgently needed are ways of helping one another in the terrible predicament of here and now by the courage to believe that the word of the Lord endures forever as well as here and now; to cooperate in trying to bring about a resurrection of sensitivity, a revival of conscience; to keep alive the divine sparks in our souls, to nurture openness to the spirit of the Psalms, reverence for the words of the prophets, and faithfulness to the Living God.[14]

---

14. "No Religion is an Island," *Union Theological Seminary Quarterly Review* 21:2:1 (Jan. 1966): 133.

Heschel viewed us as dependent on and impacting one another. However, there are still limits. When he heard that Vatican II expressed eschatological hope that Israel would be united with the Church, he "declared that, faced with the choice of conversion or death in the gas chambers of Auschwitz, he would choose Auschwitz."[15] Feeling that this was a life-or-death issue, he even met with Pope Paul VI on Yom Kippur night in order to persuade him to strike the phraseology about the mission to the Jews. He succeeded.

Rabbi Joseph B. Soloveitchik, in his landmark essay "Confrontation," presented a less ambitious approach. What Heschel argued for dependence, he did for independence. Phenomenologically, every religion *is* an island that can be understood only on its own terms, and not on the basis of any features it may share with another religion. In an appendix to the article, Soloveitchik distinguished between religious or theological dialogue, which he deemed unproductive, and dialogue of universal concerns. Such a distinction presumes that these can in fact be separated, in the same way that the Torah and theology can be disentangled from this-worldly matters.[16] On the strength of Soloveitchik's analysis, in 1964 the Rabbinical Council of America issued a declaration that avowed "the uniqueness of each religious community" and opposed interfaith dialogue on intimate religious matters, limiting interreligious discussion to humanitarian and cultural issues.

Note that both Heschel and Soloveitchik use the same scriptural verse to support their approach: "For all the peoples shall walk, each in the name of its god, but we shall walk in the name of the Lord our God, forever and ever" (Mic. 4:3). Neither adduces the verse, "For then I will transform peoples with a pure language, for them all to call in the name

---

15. Reuven Kimelman, "Rabbis Joseph B. Soloveitchik and Abraham Joshua Heschel on Jewish-Christian Relations," *The Edah Journal* 4:2 (2004): 6.

16. This division is reminiscent of the Brisker analytical approach, which posits a rigid distinction between historical, sociological, and psychological processes, on the one hand, and theology and religion, on the other, given that the latter are transcendental and therefore incommensurable. See Rabbi Shimon Gershon Rosenberg (Shagar), *"In His Study He Meditates": The Study of Talmud as a Quest for G-d* [in Hebrew], ed. Zohar Maor (Alon Shevut: Mekhon Kitvei HaRav Shagar, 2008), 73–77.

of the Lord, to serve Him shoulder to shoulder" (Zeph. 3:9).[17] Even Heschel, who encouraged substantial interfaith dialogue, did not view it as critical to the ultimate redemption.

One of the goals of this volume is to stake the claim that beyond achieving the noble goals of mutual tolerance, respect, and positive influence, adopting a new attitude is necessary for the final redemption to progress. We may fervently pray for the Lord to be one and His name one, but that day will not come until we reimagine interfaith dialogue with our non-Jewish brothers and sisters. Here there is a major role for the Jewish people, because the revelation we merited is foundational for Christianity and Islam, whose adherents cover most of the globe. Smaller religions like Sikhism, as well as massive Eastern ones, have been influenced by these Abrahamic faiths through globalization. Furthermore, it is part of the Jews' mission to be a "light for the nations" (Is. 46:9) and to spread the Torah's teachings. The message of Judaism can be conveyed directly or transferred osmotically through the world wide web of humanity. The Jewish people ought to assume this calling with humility. A Hasidic story has it that a certain devotee once told his rebbe that he had experienced a dream in which the pupil became the master. The rebbe responded cynically, "Now all that's left is for everyone else to have the same exact dream." We cannot expect the world to recognize our unique position, but we can demand of ourselves to be the guiding light for the gentiles and hope that they are drawn to this truth like moths to a flame. Rabbi Lord Jonathan Sacks exemplified this in his life's work, and after his death there was an outpouring of eulogies, columns, and tweets by non-Jews that described him as a beacon of light for all humanity. Emmanuel Levinas defined being chosen as involving "a surplus of obligations for which the 'I' of moral consciousness utters."[18] So instead of seeking recognition, we should focus on increasing light and blessing in this world. Recognition will come of its own accord.

---

17. It appears once in Heschel's article, but it is embedded within a quote from Rabbi Moses Maimonides and not part of his own approach.

18. Emmanuel Levinas, *Difficult Freedom: Essays on Judaism*, trans. Seán Hand (Baltimore: Johns Hopkins University Press, 1990), 177.

The Jewish people aspire to more than having every nation and religion be able to be in the same room together, to tolerate one another. More than we want firm handshakes we want our souls to hold hands. The connection envisioned is not imperialistic, foisting one identity on others, but a unity that preserves diversity. Rabbi Yehuda Léon Ashkenazi (Manitou) imagined the Jewish people as the floral wire that holds the bouquet of nations together, retaining their uniqueness to create the composition. While he was speaking of nations, the same image can be applied to Judaism and other religions. This profound lesson of Judaism should not only be spread by men and women of the cloth. It ought to be included in educational lesson plans and implemented in field trips, where adults and children meet members of other faiths and nationalities. The various media are also a vital tool for breaking conceptual molds. They have proven immensely powerful in overtly or subliminally implanting messages, although too often with the opposite effect of weakening religious or other identities. Broadcasting this notion of unity within diversity through the mainstream media and making it viral on social media will be crucial for effecting this global change in consciousness.

PART IV:
DIVINE SERVICE OF GENTILES:
TORAH, TEMPLE , AND SABBATH

Sharing Torah with the World: The Jewish People's Responsibility to Non-Jews

Yakov Nagen

BEING A LIGHT TO THE NATIONS: THE VISION AND THE COMPLEXITY

An inextricable part of the prophetic vision is building connections among all nations. This includes spreading the Torah to the many nations that make up humanity:

> In the end of days, the Mount of God's House will stand firm above the mountain and tower above the hills; and all the nations will gaze on it with joy. Many peoples will go and say: "Come, let us go up to the Mount of the Lord, to the House of the God of Jacob, that He may instruct us in His ways, and that we may walk in His paths." For Torah will come out of Zion and the word of God from Jerusalem. (Is. 2:2–3)[1]

Torah does not go forth by itself from Zion, nor does the word of God from Jerusalem. The Jewish people have a crucial role in spreading Torah,

---

1. See the parallel prophecy of Micah (Mic. 4:2).

because, as we see elsewhere in Isaiah, the Jewish people is destined to be "a light to the nations" (Is. 42:6). Being a light to the nations refers not only to exemplary ethical behavior, as the biblical phrase is sometimes understood, but also, as Radak writes, to spreading Torah: "And the light is the Torah that will go forth from Zion."[2] Radak's interpretation meshes well with other biblical instances of light referring to Torah: "For the mitzva is a lamp, and the Torah is light" (Prov. 6:23), as well as with the vision of the prophets Micah and Isaiah that the nations will seek Torah in Zion.

The founders of the State of Israel were profoundly aware of this role of the Jewish people. In Israel's Declaration of Independence, they declared in the name of the entire nation:

> The Land of Israel was the birthplace of the Jewish people. Here ....they...created cultural values of national and universal significance and gave to the world the eternal Book of Books.

Part of the justification and motivation to establish the State of Israel was to fulfill the Jewish vision, expressed by many generations of prophets, to be a "light to the nations," a vision that also inspired the first Prime Minister of Israel, David Ben-Gurion.[3] One of the reasons for choosing the Menora as the symbol of the State of Israel also relates to this vision.[4]

The essence of Zionism is to take an active role as partners in fulfilling the prophets' vision. This partnership is not limited to the physical return to Zion – to making the wilderness bloom and establishing

---

2. Radak's tying the expression "light to the nations" to the Torah accords with the continuation of the second chapter in Isaiah: "House of Jacob! Let us walk by the light of the Lord" (Is. 2:5).

3. "History did not pamper us with power, wealth, large lands, or great numbers. But history gave us a rare moral and intellectual quality that confers on us the privilege and the responsibility of being a light to the nations." David Ben-Gurion, *Yehud VeYe'ud: Devarim al Bitaḥon Yisrael* [Hebrew] (Ministry of Defense Publications, 1980), 35.

4. See Alec Mishory, *Secularizing the Sacred: Aspects of Israeli Visual Culture* (Leiden: Brill, 2019), ch. 7.

a state – but also includes actively fulfilling the vision of the Jewish people's universal impact. Rabbi Lord Jonathan Sacks was a particular exemplar in this area, recognized in the eyes of non-Jews as "a light to the nations," as then-Prince Charles eulogized him.[5]

Yet when we begin to analyze this vision more closely, the picture becomes more complex. Surprisingly, we find statements in the Talmud forbidding a non-Jew to study Torah or a Jew to teach Torah to a non-Jew. This chapter aims to deepen and clarify our understanding of the role of the Jewish people in spreading Torah to the nations in keeping with the prophetic vision, by looking closely at the meaning of the Talmudic prohibition against a non-Jew studying Torah.

TORAH STUDY FOR NON-JEWS: THREE FOUNDATIONAL PRINCIPLES

This chapter posits that in order to reconcile the tension between the prophetic vision and the talmudic and halakhic discussion that followed, we must adhere to three foundational principles:

The first principle addresses the *presumptions* inherent in the very language with which we approach this discussion. In the prior generation, many discussed the issue of non-Jews studying Torah using language that highlighted the prohibition rather than the prophetic vision and the Jewish people's mission. Even those who found ways to be lenient regarding this issue were motivated by liberalism and equality rather than the mission of the Jewish people. However, I would argue that the presumption for this discussion should be the opposite: the Jewish people have a spiritual responsibility, a mission to teach Torah to non-Jews. This understanding arises not only from the words of the prophets, but throughout the Bible, and even, as we will see later, from

---

5. "Prince Charles, a student of Jonathan Sacks, eulogized him as 'a light unto this nation,'" https://forward.com/fast-forward/458428/prince-charles-a-student-of-jonathan-sacks-eulogized-him-as-a-light-unto/. Note that he added "this" to stress Rabbi Sacks's contribution to England. It is worth noting that much of the special quality of the teachings of Rabbi Jonathan Sacks was his ability to integrate the Torah with the wisdom of the world. The Jewish people must learn not only to give to others but also to learn from others.

tannaitic teachings. Admittedly, in the generation of the *Amora'im* we see a prohibition against non-Jews studying Torah – a prohibition that we must clarify and penetrate – but we must start from the idea that "Torah goes forth from Zion." If non-Jews are prohibited to study Torah, to where can the word of God go forth from Jerusalem?

Changing our starting point means recognizing that interpreting this prohibition broadly is more than a stringency; it impairs the Jewish people's ability to fulfill our mission. In other words, the question is what is the "rule" and what is the "exception to the rule." If the rule is the prohibition, as it appears in the Talmud, we might look for exceptions to the rule, cases in which it is nevertheless permitted to teach Torah to non-Jews. But if the rule is the opposite, that the Jewish people are called and obligated to be a light to the nations and to disseminate Torah to non-Jews, we need only seek the proper ways to do so and identify the particular situations in which we limit this teaching.

The second principle is *to place this issue in our current historical context*. Different historical circumstances fundamentally impacted the Jewish people's ability and responsibility to disseminate Torah to non-Jews. Rabbi Abraham Isaac Kook explains that in the Diaspora, the Jewish people focuses on itself and its own survival, whereas following their redemption, the Jewish people can also attend to the nations and fulfill the vision of being "a light to the world":

> In the Diaspora, which is likened to the evening, the focus of our actions is ourselves.... but in the time of redemption, when the light of Israel is raised, the time will come for enacting [the words in the blessing before] the morning *Shema, Ahava Rabba* (Great Love), when all the nations will say that the light of Israel will become "the light of the world."[6]

---

6. *Ein Aya Berakhot* 2a. See also later: "In the Exodus from Egypt, the Jewish people merited their own freedom, which represented their own completeness, but only in Messianic days will they merit the universal completeness of humanity." In the future, "because it is impossible to continue the universal *tikkun* (repair) without the Torah and mitzvot of the Jewish people, the central purpose of most actions will be for all of humanity" (*Ein Aya Berakhot* 12b).

Rav Kook's argument implies that the process of redemption requires a change in the way we study Torah and understand its place in the world. He writes that a similar change has occurred with regard to Kabbala and Jewish mysticism, which had been reserved for a limited few; they are now shared with all of the Jewish people, as they are understood to be necessary in contending with the challenges of this generation.[7] So too, our modern circumstances demand a parallel change with regard to sharing Torah with the nations.

The current time period is different for an additional reason: the process of globalization generates multicultural encounters, mutual influences, and inspiration, along with new opportunities and possibilities. These obligate the Jewish people to clarify its role within humanity.

The third principle concerns *the nature of the prohibition*. Is this a universal, fundamental prohibition, or a prohibition that applies only in a certain context? Many medieval rabbinic authorities interpreted this *prohibition as dependent on context*, which seems to accord with the straightforward understanding of the relevant passages. But even if we accept the opinions of those who interpret the prohibition as a fundamental one, we must analyze what exactly is the nature of the prohibition and what it includes. If we continue the parallel with spreading Jewish mysticism more broadly and publicly, perhaps the prohibition at its core relates to ensuring an appropriate and constructive way of bringing Torah from being wholly internal, within the Jewish people, to being external, to a public space.

EARLY SOURCES FOR BEING A LIGHT TO THE NATIONS

This vision, in which the nations are blessed with Torah going forth from Zion and the word of God from Jerusalem, does not relate solely to the future. Rather, it is anchored in the very beginnings of the Jewish people. The lives of the patriarchs were directed toward all of humanity: starting from Abraham, whose life was based on the promise, "Abraham will become a great and populous nation, and all the nations of the earth will be blessed through him" (Gen. 18:18); through Isaac, to

---

7. See *Shemona Kevatzim* 2:2.

whom God said: "All the nations of the earth will bless themselves through your descendants" (Gen. 26:4); and to Jacob, who was blessed: "All the families of the earth will bless themselves through you and your descendants" (Gen. 28:14).

God's selection of Abraham is connected to His desire that Abraham's children follow him in walking in His ways and pursuing justice and righteousness: "For I have singled him out, that he may instruct his children and his posterity to keep the way of God by doing what is just and right (*tzedaka umishpat*)" (Gen. 18:19). The choice of Abraham, "for I have singled him out," is linked to his and his descendants' role, "to keep the way of God by doing what is just and right." Isaiah's vision of the end of days describes a concrete fulfillment of Abraham's ancient calling. In his vision, as we saw, the nations say, "'that He may instruct us in His ways, and that we may walk in His paths.' For Torah will come out of Zion and the word of God from Jerusalem" (Is. 2:3). As in Genesis, "the way of God," which the nations come to learn in the House of God, is connected to *mishpat*, as we see in the next verse there: "He will judge (*shafat*) among the nations and arbitrate for the many peoples" (Is. 2:4). In many ways, Abraham is the father of humanity even more than Noah, because he transmitted a way of living that became a compass for many peoples, who walk in his path and see themselves as his children.[8]

The first words that God tells the people of Israel when they come to Mount Sinai to receive the Torah relate to their destiny: to be "a kingdom of priests and a holy nation" (Ex. 19:6). The mission of the Jewish people among the nations is parallel to the role of the priests among the Jewish people. The priest's role is to be an emissary, to serve the wider circle that comes to seek Torah from him.[9] The previous verse in Exodus, which describes Israel as "My treasured possession among all the peoples" (Ex. 19:5), alludes to the entire Jewish people being

---

8. Sanhedrin 56a, which discusses the seven Noahide laws, derives the commandment of establishing courts of justice from the verse that presents the mission of Abraham and his descendants as being about doing *tzedaka umishpat*, what is just and right.

9. "For the lips of a priest guard knowledge, and men seek rulings from his mouth, for he is a messenger of the Lord of Hosts" (Mal. 2:7).

singled out like Abraham had been singled out, for a unique destiny. The Sforno explains:

> "You will be to Me a kingdom of priests" – thus you will be a treasured possession among them all, because you will be a kingdom of priests, *understanding and teaching all of humanity to call in the name of God, and to serve Him together,* just as the Jewish people will be in the future, as it states: "You will be called priests of God" (Is. 61:6), and as it says, "Torah will go forth from Zion" (Is. 2:3). (Sforno, Ex. 19:6)

The Sforno connects charging the Jewish people to become a "kingdom of priests" with the prophetic vision of all the nations serving God together.

When the people of Israel enter the Land of Israel, their destiny vis-à-vis the nations becomes apparent once again. The people of Israel do not enter their land in order to build a legacy disconnected from the other nations. Just the opposite: according to the Sages, when the Torah was written "very clearly" on the stones immediately following the entrance into the land (Deut. 27:8), this means *that the Torah was written in seventy languages* so that all the nations could understand.[10] The nations were tasked with learning the Torah that was written for them. The Talmud even points out that they were punished for failing to learn the words of Torah, as was expected of them.[11]

In several places, the Netziv links writing the Torah in seventy languages with Israel's role as "light to the nations," a mission which he sees as the purpose of all Creation:

> To be a light to the nations regarding how to live, *this is the purpose of Creation*...and this began with the days of Joshua, with the stones on which we were commanded

---

10. Sota 32a and 36a.
11. "They should have learned, and they did not learn" (Sota 35b).

to write the Written Law in seventy languages. (*Harḥev Davar* on Gen. 17:4)[12]

The Temple is also intended for the nations, and this is evident not only in prophetic visions for the future, but in descriptions of the past as well. The First Temple, which Solomon built, was intended to have profound significance even for the nations, endowing them with knowledge of God, which is connected to learning Torah in its broader sense: "So that all the peoples of the earth will know Your name and revere You as does Your people Israel" (I Kings 8:43).[13]

Spreading God's Torah to all of humanity through the people of Israel is more than a prophetic vision; it is a deep part of the destiny of the people of Israel from its beginning, and it accompanies the people throughout all the foundational events that shaped its character. This understanding needs to undergird any discussion of this issue.

NON-JEWS STUDYING TORAH: FOUNDATIONAL SOURCES

When discussing non-Jews studying Torah, people often quote sources that forbid and limit this study. However, the earliest source regarding this issue actually looks favorably upon a non-Jew who studies Torah:

> R. Meir would say: From where is it derived that even a non-Jew who studies Torah is considered like a High Priest? It is derived from: "You shall therefore keep My statutes and My ordinances, which, if a person performs,

---

12. Compare this to *HaAmek Davar* on Deut. 27:5: "'And you shall build there an altar' – as God did on Mount Ebal, when they were chosen as a covenantal people, and as Isaiah the prophet said: 'I created you, and I appointed you a covenantal people, *a light to the nations*' (Is. 42:6)…to establish a covenant regarding every nation's beliefs, that they should abandon their belief in other gods and believe in one God. A covenant has already been made with our forefather Abraham in this regard…and regarding this it is written, '*You will be a father of many nations*,' and today this covenant is established with all of Israel. This began on Mount Ebal when they wrote the Torah in seventy languages."

13. In the context of the earlier verse: "If a foreigner who is not of Your people Israel comes from a distant land for the sake of Your name" (I Kings 8:41).

he shall live by them" (Lev. 18:5). The phrase: "which, if priests, Levites, and Israelites do they shall live by them," is not stated, but rather: "a person." You have therefore learned that even a non-Jew who studies Torah is considered like a High Priest. (Sanhedrin 59a)[14]

The Talmud emphasizes, "which if a person performs, he shall live by them," meaning any person, a non-Jew as well as a Jew. Unlike priesthood, which is inherited, the crown of Torah is left aside, and anyone who wants to take it can come and do so.

The Sifra quotes at great length a similar interpretation, which interprets many verses regarding the possibility of becoming close to God and walking in His ways as directed toward all humanity, not just Israel:

> "He shall live by them" (Lev. 18:5) – R. Yirmeya would say: You say, from where is it derived that even a non-Jew who fulfills the Torah is considered like a High Priest? The verse teaches: "Which if a person performs, he shall live by them." Similarly, he says: It does not state: "May that be the Torah for the priests, Levites, and Israelites," but rather: "May that be the Torah for the people, O Lord God" (II Sam. 7:19). So too, he says, it does not state: "Open the gates, and let the priests, Levites, and Israelites enter," but rather: "Open the gates, and let a righteous nation that keeps faith enter" (Is. 26:2). So too, he says, it does not state: "Do good, O Lord, to the priests, and the Levites, and the Israelites," but rather: "Do good, O Lord, to the good" (Ps. 125:4). Thus, even a non-Jew who fulfills the Torah is like a High Priest. (*Sifra, Aḥarei Mot* 9:13)

Yet alongside these tannaitic sources – the *Sifra* and R. Meir – we also find the statement of the *Amora* R. Yoḥanan in Sanhedrin:

---

14. Parallel passages appear in Bava Kamma 38a and Avoda Zara 3a.

> R. Yoḥanan says: A non-Jew who studies Torah is liable
> to receive the death penalty, as it is stated: "Moses com-
> manded us a Law [Torah], an inheritance of the congrega-
> tion of Jacob" (Deut. 33:4), indicating that it is an inheri-
> tance for us, not for them. (Sanhedrin 59a)

From that point on, throughout the generations, the discussion has primarily revolved around these words of R. Yoḥanan while almost entirely
ignoring the words of the *Tanna* R. Meir. This is despite the fact that
while R. Yoḥanan's words appear only once in the Talmud, R. Meir's
words appear in three different places.

Elsewhere, R. Ami, R. Yoḥanan's student in the Land of Israel,
also expresses reservations about Torah study for non-Jews:

> R. Ami said: The secrets of the Torah may be transmitted
> only to one who possesses the following five characteris-
> tics…and R. Ami said further: The words of Torah may
> not be transmitted to a non-Jew, as it is stated: "He has not
> dealt so with any nation, and as for His ordinances, they
> have not known them" (Ps. 147:20). (Ḥagiga 13a)

The Talmud itself acknowledges the tension between the statements of
R. Meir and R. Yoḥanan. It explains that the statement of R. Meir, that
a non-Jew who studies Torah is like a High Priest, refers to studying the
seven Noahide laws, not the entire Torah. But in light of our discussion
thus far, this explanation is problematic. It is difficult to understand study
of the seven Noahide laws – which mostly address protection from harm
in various life situations – as a fulfillment of the great vision, "Torah will
go forth from Zion and the word of God from Jerusalem." The Noahide
laws do not relate to a person's relationship to God, and they certainly
seem narrower than the great vision of the word of God that goes forth
from Jerusalem to all the nations.[15]

---

15. There are attempts to deal with the relative paucity of the seven commandments by
arguing that these commandments are just general principles, from which we can
derive many more details. As the *Sefer HaHinnukh* says, "Truly those seven are general

PROHIBITION OF NON-JEWS STUDYING TORAH AS DEPENDENT ON CONTEXT

Let us closely analyze the foundations for the prohibition against non-Jews studying Torah as well as how the prohibition has been understood, so that the relevant sources can provide halakhic and philosophic guidance to situations that extend beyond non-Jews studying the Noahide laws.

There are two models with regard to the prohibition against dissemination of Torah. The first model is a prohibition that is *dependent on context*. One example of this model is the prohibition against women studying Torah (Sota 21b).[16] Many post-medieval authorities argue that this prohibition is dependent on context, and that in today's reality, with the change in women's place in Jewish life, it is actually a great mitzva for women to study Torah.[17]

The second model is that the prohibition reflects *a fundamental problem*. For example, the prohibition against writing down the Oral Law can be understood in this way (Gittin 60b).[18] Writing down the Oral Law undermines its essence and changes its character. Nevertheless, despite the fact that there is a fundamental prohibition, the Sages

---

types, but they contain numerous details" (416). However, even if we significantly expand the number of commandments, they are still limited to particular areas of life and do not relate at all to the key question of worshipping God.

16. The Talmud quotes a proof text: "As it is written, 'I, wisdom, dwell with cunning' (Prov. 8:12). When wisdom enters a person, cunning enters with it." Similarly Maimonides writes, "One should not teach one's daughter Torah, because most women cannot concentrate their attention on study and therefore transform the words of Torah into idle matters because of their lack of understanding" (*Mishneh Torah, Talmud Torah* 1:13).

17. For example, the Hafetz Hayim famously says: "It seems that all this applies to previous times, when each person lived in the place of their parents and it was a very strong assumption that everyone would follow what their parents passed down to them. In that case, we would say not to teach Torah [to women] ... but today, there is a great mitzva to teach them" (*Likkutei Halakhot*, Sota, ch. 3, 21–22).

18. "It is written: 'Write down these words' (Ex. 34:27), and it is written: 'According to these words' (ibid.) [about the verbal covenant]. How so? Written words may not be said verbally, and spoken words may not be written."

permitted writing down the Oral Law in a situation where "it is a time to act for God; they have violated [literally, uprooted] Your Torah" (Ps. 119:126):

> They said: It is better to uproot the Torah, so that Torah is not forgotten from the Jewish people. "It is a time to act for God; they have violated Your Torah." (Temura 14b)

Is R. Yoḥanan and R. Ami's prohibition of a non-Jew studying Torah dependent on context, or does it reflect a fundamental problem? I would argue that both logic and analysis of the relevant passages lead to understanding this prohibition as being dependent on context. First, and most importantly, the broader picture points to this understanding; the Torah and the prophets' visions describe teaching Torah to non-Jews as a destiny that we long for, certainly not as a prohibited act. So too, the fact that the Rabbis draw a comparison between the prohibition against teaching Torah to a non-Jew and the prohibition against transmitting Torah to an ignorant person supports our understanding that the prohibition is not fundamental, but rather, dependent on context. Regarding a non-Jew studying Torah, the Talmud says:

> R. Yoḥanan says: A non-Jew who studies Torah is liable to death, as it is stated: "Moses commanded us a law [Torah], an inheritance [of the congregation of Jacob]" (Deut. 33:4) – it is an inheritance for us, not for them.
>
> And do we count this prohibition among the seven mitzvot? According to the one who says [the verse is referring to the Torah as] an inheritance [*morasha*], [this prohibition is included in the prohibition of robbery, as a non-Jew who studies Torah robs it]. And the one who says [the verse is referring to the Torah as] betrothed [*me'orasa*], the punishment is like [one who engages in intercourse with] a betrothed young woman, which is stoning.[19] (Sanhedrin 59a)

---

19. The Talmud is asking if R. Yoḥanan's statement implies that this prohibition is among

The Talmud asks: Why is the prohibition against a non-Jew studying Torah not included in the seven Noahide laws? It answers: This prohibition is already included in the prohibition of robbery, or, alternatively, of having intercourse with a betrothed young woman. This interpretation also appears in Pesaḥim, regarding studying Torah in the presence of an ignorant person:

> Anyone who engages in Torah study in the presence of an ignorant person is considered as though he had sexual relations with the ignorant person's betrothed bride in his presence, as it is stated: "Moses commanded us the law [Torah], an inheritance [*morasha*] for the congregation of Jacob" (Deut. 33:4). Do not read it as inheritance [*morasha*]; rather, read it as betrothed [*me'orasa*]. (Pesaḥim 49b)

The comparison of the Torah to Israel's "betrothed young woman" implies that there is a prohibition against "betraying" the Torah by exposing the Torah to foreign eyes that will defile it, similar to one who engages in intercourse with another man's betrothed. The aggadic literature uses this metaphor to issue a severe warning regarding defiling the Torah, not necessarily to express a fundamental, across-the-board prohibition of non-Jews studying Torah in any form.[20] Indeed, throughout the generations, rabbinic authorities interpreted the prohibition against non-Jews studying Torah as applying in a certain context, and even explained the precise context in which that study was forbidden.

---

the seven Noahide mitzvot: either in the category of robbery, as a non-Jew who studies Torah robs the Jewish people of the exclusive inheritance of the Torah; or in the category of adultery, if the verse is read likening him to one who engages in intercourse with a betrothed young woman, which is punishable by stoning.

20. The aggadic nature of this warning is highlighted by the parallel statements in the passage in Pesaḥim: "It was taught in a *baraita* that Rabbi Yehuda HaNasi says: It is prohibited for an ignorant person to eat meat, as it is stated: "This is the law [*torah*] of the beast and of the fowl" (Lev. 11:46). He expounds: Anyone who engages in Torah study is permitted to eat the meat of animals and fowl, and anyone who does not engage in Torah study is prohibited to eat the meat of animals or fowl. R. Elazar said: It is permitted to stab an ignorant person to death on Yom Kippur that occurs on Shabbat.

A. *Seridei Esh*: The Prohibition Depends on the Context of "Robbing the Torah"

Rabbi Yehiel Yaakov Weinberg explains in his work of responsa, *Seridei Esh*, that the Talmud's comparison of the prohibition against a non-Jew studying Torah to the prohibition of robbery indicates that the prohibition applies only when the non-Jew intends to "rob" the Torah by denying that it belongs to Israel:

> In truth, R. Yoḥanan's teaching in Sanhedrin 59a: "'Moses commanded us a law [Torah], an inheritance of the congregation of Jacob' (Deut. 33:4), indicating that it is an inheritance for us, and not for them," whether we follow the rationale regarding a betrothed women or the rationale regarding robbery, applies only to the case of a non-Jew who says that the Torah is his and does not belong uniquely to Israel, for such a person "robs" Israel of its birthright and preferential status. However, the teaching does not apply to one who reads the books of Israel in order to gain knowledge and wisdom. (*Seridei Esh* 2:55)

The halakhic conclusion from this understanding of R. Yoḥanan's teaching is that the prohibition applies only to non-Jews who are likely to deny that the Torah belongs fully to Israel, similar to the way a betrothed young woman belongs to her betrothed:

> It seems that the essence of the prohibition against a non-Jew studying Torah is the concern that he might take the Torah from Israel by denying that Israel has a preferential status with regard to the Torah. This is what the Sages meant when they described the Torah as similar to a betrothed young woman or a man's wife (the language of the *Sifrei*), or the prohibition as similar to robbery. These different comparisons all refer to one thing: "robbing" the covenant that God made with His people to single them out and distinguish them from all other nations. (*Seridei Esh* 2:55)

The prohibition is "robbing" Israel's covenant with the Master of the Universe, which is expressed through God having given the Torah to Israel. The prohibition, therefore, does not apply in a situation where there is no concern that the non-Jew will deny or "rob" this covenant. Rabbi Weinberg's words were very relevant historically, because early Christians exploited their knowledge of Torah to claim that God had nullified His covenant with Israel and replaced it with a covenant with the "spiritual Israel" (meaning Christianity). This amounted to "stealing the identity" of the Jewish people. In another passage, Rabbi Weinberg mentions "a certain sage" who argues that the statements of R. Yoḥanan and R. Ami are referring to early sects of Christianity.[21]

According to this understanding, it is clear why the Talmud relates so stringently to this prohibition: It goes beyond sharing Torah recklessly, to stealing the most essential, inner part of a person, the core of our identity as Jews. The Torah is not just *morasha*, meaning our inheritance or money, but, rather, *me'orasa*, meaning it belongs to us in an absolute, elemental way. Taking the Torah thus constitutes the most heinous desecration of the covenant. And therefore, the issue of a non-Jew studying Torah is dependent on the historical context of stealing and denying the Jewish people's identity. In a time and place where this "stealing" does not happen, preventing a non-Jew from studying Torah is merely a matter of the Talmudic principle (Bava Kamma 20a): "This one benefits, and that one is not harmed." The Christian benefits from the Torah study without harming Jews or Judaism.

Similarly, the Meiri explains that the context of this prohibition is the concern that Jews will be led astray because of the non-Jew's knowledge of Torah:

---

21. "And I will not hold back from saying to his honor that more than thirty years ago I found in a certain book in the name of a certain sage, that the statements in Sanhedrin regarding a non-Jew who observes the Sabbath and who studies Torah, were referring to a sect of early Christians, who violated the covenant of circumcision but observed the Sabbath and studied Torah, and they would mix with the Israelites on Sabbath and holidays, and would listen to everything the Israelites said, and later they would go and slander them to the authorities."

> He will look like one of our people, and others will learn
> from him…they will think he is one of us, since they see
> that he has knowledge, and they will be led astray. (*Beit
> HaBeḥira*, Sanhedrin 59a)

A corollary of this, according to the Meiri, is that it is a great virtue for
a non-Jew to study Torah in the right way, as we will see later.[22]

B. Maimonides: The Context Is Using the Knowledge against the Jewish People

In the Responsa of Maimonides (149), we find an instructive responsum
in which Maimonides limits the prohibition against non-Jews studying
Torah to applying exclusively to Muslims. This reflects Maimonides'
understanding that at its root, the prohibition is intended to avoid placing a stumbling block before Jewish people living under Muslim rule, i.e.,
to prevent them from being led astray by Jewishly knowledgeable Muslims. The context for Maimonides' words is the Muslim-Jewish polemics that took place in the Middle Ages, in which the Muslims claimed
that the Torah had been fundamentally corrupted. The Muslims' Torah
study was intended to find fault in the Torah:

> It is permitted to teach mitzvot to Christians in order to
> draw them to our religion, but it is not permitted to teach
> any of this to the Ishmaelites, because of what is known
> about their beliefs, that Torah is not from Heaven. When
> they learn something from the biblical verses that contra-
> dicts what they made up themselves on the basis of their

---

22. "But we do not prevent them from doing other mitzvot, since it is said that their
sacrifices and acts of righteousness are accepted…Nevertheless, we respect a person
who studies the seven commandments and the details thereof, and all that is derived
from them – even though most of the principles of Torah are included in them – as
if that person is the High Priest, because there is no concern that he will lead people
astray…and all the more so if his study is intended to understand the purpose and
perfection of our Torah, so that if he finds the Torah is perfect, he will go back and
convert, and all the more so if he studies and fulfills the fundamental commandments
for their own sake, even the parts that are not derived from the seven Noahide laws."

mixed-up stories and confused ideas, the biblical verses will not prove to them that they made a mistake. Rather, they will interpret the verses according to their mistaken assumptions, and they could respond to us using these verses, according to their claims, and lead astray all Jewish people and converts who do not have knowledge. This will be a stumbling block for Israel, who are imprisoned among them due to their sins. (Responsa Maimonides 149)

If Muslims learn Torah, it will not function as a "light to the nations" for them, but, rather, it will be exploited as a weapon for leading astray the Jewish people, who live dispersed throughout Muslim lands in the Diaspora.

Maimonides is not similarly concerned about Christians, who believe in the verity of the Torah text, because in their case the context in which the Torah is transmitted does not create a stumbling block for Israel:

> But the uncircumcised (=the Christians) believe in the unchanging text of the Torah, they just discover different aspects of it according to their mistaken interpretations, and make their own explanations, for which they are known. Yet if we convince them of the correct interpretation, we might be able to return them to good, and even if they do not return when we want them to return, this will not create a stumbling block for us, and we will not find in their text anything different than our texts.

This responsum of Maimonides seems to have far-reaching halakhic implications: "It suggests that by Maimonides' time, the Talmudic prohibition against non-Jews studying Torah was to be applied only to Muslims." Furthermore, it indicates that there is no fundamental prohibition, even for the Muslims, because in R. Yohanan's time, when this prohibition first appeared, Islam did not yet exist. Maimonides' responsum implies that the prohibition is dependent on context, and that in each generation we must determine whether there is a danger in non-Jews studying Torah, and under what circumstances.[23]

It is interesting to note that in the laws of Umar, which delineate the status of the non-Muslim minority in lands under Muslim rule, Christians and Jews are forbidden to teach their children the Quran. The reason seems to be a concern that they will denigrate the Quran.[24]

Elsewhere Maimonides seems to indicate that studying Torah can be a stumbling block for the non-Jew himself, because it might threaten his unique identity:

> A non-Jew who studies Torah is punishable by death. The non-Jew can study only the seven Noahide laws…. The general principle is that we cannot allow a non-Jew to make up his own religion and perform mitzvot for their own sake, of his own accord. The non-Jew must either be a righteous convert and accept all the mitzvot or keep his own religion without adding or subtracting from it. (*Mishneh Torah, Hilkhot Melakhim* 10:9)

---

23. Rabbi Barukh Oberlander explains that this statement of Maimonides, which indicates across-the-board permission to study Torah with any non-Jew who is not Muslim, barely impacted halakhic discussion on this issue, because the halakhic decisors had a different, corrupted version of the manuscript of Maimonides: "It is very surprising that despite all the halakhic decisors' long discussions regarding permitting non-Jews to study parts of the Torah, no one relies on the across-the-board permission found in Maimonides' responsum above. According to Maimonides, only studying Torah with Ishmaelites [i.e., Muslims] is forbidden, but it is permissible to teach Torah to Christians. The explanation for this is simple. Until the previous generation, Maimonides' words were known only through the responsa printed in *Pe'er HaDor* (Amsterdam 1764–1765, 50), and in this edition there was an incorrect version of his words, and therefore this permission was not known." Rabbi Barukh Oberlander, "*Limmud Torah LeNotzerim,*" *He'arot UVei'urim,* http://www.haoros.com/Archive/index.asp?kovetz=943&cat=9&haoro.

24. Jacob Marcus, *The Jew in the Medieval World: A Sourcebook, 315–1791* (JPS: Philadelphia, 1938), 13–15.

SHARING TORAH APPROPRIATELY

The understanding that the prohibition against non-Jews studying Torah is dependent on context does not signify that teaching them Torah is entirely acceptable. As R. Yoḥanan's statement in Sanhedrin implies, the Torah is the heart of Jewish existence. The Torah is potent and powerful; it is connected to our very existence like a flame to an ember. Clearly, teaching Torah beyond the Jewish people demands caution. However, once we understand that the prohibition is intended to prevent a particular problem, we must examine whether or how the prohibition is relevant to our current, precise context.

The variety of directions taken by the medieval and post-medieval authorities shows us that we need to understand the problem addressed by the prohibition in the unique context of each particular period. In the time of early Christianity, the threat came from blurring the distinction between Jewish and Christian identities and using Torah knowledge to deny the Jewish covenant with God. Christians usurped the Jews' connection to the Torah, claiming it for themselves instead. In the lands of Islam, the danger lay in providing "ammunition" to Islam in its polemics to claim that the Torah was fundamentally corrupted. In every generation, we must determine anew whether teaching non-Jews Torah is still problematic, just as Maimonides did when he analyzed the damage that could result from this study in his generation and permitted it to Christians but not Muslims. Why is this frequent reassessment necessary? The answer is that transmitting the Torah of Israel to someone from a different nation requires thinking, translating, and adapting the Torah to the language and world of the non-Jew. Part of the greatness of the former Chief Rabbi of England, Rabbi Lord Jonathan Sacks , was his ability to teach and share Torah with the world in a way that gave humanity insights and tools for dealing with the burning problems of today, problems with which many nations are concerned.[25] This is difficult to do

---

25. My friend Assaf Malach suggests that just as Rabbi Kook, in his time, wrote *Maamar HaDor* ("Essay for This Generation"), which addresses the question of how to "translate" the Torah to meet the needs of his generation, so too we need some kind of "Essay for this Generation Regarding Non-Jews," which will provide guidance on appropriate ways of creating an encounter between a person from a different culture and the Torah. According to Rabbi Kook, part of loving humanity is getting

effectively, as cultures that have "a little of this and a little of that" may sow confusion and create a Tower of Babel-like mixture of identities.

One example of this idea is found in a passage in Megilla 9a that recounts the story of King Ptolemy II assembling seventy-two Jewish Sages to translate the Torah for him. God bestows wisdom upon them so that they all change the translation of certain words identically, in order to make the translation acceptable according to the worldview and opinions of the non-Jewish king. These seventy-two Sages bring to mind the seventy nations and seventy languages in which the Torah is to be written and explicated.[26] The story teaches us that sharing the Torah requires us to consider our audience, to ensure that the Torah can truly be "a light to the nations." In effect, writing the Torah in seventy languages, which occurs when the people of Israel enter the Land of Israel, teaches us that we need to adapt the Torah to "the language of each person," to each nation according to its language and speech.

I learned this lesson from personal experience in my travels to China. I was invited by a group of Chinese people to give lectures on Torah-related topics. Through examining Chinese culture, I tried to identify which topics would be relevant and helpful for Chinese people and which would not. Among other things, I learned from a preliminary discussion that the Chinese see great importance in the Jewish understanding of disagreement as positive, represented by the statement: "These and those are the words of the living God." As the Chinese culture prescribes self-deprecation in the face of authority and has a negative attitude toward disagreement, it was a novel idea for them to see diversity of opinions as a blessing, as seventy faces that express the name of

---

to know the other nations, their ways of life, and their characters: "The higher level of loving creation must spread love of humanity to all people, despite all differences in opinion, religion, and belief, and despite divisions of race and climate. *The right thing to do is to deeply understand the ideas of the different nations and groups, to learn as much as possible about their characters and their qualities, in order to know how to base love of humanity on foundations that approach the practical* " (*Middot HaReiya, Ahava* 10). Thank you to my friend Rabbi Yitzchak Blau for this reference.

26. The later commentators explain that the Talmud is speaking about the seventy Sages of the Sanhedrin, plus the President and Chief Judge of the court (see *Rashash* on Sanhedrin 16).

God in diverse ways. They were also struck by the importance and value that Judaism attaches to each individual within society.[27]

Perhaps this can also help us understand the Talmud's answer with which we opened our discussion: A non-Jew who studies Torah is like the High Priest when he studies specifically the seven Noahide laws, because these commandments symbolize and represent the parts of Torah that are relevant to everyone. There are other parts of Torah, those that are unique to the covenant between Israel and God, which the non-Jew should not study.

On the other hand, we can also identify times in which people use certain content from the Torah for harmful purposes. An example would be New Age movements that use kabbalistic sources to engage with sexuality in an immodest way; instead of increasing holiness, they desecrate the holy.

PROHIBITION OF A NON-JEW STUDYING TORAH AS FUNDAMENTAL

Non-Jews Studying Torah as Damaging the Covenant

Until now we have discussed the words of authorities who see the problem as dependent on a particular historical context. However, there are also those who understand the prohibition as fundamental, independent of any particular context. For example, the *Rash MiShantz* comments on a Tosefta about a case where an abandoned baby is found, and it is unknown whether the baby is a Jew or non-Jew. He says that the baby must follow the stringencies of both sides: the stringency for a Jew, that he is obligated in mitzvot, and the stringency for a non-Jew, that he is forbidden from studying Torah.[28]

Similarly, in a practical discussion regarding a case that came before him, Rabbi Akiva Eiger makes an even more far-reaching ruling based on his understanding of a nuance in the words of *Tosafot*. He rules that the prohibition is so fundamental that even if a non-Jew comes to

---

27. The story of my travels to China and what I learned from them appears in my book, *Ha-Hayim KeSippur* (Otniel: Gilui, 2019) [Hebrew] in the chapter, "Journey to China."
28. *Rash MiShantz* on Mishna Makhshirin 2:7.

convert, there may be a prohibition to teach him Torah until he actually converts. In this case, the non-Jew lived in a place where the law forbade conversion. The rabbi asking the question wanted to teach the non-Jew Torah in the meantime, until he could move to a country where conversion is permitted, and then he would complete the process. Yet Rabbi Akiva Eiger concluded: "It is not in my power to permit. Your loving son-in-law, Akiva."[29]

Yet even according to these opinions, which see this prohibition as independent of context, we can ask: what is the reason for and the nature of the prohibition?

The Talmud in Sanhedrin indicates that the reason for the prohibition is that the connection between the Jewish people and the Torah is understood as intimate and unique, as expressed in the separateness of the Jewish people, as we see in the verse:

> You shall be holy to Me, for I the Lord am holy, and I have
> set you apart from other peoples to be Mine. (Lev. 20:26)

R. Yoḥanan, the author of the statement prohibiting a non-Jew studying Torah, elsewhere sees the essence of the intimate covenant between Israel and God to be revealed in the Oral Law:

> R. Yoḥanan says: The Holy One, blessed be He, made a
> covenant with Israel only for the sake of the matters that
> were transmitted orally [*be'al peh*], as it is stated: "For on
> the basis of [*al pi*] these matters I have made a covenant
> with you and with Israel" (Ex. 34:27). (Gittin 60b).[30]

---

29. Responsa Rabbi Akiva Eiger, 1st ed., 41. We should point out that Rabbi Akiva Eiger himself explained that his reading of *Tosafot* is in opposition to *Maharsha*'s words. *Maharsha* learns from the story of Hillel and a non-Jew who comes to him to convert that it is permitted to teach Torah to a non-Jew who is studying Torah in order to convert.

30. Thank you to Rabbi Sarel Rosenblatt for connecting these two statements of R. Yoḥanan.

The Oral Law expresses a unique, intimate connection between Israel and their Father in Heaven, and it expresses the communion and covenant to which no foreigner can come near. From this, we can also understand those opinions that limit the prohibition to the Oral Law alone: the prohibition applies only to the special space where the covenant could be harmed.[31]

According to this approach, R. Yoḥanan takes a fundamentally different approach than R. Meir and the Sifra, who emphasize the "Torah of Humanity," which belongs to every person and not just to Israel. Both of these approaches – emphasizing that the Torah is part of the unique covenant with Israel, and seeing the Torah as addressing every person as they are – are valid, as we say: "These and those are the words of the living God."

These two approaches are both reflected in Shabbat. In Exodus, Shabbat appears as a "sign of the covenant" (Ex. 31:16) between the Jewish people and God, and consequently the non-Jew has no part in it. Quite the opposite, a non-Jew who keeps Shabbat undermines the unique covenant with the people of Israel. In contrast, in Genesis, Shabbat is universal and addresses the entire world (see Gen. 2:1–3). Similarly, the Talmud states that "a non-Jew who keeps Shabbat is punishable by death" (Sanhedrin 58b), but R. Akiva states that a non-Jewish resident of Israel must keep the prohibitions of labor on Shabbat on the same level that a Jew is required to keep the prohibitions of labor on a festival (Keritot 9a).

Fulfilling the Covenant: Exclusivity or Uniqueness?

Yet does keeping the unique covenant between Israel and God indeed obligate us to be separate and isolated? There were time periods in which this was certainly the case, when cooperating with the nations too closely would have been harmful to the Jewish people. However, we can suggest another alternative: Fulfilling Israel's mission with regard to the nations, being a "light to the nations," does not blur Israel's uniqueness but actually strengthens it.

---

31. See, e.g., Netziv, Responsa *Meshiv Davar* 2:76.

According to this approach, the unique status of Israel is actually derived from its destiny and mission vis-à-vis all of humanity. We can already see the roots of this approach at Mount Sinai, where Israel is described as a "treasured possession among all the peoples" (Ex. 19:5). The verses there emphasize that Israel belongs to God precisely because Israel is a "kingdom of priests and a holy nation," a people who fulfills their mission regarding the Torah by teaching Torah to the world. Israel is treasured, in this context, not as a special race, but depending on its actions in the framework of its covenant with God.

The covenant is thus composed of two circles. In the inner circle, we are a "treasured possession among all peoples." We keep our covenant with God, and, as a result, we bring the voice of Torah to the world, which is part of our mission and uniqueness. In certain generations, the uniqueness of the covenant lies in this first circle, which emphasizes exclusivity, and, consequentially, the prohibition of non-Jews studying Torah. However, this very same covenant, the covenant of our destiny, obligates our generation, in which information is free and accessible, to open up new possibilities for fulfilling the covenant by spreading Torah. Doing so restores us to our original destiny of being a kingdom of priests and a holy nation.

Parallel between the Prohibition against Non-Jews Studying Torah and the Limits Regarding Jewish Mysticism

Another way of understanding the nature of the prohibition comes from the context in which R. Yoḥanan's statement appears: a passage in Ḥagiga that discusses limits on sharing Jewish mysticism. The Mishna (Ḥagiga 2:1) discusses the prohibition against transmitting the story of Creation or the story of the Chariot (Ezekiel's vision, which is a foundational text of Jewish mysticism) to the wrong people or inappropriately. In this context, the *Amora'im* forbid transmitting words of Torah to a non-Jew:

> R. Ami said: The secrets of the Torah may be transmitted only to one who possesses the following five characteristics: "The captain of fifty, and the man of favor, and the counselor, and the cunning charmer, and the skillful enchanter" (Is. 3:3). And R. Ami said further: The words of Torah may not

be transmitted to a non-Jew, as it is stated: "He has not dealt so with any nation, and as for His ordinances, they have not known them" (Ps. 147:20). (Ḥagiga 13a)

The essence of the prohibition, then, is about our approach to content that must remain esoteric, limited to the inner circle of people, who know how to respect and safeguard its transmission.

Change in Status of Jewish Mysticism

However, comparing the prohibitions against teaching non-Jews Torah and against sharing Jewish mysticism demands that we also compare the changes taking place regarding the dissemination of such content. In our time, Jewish mysticism has been shared more widely than ever before, at least in part because the greater intellectual sophistication of recent generations requires a corresponding sophistication in understanding and relating to divinity. This tension – between revealing secrets inappropriately and not revealing them at all, thus denying many people the light of Torah – always accompanies the teaching of Jewish mysticism. Even in the Zohar itself, R. Shimon bar Yoḥai says: "Woe to me if I reveal, and woe to me if I do not reveal" (Zohar III:127b).

We may suggest that a similar process needs to take place, recognizing a similar tension, regarding sharing Torah with non-Jews. The hidden Torah for Jews is parallel to the revealed Torah for non-Jews. This tension – between the need for secrecy, intimacy, respect, and the covenant, on the one hand, and the need to share and influence, on the other – must always accompany the important process of teaching Torah to non-Jews.

Rabbi Yitzchak Ginsburgh, who has expressed extremist views against non-Jews, quite remarkably takes an even broader perspective on the question of non-Jews studying Torah.[32] In the context of opening the circles of Torah, he argues that there are four revolutions regarding

---

32. While I am adamantly opposed to the extreme statements and views Rabbi Ginsburgh has expressed in the past regarding non-Jews, it is my hope that his open approach to sharing Torah with humanity is reflective of a change in his general approach to the non-Jewish world. He is cited here in order to illustrate that even a rabbi who

Torah study, four essential changes in our halakhic approach. Three of these revolutions have already occurred or are at an advanced stage in the process: writing down the Oral Law, nullifying the prohibition of receiving payment for Torah study, and women's Torah study. Following these three, Rabbi Ginsburgh calls on us to advance the fourth revolution: Torah study for non-Jews.

According to Rabbi Ginsburgh, Torah study for non-Jews does not need to be limited to the seven Noahide laws (as some understand the simple meaning of the Talmud that we mentioned earlier). Rather, this study should also include "the entire expanse of Torah teachings. This should begin with the wealth of spiritual and psychological ideas that are available through the Torah's inner dimension – Kabbala and Hasidism – without skipping over the laws relevant to all of mankind that exist in the revealed dimensions of Torah."[33]

BEING A LIGHT TO THE NATIONS: PRACTICAL HALAKHA

As I wrote in the beginning of this chapter, we are living in a time in which it is imperative that non-Jews study Torah; it is part of fulfilling the prophetic vision that "they all invoke the Lord by name and serve Him with one accord" (Zeph. 3:9) and that "Torah will go forth from Zion and the word of God from Jerusalem."

Our analysis here of the Talmud and the commentaries on the topic of Torah study by non-Jews indicates that the process of sharing Torah, of being a light to the nations, does not constitute a violation of the covenant and of the uniqueness of the Jewish people. That said, close reading of the texts and striving to discover the will of God in our time lead to the conclusion that the serious reservations that exist about non-Jews studying Torah should be translated today into caution, into

---

espouses extremist views against non-Jews makes a broad argument for non-Jews to study Torah. His argument is all the more significant to note, given his extremist views.

33. "*Heferu Toratekha* – The Fourth Revolution in Torah Learning," in *Gal Einai, Parshat Bemidbar*, No. 25, Shevuot.

sharing Torah that is adapted to the particular audience, so that it does not harm the recipient or harm the uniqueness of the giver.

In halakhic language, we can permit teaching Torah to non-Jews – even though doing so is, at first glance, against the simple meaning of the Talmud – by relying on a number of approaches and considerations:

1. *The approach that there is no fundamental prohibition, but only a prohibition dependent on context.* As we said, this approach is derived from the simple meaning of the talmudic passage. Maimonides also espouses this approach by limiting the prohibition to Muslims, as does the *Seridei Esh* by limiting it to early Christians. Accordingly, each generation must examine its own circumstances in order to determine how now-Jews may study Torah in that generation.

2. *The Talmud itself permits studying the seven Noahide laws, and some medieval authorities significantly expand the definition of these seven commandments.* The Meiri (*Beit HaBeḥira Sanhedrin 59a*) writes: "Nevertheless, as long as he is studying the principles of the seven commandments and their details, and what is derived from them, even though this includes most of the principles of Torah, we respect him even as if he were the High Priest." The Noahide laws can be expanded to include fear of God, knowledge of God, charity, and repentance, as we see in the prayer of Solomon, which invites the non-Jew to come and pray in the Temple out of fear and knowledge of God.

3. *Later authorities who limit the prohibition to Oral Law alone.*[34] The rationale behind this limit is to prevent study that could harm the intimacy of the covenant between Israel and God.

In addition to these fundamental distinctions, some later commentators outline other directions for severely limiting the prohibition. Rabbi Yissakhar Ber Eilenberg suggests that the entire passage in Ḥagiga does not reflect the halakha, and that this is why many rabbis teach Torah to non-Jews.[35] In a much more limited interpretation, the

---

34. Netziv, Responsa *Meshiv Davar* 2:76.

35. Responsa *Be'er Sheva, Be'er Mayim Hayim* 14: "I tried to understand, what do the rabbis who learn Torah with non-Jews rely on? ... And I did not see or hear anyone

Turei Even explains the passage in Ḥagiga as saying that because the root of the prohibition against a non-Jew studying Torah is, according to the Talmud, the prohibition of robbery, when the Jew chooses, of his own volition, to teach the non-Jew, this does not constitute robbery.[36]

Another exception found in the sources is the non-Jew who studies in order to reach the source of truth and who is prepared to accept the conclusions and convert if he "finds the Torah is perfect."[37] Alternatively, there are those who limit the prohibition to actual idolaters and do not apply it to every non-Jew.[38] Similarly, others define the prohibition as applying only to certain kinds of study – only in-depth study is forbidden, and not superficial,[39] or only regular and not occasional study.[40]

These permissions are not just dubious loopholes. Fear and stringency today can impair our ability to fulfill God's will regarding the destiny and mission of the Jewish people. "The humility of R. Zekharia ben Avkolas destroyed our Temple" (Gittin 56a), and we cannot "sit on the fence" without making a decision. The prophetic vision and the vision of the Temple as the heart of all humanity, from which the Torah goes forth to many nations, call upon us to harness our spirit and to find the paths – which are not always simple – to disseminate and teach Torah to non-Jews in a way that is appropriate, accurate, and illuminating. In doing

---

who mentions this. Why does not a single author from all the halakhic decisors, whether earlier or later, bring this ruling of R. Ami? This question is particularly strong regarding Maimonides, for it is well known that he does not leave out any ruling taught in the Talmud that is reflected in the halakha. Because of all this I would say, were I not afraid of my friends, that the halakhic decisors did not bring R. Ami because the halakha does not go according to him."

36. "Therefore, he says that R. Ami follows those who say 'inheritance' [our inheritance and not theirs] and because it is robbery, but in a case where a Jew transmits and teaches of his own will, there is no robbery" (*Turei Even*, Ḥagiga 13a).

37. "All the more so if his study is intended to understand the purpose and perfection of our Torah, so that if he finds the Torah is perfect, he will go back and convert, and all the more so if he studies and fulfills the fundamental commandments for their own sake, even the parts that are not derived from the seven Noahide laws" (Meiri, Sanhedrin 59a).

38. *Hatam Sofer HaShalem*, Meiri, Ḥagiga 13a.

39. Rabbi Nachum Rabinovitch, *Yad Peshuta*.

40. Responsa *Seridei Esh* 2:56.

so, we respond to the divine call to us: "I, the Lord, in My grace, have summoned you, and I have grasped you by the hand. I created you, and I appointed you, a covenantal people, a light to the nations" (Is. 42:6–7).

"A House of Prayer for All Peoples": Non-Jews and the Temple

Yakov Nagen

The affiliation of gentiles with the Jewish Temple has roots that penetrate deep into antiquity. Non-Jews were involved with both the First and Second Temples, and when it will be built, they will share in the Third Temple as well.

When King Solomon was planning God's first permanent abode in this world, he shared his vision with Hiram, King of Tyre, and requested his assistance in its construction. The latter obliged out of solidarity with Solomon's father, David.[1] According to rabbinic tradition, Hiram was one of seven people who merited entering the Garden of Eden in their lifetimes: "Why did he merit this? Because he, like Moses, fashioned a tabernacle."[2] At the Temple's inauguration, Solomon recited a lengthy prayer, in which he specifically prayed that God should respond to non-Jews who come the Temple: "And to the foreigner who

---

1. I Kings 5:15–21.
2. *Kalla Rabbati* 3. The simple reading of the verses speaks of Hiram of Tyre, son of the widow, and not King Hiram; see I Kings 7:13–14.

is not from Your people Israel and comes from a distant land for the sake of Your name.... You shall hearken from your heavenly abode and do according to all that he shall ask of You" (I Kings 8:41, 43).

The involvement of non-Jews in the construction of the most sacred Jewish site repeated itself with the Second Temple. First King Cyrus and later Artaxerxes promoted the rebuilding of the Temple.[3] A rabbinic homily takes the "voice of the turtledove" that is "heard in our land" (Song. 2:12), a harbinger of redemption, as belonging to Cyrus.[4]

These are historical facts. In addition, there is an aspirational element to the Temple service on an annual basis that seems to take its cue from Solomon's prayer in its consideration of non-Jews. On the harvest festival of Sukkot, seventy bulls used to be slaughtered on behalf of the seventy nations of the world.[5] This holiday, on which the world is judged for how much water it will receive for agriculture, was centered in Jerusalem, but its embrace extended around the entire globe to secure the sustenance of non-Jews.

The recognition by Kings Hiram and Cyrus of the respective Temples and their contributions to them call to mind the unfolding process of redemption today. The nations of the world have recognized the State of Israel, whose Declaration of Independence identifies it as the Jewish homeland, and this has provided an international boost for Jews to return to Zion.[6]

In the future, non-Jews will be even more involved in the Temple on an ongoing basis, as foretold in biblical prophecies. The Temple

---

3. See Is. 44:28, Ezra 1:1–3, 6:3–5, 7:12–27, and II Chr. 36:23.
4. *Shir HaShirim Rabba* 2. Alongside this praise, there is rabbinic criticism of Cyrus for not doing enough. According to this opinion, he should have been the one to build the Temple; see Megilla 12a.
5. See Sukka 55b.
6. President Harry Truman, who recognized the State of Israel immediately after its declaration, said in 1948: "It was my father's custom to read from the Bible every Sunday. When we read about Cyrus, King of Persia, who granted the Jews permission to return to the Land of Judea and rebuild the Temple, I thought to myself: 'The day will come when I'll be President of the United States ("the dream of every American boy") and I, too, shall do what Cyrus did in his day'" (https://www.chabadaz.com/templates/viewemail_cdo/aid/3429741). See also https://www.commentary.org/articles/meir-soloveichik/i-am-cyrus/.

will be a place to which the nations stream to learn about God and His Torah, and a place where they will bow before Him and pray to Him.[7] Rabbi Saadia Gaon believed that the nations will build the Temple walls, as it says, "And the sons of foreigners will build your walls" (Is. 60:10).[8] Rabbi Moses Nahmanides, however, thought that the Third Temple will be built "without strife or dispute, and God will enlarge our borders," in which "all peoples will worship Him shoulder to shoulder."[9]

This vision of the future establishes continuity between all three Temples. Non-Jews have always had a relationship with the Temple, and the opinions above augment it for the final Temple. The abode for God in this world, where His presence fully rests, has been and will continue to be a fountain of blessing for all of humanity, "a house of prayer for all peoples" (Is. 56:7).

THE TEMPLE AND THE TORAH

The Temple was always inextricably bound up with the Torah. In its innermost recesses, the Holy of Holies, lay the Ark of the Covenant, which contained both the first, broken set of tablets and the second, intact pair of tablets.[10] The Sanhedrin, who were the "mainstay of the Oral Torah and pillars of instruction,"[11] convened at the Chamber of Hewn Stone, which was "half inside the sanctuary and half outside the sanctuary."[12] The biblical Mount Moria, identified with the Temple Mount, was so called because "thence do they give instruction to Israel."[13] The *Hak'hel* assembly that reenacted the assembly at Mount Sinai took place at the Temple during Sukkot, when the pilgrims came to visit it.[14]

---

7. See, respectively, Is. 2:3–5, 66:20–23 (with *Metzudat David* ad loc.), and 56:7.

8. *Emunot VeDei'ot* 8.

9. *Commentary on the Torah*, Gen. 26:20.

10. Menahot 99a.

11. To use the language of Rabbi Moses Maimonides in *Mishneh Torah, Hilkhot Mamrim,* 1:1.

12. Yoma 25a.

13. *Pesikta Zutarta* (*Lekah Tov*), *Shir HaShirim* 4. See also *Midrash Aggada* (ed. Buber), *Vayera* 22.

14. *Mishneh Torah, Hilkhot Hagiga*, ch. 3. In 3:6, Maimonides equates the *Hak'hel* assembly with the assembly at Mount Sinai for the giving of the Torah.

And, of course, at the end of days, all the peoples of the world will throng to the Temple, from which the Torah proceeds to the entire world.

A fine expression of the connection between the Torah and the Temple appears at the end of Tractate Taanit of the Mishna. It draws parallels between the Torah and the Temple in its enumeration of the reasons for mourning on the seventeenth of Tammuz, and those for celebrating on the two most joyous days of the year, the fifteenth of Av and Yom Kippur. It concludes with a homily about such joyous days: "'On his wedding day' (Songs 3:11) – this is the giving of the Torah; 'and on the day of the gladness of his heart' (ibid.) – this is the building of the Temple, may it be rebuilt speedily in our days." Yom Kippur is the day when all eyes were on the Temple and its life-changing service, and when the Torah, in the form of the second tablets, was given at Mount Sinai. The most rapturous joy combines the Torah with the Temple.[15]

Just as non-Jews participated in the building of the Temple and in its rituals, they are also partners in Torah study, as we illustrated in the previous chapter. Our Torah is for all the peoples of the earth, "for from Zion shall the Torah go forth, and the word of God from Jerusalem" (Is. 2:3), and our Temple, the navel of the world, invites them to come call out to the Lord, in order "to serve Him shoulder to shoulder" (Zeph. 3:9).

THE TEMPLE AS CONNECTOR

The Temple unites the world because that is one of the characteristics of holiness. It is the great unifying theory of all reality, an edifice that makes manifest the unity that will lead to a day when "the Lord shall be one and His name one" (Zech. 14:9). The portal to heaven where above meets below condenses everything in our world into the space between its walls, in order to establish a connection to the *Shekhina*, the Divine Presence.

Faith is sometimes seen as divisive, but monotheism has a tremendous power of connection that can repair the world. The intense interest that the site of the Temple attracts across the world and the ceaseless

---

15. See the commentary of Rabbi Obadiah of Bertinoro ad loc.

friction generated by the Temple Mount are not only bad news. If one digs beneath them one finds a spiritual inscription: herein lies the root of all-encompassing unity. In a certain sense, if the world were indifferent to news about the Temple Mount, the ultimate redemption would be further away. Today, at least the site of the Temple is on the radar screen of most people, even if not in the way we would like.

Thinking about the Temple in such universal terms also strengthens our own connection to it. If the Temple is the great connector of nations and peoples, it reminds us that world peace begins at its gates, where all humanity stands as one before the Source of all being: "For then I will transform peoples with a pure language, for them all to call in the name of the Lord, to serve Him shoulder to shoulder" (Zeph. 3:9). Contemplating this idea reconnects us to the Temple and renews our longings for its rebuilding. While cultivating this conception is of practical value, it is much more than that. The construction of the third and final Temple will heal the world, making peace between everyone and connecting us all to the One above.

FROM FLASHPOINT TO RALLYING POINT

To this point, we have discussed the history of the non-Jews' relationship to the two Temples and how the Temple has the theoretical capacity to unify us all. In today's reality, though, the competing claims of the Muslims to the Al-Aqsa complex and the Jews to the Temple Mount appear to shrug off all attempts at dialogue, let alone coming to any understanding.

For Jews, the Temple Mount is the site of the ancient Temples and the most sacred spot on the planet. It is the place that the Lord "chose," as Deuteronomy reminds us repeatedly. The location was hallowed when the Temples were standing, and the holiness persists today and will endure forevermore. According to halakha, a Jew may not ascend the mount without spiritual preparation, including immersion in a mikveh. Moreover, our national hopes for a rebuilt Temple have continued burning for millennia, and wherever we have been dispersed in the world, we have never stopped praying toward where it once stood.

Many Muslims, for their part, ignore this Jewish connection to the holy mountain. In extreme cases, some even deny that a Jewish

Temple existed there. Others who do not deny the historical connection or indisputable archaeological findings argue for their irrelevance; today, they assert, the Jewish people no longer have any claim to the Temple Mount. The site is holy to Islam and that is all that matters. The seventeenth *sura* describes Muhammad's ascent to heaven and mentions his night journey to *al-masjid al-aqṣā*, literally "the farthest house of prayer." The accepted interpretation today is that this place of worship so far from Mecca is none other than the hill on which the Al-Aqsa Mosque was later built. It was there that Muhammad is said to have gone up to heaven and received prophecy. For that reason, millions of Muslims annually visit the large mosques on the Temple Mount.

I believe that this mountain must become a hub that connects the spokes of Judaism and Islam (and of other religions). The modern Italian kabbalist Rabbi Elia Benamozegh, to whom we have devoted an entire chapter, explained the concluding verse of the Prophets, "And he shall reconcile parents with children and children with parents" (Mal. 3:24), as a symbolic reference to reconciliation between Judaism and its daughter religions, Christianity and Islam. What better location than the Temple Mount and the Al-Aqsa Mosque is there to effect this unification?

THE TEMPLE MOUNT AS AL-AQSA

One of the most emotional moments I experienced at a joint study session of rabbis and sheikhs occurred when one of the former read Solomon's aforementioned prayer at the completion of the Temple. This supplication ties the people of Israel to the nations of the world at this locus of supreme holiness:

> And to the foreigner who is not from Your people Israel and comes from a distant land for the sake of Your name – for they shall hear about Your great name, Your strong hand, and Your outstretched arm, and come pray at this house – You shall hearken from your heavenly abode, and do according to all that he shall ask of You. (I Kings 8:41–43)

When the rabbi read these verses aloud and explained how Solomon linked the Temple to the prayers of far-off peoples, meaning that the Temple gathers in all of humanity, one of the sheikhs was visibly moved. He rose and explained that from a Muslim perspective, Solomon's prayer prophetically anticipated words of the Quran uttered thousands of years later in the seventeenth *sura*. Solomon speaks of non-Jews coming from "a distant land," and Muhammad journeyed to the "farthest" mosque. According to him, Muhammad visited this prayer house of the Jews because he expected, as Solomon had prayed, that God would favorably answer a non-Jew who came all the way from a distant land to pray at His Temple. The continuation of the *sura* discusses the children of Israel and the two destructions of the Land.[16] Based on context, the reference strongly appears to be to the First and Second Temples.

This is no mere homily. The interpretive method that produces it is ironclad: large tracts of the Quran are in direct conversation with Scripture or rabbinic literature. Muhammad's journey to Jerusalem, here referred to as "the farthest house of prayer," pulls together Solomon's prayer that God should hearken to peoples who come from afar and the Islamic belief that Muhammad went to the site of the Temple to pray.

There is even archaeological evidence that early Muslims identified "the farthest house of prayer" with the Temple Mount precisely because it was the location of the Jewish Temples. This evidence in the form of coins minted by Umayyad caliphs in the seventh and eighth centuries. They bear Arabic script and are adorned with depictions of the Temple Menora (see the figure at the end this chapter). One concludes from this that there were periods in which the holiness of the Temple Mount for Jews did not stand in contradiction to its reverence by Muslims. This offers a ray of hope that the site of so much conflict can become a center of world peace, where Jews and Muslims can find a common path to the God they both believe in.

The interpretation linking Muhammad's journey to Solomon's prayer puts the contest over the site in new perspective. The competing claims derive not from some incidental clash, historical accident, or

---

16. "They will make wretched your faces, and enter the Temple as they entered it the first time, and utterly ruin whatsoever they overtake" (v. 7).

frustrating coincidence. Muslim tradition continues the ancient Jewish connection to the place that God chose, and the fervent Jewish desire, worded so eloquently by King Solomon, for it to be a sanctuary where all peoples can reach God.

The rabbi's teaching and the sheikh's associations within his own faith tradition demonstrate that beneath the turbulent waves of conflict are still waters from which the two religions can drink. Judaism and Islam want to realize Solomon's wish and turn the Temple into a holy site for the whole world. Islam is indebted to Jews and Judaism for its monotheism and belief in the sacredness of the Temple Mount.

This world of religious harmony seems impossibly remote at the moment. But we hold out hope that, over time, it will slowly morph into reality. An understanding that the presence and prayers of others enhance the sanctity of the site, rather than detract from it, can turn the Temple Mount into a centripetal force that draws in all religions and nations in unity.

COINS FROM THE UMAYYAD DYNASTY

Shabbat for the Jews and Shabbat for the Nations

Yakov Nagen

The preceding chapter discussed the presence of non-Jews in sacred Jewish space, namely the Temple in Jerusalem. We observed an inherent tension between the particular relationship between the Jews and the Temple and the universal valence of the Temple to all of humanity. This chapter continues to explore this theme by looking at the inclusion of non-Jews in sacred Jewish time.

Shabbat is essential to Jewish existence and identity. Several times, the Torah underscores the special connection Jews enjoy with Shabbat. The second time Shabbat appears in the entire Torah it is described as a unique gift to the Israelites (Ex. 16:29). Moreover, it is a "covenant" between them and God (Ex. 31:16–17). When we sanctify Shabbat in Kiddush, we state that this covenant relates to the election of Israel: "For You chose us, and you sanctified us from among all the peoples." The *Amida* recited on Shabbat accentuates this even more, introducing an exclusivist element:

> You, the Lord our God, did not give it to the nations of the
> lands, nor did our King bequeath it to idol worshippers,
> neither will the uncircumcised enjoy its rest – because You
> gave it to Your people Israel out of love, to the progeny of
> Jacob whom You have chosen.

Given its prominence for Jews, it is perhaps unsurprising that certain
Jewish sources forbid non-Jews from observing Shabbat. This prohibition magnifies the covenantal dimension of Shabbat, the special, intimate
bond between God and His people that makes it off-limits to strangers.
And yet, verses in the Torah do extend Shabbat beyond the Jewish people,
and Philo and Josephus report that during the Second Temple era entire
non-Jewish communities kept Shabbat because it was understood as an
institution for all humankind.[1] Here, too, there is a tension between the
particularistic and universalistic dimensions of Shabbat, which raises
the broader question of the relationship between the divine service of
the Jewish people and that of the nations of the world.

GENTILES AND SHABBAT IN SCRIPTURE

Shabbat first makes an appearance in the Torah at the end of the Creation narrative, after the creation of Adam on the sixth day. God rests
on the seventh day, which He blesses and sanctifies. The seventh day is
imbued with this unique status long before the Jewish people come into

---

1. See Mordechai Arad, "Shabbat Observance as a Sign of Jewish Identity in the Hel-
   lenistic and Roman Periods" [in Hebrew], https://schechter.ac.il/article/sabbath-
   second-temple/. He cites Philo and Josephus: "But this is not the case with our
   laws which Moses has given to us; for they lead after them and influence all nations,
   barbarians, and Greeks; the inhabitants of continents and islands; the eastern nations and the western; Europe and Asia; in short, the whole habitable world from
   one extreme to the other. For what man is there who does not honor that sacred
   seventh day" (*Life of Moses*, 2:20–22); "What is more, even among the masses for
   a long time there has been much emulation of our piety, and there is not one city
   of the Greeks, nor a single barbarian nation, where the custom of the seventh day,
   on which we rest, has not permeated" (*Against Apion*, 2:39 [ed. Mason and Barclay,
   327–328]).

the world and are commanded to observe it. In this sense, the sanctity of Shabbat has a universal quality to it.

When the Jewish people are given Shabbat as one of the Ten Commandments, the account in Exodus says it is in response to the divine rest:

> For in six days the Lord made heaven and earth, the sea, and all that they contain, and He rested on the seventh day; therefore, the Lord blessed the day of Shabbat and sanctified it. (Ex. 20:11)

Note the anthropomorphic imagery used here to enable human beings to emulate God: God works and then rests, so human beings must work and then rest. This rationale of *imitatio Dei* applies to everyone fashioned in the "divine image" – all human beings. That explains the extension of the mitzva beyond the Jewish people to "the stranger (*gerekha*) within your gates" (Ex. 20:10), which on the face of it refers to the *ger toshav* (resident alien), a non-Jew living amongst Jews in the Land of Israel.[2]

In the book of Deuteronomy, however, the second version of the Decalogue presents another reason for keeping Shabbat, namely to remember the Exodus from Egypt:

> You shall remember that you were a slave in the Land of Egypt and the Lord your God took you out of there with a strong hand and an outstretched arm; therefore, the Lord your God commanded you to observe the day of Shabbat. (Deut. 5:15)

Each rationale distinctively colors the labor to be ceased on Shabbat. In Exodus, labor is an expression of the human being's greatness, doing as God does. In Deuteronomy, labor is associated with weakness because

---

2. See the commentary of Rabbi Moses Nahmanides ad loc.: "According to the simple reading, the stranger of the gate always refers to the resident alien who comes to live in the gates of our cities and accepts upon himself the seven Noahide laws. He is called 'the stranger who eats unslaughtered meat.'"

toiling under the hot sun is the unfortunate lot of the enslaved. This latter import of Shabbat should only resonate with the Jewish people, since the foundational event was experienced by this nation and no other. And yet, here too the command to rest is extended to "the stranger within your gates" (Deut. 5:14).

One could understand the inclusion of this non-Jew in the observance of Shabbat because being "a stranger of the gate" means that he or she lives in a Jewish domain. Since everyone else is resting, the gentile should follow suit and not disrupt the Shabbat atmosphere. But a third verse indicates that there is more to it:

> Six days you shall do your work, but on the seventh day you shall cease from labor, in order that your ox and your donkey may rest, and that the son of your handmaid and the stranger (*hager*) may be refreshed. (Ex. 23:12)

The handmaid's son and the non-Jew do not rest because they have some connection to Jews but because that is the very purpose of Shabbat. The day is not exclusive to Jews. This expansion of Shabbat from the Jewish people to the nations of the world embodies the oft-repeated Torah value that we should recall and learn from the harsh experience we endured in Egypt, and implement those lessons in our treatment of the poor and downtrodden.

In Isaiah's vision of the end times, this linkage between the nations and Shabbat recurs. The prophet addresses the Shabbat observance of "foreigners who attach themselves to the Lord" (Is. 56:6). While some commentators believe he means converts, context indicates otherwise.[3] Since the next verse mentions that the Temple is a "house of prayer for all peoples" – not only for converts who have become Jews – one can deduce that the "foreigners" referred to are not converts in the strict sense. At the conclusion of the book of Isaiah, one finds another reference to non-Jews and Shabbat, this time concerning the Temple, to which all humanity will come every month (Is. 66:23). This instance is part of a general theme of the book: the future relationship

---

3. See Rashi's comment on Is. 56:3.

between non-Jews and the Temple. Now, the Temple itself is linked to Shabbat; the Torah cautions, "You shall keep my Shabbatot and fear My temple" (Lev. 19:30). Isaiah is therefore conveying that non-Jews also partake of the holiness that spans from the Temple to Shabbat, as part of the yearning of all humanity to encounter God in both space and time.[4]

NON-JEWS AND SHABBAT IN RABBINIC LITERATURE

No verse explicitly excludes non-Jews from keeping Shabbat, but the Torah does stress the day's importance to the Jewish people. Halakhic discourse, though, takes no heed of this. Certain sources do prohibit non-Jews from keeping Shabbat, but none do so on the grounds of Jewish exclusivism expressed in the above sources – election, uniqueness, covenant. Moreover, some even obligate non-Jews to observe it to some degree.

A discussion of the issue in Tractate Keritot contains a range of opinions.[5] Rabbi Akiva rules that a *ger toshav* should observe Shabbat to the degree that Jews observe Yom Tov. This is a rather high bar, as it would mean that the non-Jew may not perform any kind of halakhic labor on Shabbat unless it involves food preparation. An anonymous opinion sets a much lower bar: the non-Jew may not do anything prohibited to a Jew on Ḥol HaMoed, the intermediate days of the festival, which are much closer to a regular weekday than they are to Yom Tov. Other authorities – Rabbis Yose and Shimon – permit non-Jews to do all work on Shabbat, and "permit" is the key word. Under no circumstance are they prohibited from resting. Through the end of the tannaitic period, not a single source prohibits non-Jews from observing Shabbat, and multiple opinions require it to some degree or other.

In another talmudic discussion we do encounter the expression, "A gentile who observed Shabbat is liable for death," but the author of that statement is Reish Lakish.[6] He is an *Amora*, not a *Tanna*, and there is no precedent in tannaitic literature for his position. Beyond this, the

---

4. I thank my co-author Rabbi Sarel Rosenblatt for pointing this out to me.
5. Keritot 9a. See the parallels in Y. Yevamot 8:1 and *Mekhilta DeRashbi*, Ex. 20:10.
6. Sanhedrin 58b.

simple reading of the passage is not that gentile observance of Shabbat is a problem per se, let us say on account of Shabbat's holiness. Instead, the crux is that people have an unceasing obligation from the Torah to keep the world going, and to rest is to shirk that duty. This is the point of Resh Lakish's prooftext from the story of the Flood: "as it says, 'day and night shall not cease (*yishbotu*)'" (Gen. 8:22). God promises Noah that the daily rhythm will not be interrupted, and Resh Lakish homiletically reads *yishbotu* in the sense of resting on Shabbat. This is supported by another statement of Resh Lakish from the same passage:

> And Reish Lakish said: Why is it written, "One who works (*oved*) his land shall be sated with bread" (Prov. 12:11)? If a person makes himself like a slave (*ke'eved*) to the earth – he will be sated with bread; and if not – he will not be sated with bread. (Sanhedrin 58b)

That the continuous upkeep of the world is the issue at hand is further confirmed by the continuation there. Ravina rules that the prohibition for non-Jews to rest applies "even on Monday," and Rashi explains: "Do not say that Reish Lakish refers to resting due to an obligation [...]; he forbids them rest of any kind." In other words, Reish Lakish does not forbid them from resting on Shabbat in order to fulfill the mitzva; he criticizes lying back and kicking up one's feet more generally. This is because after the Flood, God made a covenant that nothing would cease again. First on the list of things that will continue uninterrupted are "seedtime and harvest," right before "cold and heat, summer and winter, day and night" (Gen. 8:22). God is instructing the survivors of the cataclysm in the importance of labor and its preservation of the world, and by implication turning laziness into a kind of sin.

Are Jews not part of humanity, descendants of Noah, who are bidden to work without end? The answer is that they have a second, opposing value of resting on Shabbat. For them, it overrides the norm of productivity. One can infer from this that if Jews were to establish another day of rest in addition to Shabbat, that would be equally problematic. All human beings must continue their exertions unless given special leave to lay down their tools. Based on this analysis, one could suggest that it might not be a problem for non-Jews to rest on Shabbat if they are doing so to experience its spirituality, and not because they need a daylong break from physical work.[7]

Returning to the tannaitic discussion in Keritot, the consensus is that the halakhic rest of non-Jews on Shabbat differs from that of Jews. This can be explained as the product of the tension between the universalist and particularist sides of Shabbat. The *Tanna'im* endeavor to capture this intermediate position between belonging and exclusion by drawing on other, less intense halakhic categories of forbidden work to apply to the non-Jew, like Yom Tov or Ḥol HaMoed. These are intended to prevent intensive labor and exertion, and to fulfill the Torah's directive for non-Jews to rest and be refreshed.[8] For the Jewish people, in contrast, Shabbat is not taking a breather from heavy lifting but desisting from all productive and creative physical activity.

From this perspective, we can better see why Shabbat carries special meaning for Jewish identity and separates Jews from the nations of the world. Shabbat demarcates a sacred time, separating between holy and profane, the same way the election of Israel expresses difference on the human level. Shabbat is therefore part of the unique covenant between God and the Jewish people.

---

7. Rabbi Moses Maimonides writes: "Likewise, an idolater who rests, even on a weekday, is liable for execution if they made it like Shabbat for themselves. Needless to say [this applies] if they made a holiday for themselves. *The general rule is that they are not allowed to invent a religion and to make themselves mitzvot as they see fit*" (*Mishneh Torah, Hilkhot Melakhim* 10:9; emphasis mine). This is the opposite of Rashi's opinion, upon which I am expanding, because Maimonides is not focused on the resting per se but on the religious motivations behind it. Maimonides's reasoning is not hinted at in the talmudic dicusssion, and he must consider Reish Lakish's citation of Genesis 8 as an *asmakhta*, a homiletical derivation of rabbinic force alone.

8. I again thank Rabbi Sarel Rosenblatt for his insight.

SHABBAT'S MULTIPLE FACETS

A fine encapsulation of Shabbat's multifacetedness, of its special connection to the Jewish people and its universal relationship to all of humanity, can be found in the twelfth-century compendium *Maḥazor Vitry*:

> Why do we vary the Shabbat *Amida* in the nighttime, morning, Musaf, and afternoon, instead of having a single liturgy like we have for the festivals, when we recite *atta beḥartanu* during every *Amida*? I have heard from someone from Narbonne that the Sages instituted these prayers to correspond to three Shabbatot. *Atta kiddashta* (You have sanctified) corresponds to the Shabbat of Creation, for God sanctified it, and it has retained that sanctity since the six days of Creation. *Yismaḥ Moshe* (Mose rejoices) corresponds to the Shabbat at Sinai, for the Torah was given in the early morning of Shabbat. [...] *Atta eḥad* (You are one) corresponds to the Shabbat of the future, as it says, "On that day the Lord shall be one and His name one" (Zech. 14:3), and the Jewish people will be one nation, as it says, "And Your people will be all righteous, and they shall inherit the land forever" (Is. 60:21). (*Maḥazor Vitry*, 162)

There are multiple aspects to Shabbat which the *Amida* prayers address or invoke. The first is the primeval Shabbat, the universal Shabbat established after Creation. The second is the Shabbat on which the Torah was given, and it is unique to the Jewish people. What about the third, future Shabbat of divine unity: will it be universal or particular? According to this quotation, there is an element specific to the Jewish people, as the Jewish people will be "one nation," but the prophecy of Zechariah is about all of humankind coming to God in Jerusalem. The Shabbat of the future, therefore, encompasses everyone, in what is kabbalistically characterized as "the mystery of Shabbat," being "the Shabbat that is unified through the mystery of the One."[9]

---

9. Zohar, II:135b.

Afterword

Moving Forward:
Interreligious Interaction Today

Sarel Rosenblatt

T he present volume has sought to bring the issue of Judaism's attitude toward other religions and forms of religiosity to the fore in contemplating the identity and destiny of the Jewish people.

Most of the book consists of individual chapters dedicated to the pertinent thought of Jewish luminaries throughout history. When taken as a whole, they tell the long story of continuous and considered Jewish engagement with non-Jewish religiosity. It manages to rise above the strife between nations and religions, and even to look beyond the existential threat posed by the Jewish State's neighbors. Even in its transcendence, though, it sees and does not forget them. The story recounted herein charts human history according to the perspective of Judaism, as refracted through biblical prophecies and rabbinic wisdom. This book principally has drawn on the conceptual models and terminology of Jewish law and Jewish philosophy, and its findings have halakhic and other ramifications for many areas of life. But the heart of the book is really a spiritual and intellectual journey of discovering ourselves, because considering the other has a direct impact on us. It especially shapes the encounter between the committed Jew and the religious non-Jew, which naturally provokes burning, important questions. In this afterword, I would like to collect the many insights scattered throughout the book and incorporate them into a cohesive response to such questions. How should the Jew understand and relate to the religiosity of members of other faiths? Is there one "true" religion that renders the rest false? Must there be only a single "divine religion"? How should the Jew react to the New Testament, which claims to be a continuation and realization of the Torah, and what is he or she to make of the biblical stories adapted in the Quran? How should one relate to non-Jewish figures venerated by their believers as prophets: should they be the object of learning or of criticism? Should other religions be viewed as competitors over a finite religious space, or can belief systems coexist and perhaps even cooperate? Is interfaith dialogue a waste of time, or critical to the redemption of the world? These are not esoteric problems that vex some small cadre of theologians who seriously think through interfaith issues. In the world of today, an era of hypermobility and hyperconnectivity, one encounters ideas and worldviews rooted in other religions and actual members of those faiths on a daily basis. Pretending that they do not exist – if that was ever a good strategy – is not an option. Having a robust response ready for inevitable exposure is vital. This is especially the case in Israel, where actively engaging in conversations on these issues can serve initiatives to reduce violence and bloodshed. On a deeper level, probing the boundaries of legitimate religion and religious identity puts our own beliefs and mission in this world into much sharper relief. How do we reconcile being chosen with the concept that every person is beloved to God because they are made in His image? What does God want from the nations of the world and what does He want from us? What role does the State of Israel play in all of this?

ISRAEL AS A FORCE FOR CHANGE

The return of the Jewish people to their homeland, their attainment of political independence and demonstration of military prowess, the flowering of Torah study and coalescence of Israeli culture – all of these make the contemporary encounter between Jew and non-Jew categorically different from what it had been for two millennia of exile. The Jew who comes to the table is no longer cowering from fear of physical blows, economic sanctions, or wholesale exile, nor is he trying to keep his head down and mind his own business. Held head high, confident in our people's capacity to contribute to the world, the Jew is now able to sincerely and openly engage with other peoples and religions. He or she does so in the service of humanity, to make the ancient prophecies of world peace a reality. The peace envisioned by the prophets was not merely the absence of wars, but the presence of harmony. So much so, that the rebuilt Temple will become "a house of prayer for all peoples" (Is. 56:7). This new engagement is already underway on the ground. Since the turn of the millennium, the Israeli Chief Rabbinate has convened a special committee of its members to cultivate connections and hold meetings regularly with leaders of the Vatican, the Anglican Church, and, most recently, Islam. These gatherings address the most pressing social and ethical questions of the day. In keeping with this, the one hundred ambassadors and consuls of Israel stationed throughout the world formalize – and help entrench – the story of the Jewish State as the story of an ancient people, not only to defend its sovereignty over its territory, but also to contribute the collective wisdom and experience of that people to the entire world. Concurrently, there are organizations of all kinds in Israel and around the world that are active in bringing together religious leaders of all stripes.

We should not view this engagement as a natural reaction to globalization, nor as a *hasbara* project necessitated by Israeli diplomatic concerns. We should treasure projects like these because they are part of the great restructuring of the relationship between the Jewish people and the rest of humanity.

When God told Abraham, "Through you will all the clans of the earth be blessed" (Gen. 12:3), He did not mean it solely as a supernatural promise kept without human input. God also intended that the blessing be transmissible through dialogue and personal interaction. Every encounter is another braid of fraternity that has the potential for learning from one another, for growing together, and – if we are fortunate – for criticizing one another from a place of mutual respect. For Rabbi Moses Maimonides, this is what it means to heed the truth regardless of who utters it. Rabbi Joseph B. Soloveitchik believed that it yields deeper insight into how to deal with the challenges facing one's generation. According to Rabbi Abraham Isaac HaKohen Kook, it affords us a better view of our obligation to the world and the betterment we have to offer:

> All the diverse spiritual currents of human existence have a root in the Congregation of Israel.... That is why we cannot afford to ignore any stirring when we come to investigate the spiritual power of the Congregation of Israel, the "Bride (*kalla*)" that is "crowned (*kelila*) by all colors."[1]

To really comprehend and improve our divine service as the Congregation of Israel requires opening our eyes to the spiritual stirrings of humanity, which in aggregate give expression to the full divine truth. For Manitou, interfaith dialogue is a means to unify the attributes of God as they are manifest in this world and to repair "the equation of fraternity," at long last effecting the rectification of the sin of Cain and Abel.

THE INTERFAITH ENCOUNTER IN RABBINIC THOUGHT

The source for the conventional opinion that all non-Jewish religions are illegitimate is, as we have seen, the original and singular opinion of Maimonides. It contradicts the conclusions of two earlier thinkers, Rabbi Nathaniel b. Rabbi Fayyumi and Rabbi Yehuda HaLevi, who both viewed other religions favorably. Maimonides favored a different track of spirituality: the individual's journey to find God. If a non-Jew wishes to fulfill more than the seven Noahide laws and keeps other mitzvot of the Torah, he or she does so as one who is not obligated. Such a person

---

1. *Shemona Kevatzim, Kovetz* 1:26.

demonstrates commitment to the truth – be it pronounced by Jew or non-Jew. Despite looking kindly on religious pursuits, Maimonides was not keen on organized religions. His ambivalence is evident: it is true that the resounding successes of Christianity and Islam, which have spread awareness of divine revelation and messianism, reveal God's providential hand, but they do not qualify as religions qua religion, because the only revelation that could establish a genuine religion was that of Moses. In actual instances of interfaith encounter and dialogue, Maimonides's dialectical approach poses a serious challenge, both intellectually and emotionally, for the Jew and his counterpart. How can a Jew be attentive and curious, ears pricked to hear the truth from any source, when deep down there is a tiny voice protesting that the other person's religion is illegitimate, because their prophets deceived them and their Scripture is full of falsehoods? And if a non-Jew were to get wind of this stance of scorn and dismissal, they would be disinclined to conduct a serious dialogue with Jews. This raises a practical issue: should the Maimonidean position on non-Jewish religion be publicized or kept under wraps? The latter would allow Jews to learn truths that others possess and to admire their spiritual yearnings, and non-Jews to recognize the truths of Judaism. Or perhaps the question is moot, because discussion of weighty theological tenets will inevitably end in a head-on collision? The fact that Maimonides was conflicted and the fact that it might blow up in the faces of well-meaning people are perhaps what dissuaded Rabbi Soloveitchik from supporting interfaith dialogue with devout Christians on matters of theology.[2]

The long tradition presented in this book shows that interfaith interaction need not be this way. The starting point is the Torah, with the book of Genesis and the election of Israel and its role in the final redemption in the Prophets, whence it is picked up and developed in talmudic discourse and by our greatest rabbinic leaders. These sources and thinkers were not uncritical of the contents of other religions, but they took the very existence of other religions as a fact of life. According to HaLevi, other religions are wonderful so long as they increase awareness of the one God, establish a functioning society, and reform

2. See his "Confrontation," *Tradition* 6:2 (1964): 5–9.

individual character. Rabbi Joseph Albo and Rabbi Kook went beyond conceding the legitimacy of such religions by being willing to admit non-Jewish forms of religiosity as "divine religion." Rabbi Nathaniel thought that prophets of such religions likely received divine inspiration, and Rabbi Jacob Emden argued that Christian Scripture has positive content attuned to the spiritual constitution of its believers. This line of thinking completely transforms the entire nature of interfaith interaction. A Jew can be open to the totality of the human being in front of them because not only is their religiosity not a threat, but it is what makes them allies, what promotes shared values and even the same redemptive aspirations.

But how is the devout Jew to respond to monotheistic religions that postdate Judaism and seemingly co-opted its holiest text for their own ends? The New Testament styles itself as the continuation and fulfillment of the Jewish Bible, and the Quran systematically reworks biblical narratives. Nathaniel, Emden, and Manitou offer a reframing. These other Scriptures are not a threat, a distortion of the Truth, or the product of copyright infringement, but rather adjustments necessary for the national or ethnic character of their believers. With this understanding, one can analyze divergences that reflect fundamentally different conceptions of theology and more. Nathaniel actually believed that the adaptation of Holy Writ should reinforce Jewish belief, because our Torah is a source of inspiration for billions of people around the world. In the opinions of Rabbi Moses Rivkes and Rabbi Zvi Hirsch Chajes, the religious piety of Christians and Muslims is what defines them as the pious of the nations of the world. Rabbi Elazar Fleckeles stressed that their religious observance is a fulfillment of God's will. Rabbi Jacob Zvi Mecklenburg extended this positive approach when he wrote that the Rabbis were referring to such nations in the dictum that "a gentile who studies Torah is like the High Priest." Rabbi Elijah Guttmacher rounds out these opinions by stating that one should pray for the success and peace of those nations and religions – period. Our own benefit or considerations do not factor into it.[3]

---

3. For the opinions of all these authorities. See the chapters in this volume regarding modern halakhic authorities on Christianity, pp. 121–167..

The language of fraternity and fellowship used by Rabbi Menahem Meiri and Manitou also dramatically influence the interfaith
encounter. The entire intellectual discourse is shifted from a mindset
of insiders versus outsiders to an existential consciousness of constructive opposition "within the family." Experience teaches that familial disagreements can be scathing, but they possess incredible potential. The
face of interfaith discourse is completely remolded if I know that the
other person is my brother or sister, and that their God-given destiny
is to better the world and bring about its redemption. The motivation
for and assumptions of that meeting, as well as the tone and substance
of its debate, would bear no resemblance to a similar encounter and
dialogue with a stranger, nor to the framework of a zero-sum game in
which the loss of one is the gain of the other.

Another impactful perspective introduced by Kook – and subsequently developed by Manitou – is an organic model of religions, in
which Judaism is the beating heart. The Jewish people are like the *sefira*
called *Tiferet* that lies at the center of the sefirotic tree, and that joins
all the divine *sefirot*. In this approach, establishing a platform for interfaith interaction is essential to the divine mission of the Jewish people.
The foremost goal of Judaism in this model is not to be the king of all
religions or to win glory for itself, but to unify the divine attributes and
restore the equation of fraternity in order to achieve rectification and
hasten progress. Since the nations and religions of the world are limbs
of a single organism, it is necessary to constantly maintain harmonious
relations between them. Reform and progress entail passing criticism
that requires lines of dialogue that are already open. Accordingly, Kook
and Manitou would not label dialogue and encounter as possible, but
as absolutely vital.

The story told in this volume begins with Adam and ends with
us. Our hope is that it will transform the present moment into the next
chapter. The only question is, will we seize this opportunity to realize the destiny assigned to us by God through His prophets and sages
throughout history?

The reality today is complex. Two thousand years of exile and one
hundred years of existential wars fought for our very existence in the
Land of Israel against Islamic countries and movements have led many

to develop suspicion, revulsion, and even hatred of other religions. It is only natural that Jews have developed the view that being a good Jew demands rejecting the legitimacy of all other religions. As Kook has taught us, however, this is the position adopted by the "masses" who are "narrow-minded," and is not the well-informed opinion of those whose wisdom and faith run deep.

Furthermore, the Meiri lived at the height of medieval Jewish persecution, yet he clung firmly to a positive view of his Christian brethren. The determined repetition and integration of this view across his writings show us a path out of our present circumstances and up the proverbial mountain to see the bigger picture. From that vantage point one can make out the lights lit in solidarity, identify the good people with whom one can and should become neighbors, and map out the progress made since the pagan religions of late antiquity. It is upon us to realize that circumstances have changed for the better: the Vatican has dramatically changed its position toward the Jewish people and the State of Israel, and Arab countries have begun cultivating relationships with us based on our shared traditions.

Will we succeed in internalizing who we truly are and meet the task asked of us? Will we heed the call to action that emerges from a comprehensive examination of Jewish belief and properly appreciate the positive aspects of other religious identities? Will the strength of the Jewish State produce more than economic prosperity and security and also support activities seeking to restore the equation of fraternity? Will fraternity between different religious communities around the world help us come together to overcome the hatred and racism and the bloodshed they lead to? Will Judaism and Torah scholars be a light for the nations and a blessing for all the tribes of humanity?

We believe that the answer to all of these questions must be affirmative. Action in this arena is neither a privilege nor an option, it is part and parcel of who we are and of our purpose in this world. Perhaps it is for this very reason that we have regained our national power on the world stage.

About the Ohr Torah
Interfaith Center

The Ohr Torah Interfaith Center aims to make religion part of the answer to global challenges by promoting mutual recognition and respect between Judaism and other faiths. The Interfaith Center was founded on the belief that Judaism has a significant role to play in the larger story of humanity, especially in this new era of globalization on the one hand, and the *Shivat Zion* (the Jewish People's return to their historical homeland) on the other. This work has always been as urgent as it is complex, but never more so than since October 7, 2023.

The horrific events of October 7 gave the world a close encounter with the outcomes of the weaponization of religion and the challenge it poses to global stability. We believe that as much as religion is part of the problem, it must also be part of the solution – and that there will not be a solution without fully exploring, and understanding, the religious aspect of reality.

The Center's initiatives include developing an intellectual infrastructure, garnering support within the Jewish people for interfaith work, and advancing long-term connections with leaders of other faiths. Established in 2020, the Interfaith Center is recognized by religious and political leaders nationally and globally, with associations including top leaders in Indonesia, Morocco, Kazakhstan, Saudi Arabia, Pakistan,

Germany, and the US, as well as the Israeli government and numerous Jewish, Christian, and Muslim organizations.

The Ohr Torah Interfaith Center began with the establishment of the **Blickle Institute for Interfaith Dialogue** and the Blickle Fellowship Program, which trains senior Jewish educators and organizational and community leaders to build greater interreligious understandings. Throughout the yearlong program, Blickle fellows meet Jewish, Christian, and Muslim leaders, research the approaches by the three faiths to interfaith dialogue, and explore ways they can work together to advance respectful connections across Israeli society and worldwide.

Members and graduates of the Blickle Institute give lectures on the importance of interfaith dialogue to educational institutions and participate in conferences together with other faith leaders across Israel and overseas. They thus make a unique impact on interfaith work on both the national and global levels, engaging fruitfully with other faith communities in Israel and abroad.

We are grateful to Lisbeth (may she live and be well) and Karl-Hermann Blickle (of blessed memory) for their very generous support of the Blickle Institute for Interfaith Dialogue.

In 2025, the world will mark the 60th anniversary of the *Nostra aetate* a groundbreaking declaration regarding the relationship of the Church with non-Christian religions. We would like to capitalize on this important milestone to promote a similar Jewish-Muslim proclamation, without undercutting the previous Jewish-Christian process.

Moving in this direction requires a deep intellectual and theological infrastructure that goes beyond general aspirations for peace, love, and tolerance. If we want to affect real change in human and societal behavior, we must aim to impact the world of ideas. Religious belief, thought, and tradition are key in this context. Our goal is to propel a paradigm shift anchored in the core ideas that motivate people to act in a positive and constructive manner.

To this end, one of the main initiatives of the Ohr Torah Interfaith Center is the **Beit Midrash for Judaism and Humanity**. The Beit Midrash is based on the conviction that ideas are the underlying infrastructure of human deeds. We are not reforming our religious principles to align with external values, nor do we encourage or expect our non-Jewish partners to do so. Rather, we aim to bring forward new and creative thinking rooted in our traditional sources, while creating the intellectual infrastructure for a fundamental change in approach and underlying assumptions.

As a think tank of prominent rabbis and academics, the Beit Midrash for Judaism and Humanity is the main vehicle and the production floor for the ideas that infuse our interfaith work, field-building efforts, and connections with other faith leaders. The researchers study Jewish perceptions of other religions and central ideas of other faiths while looking for potential bridges for reconciliation. Members of the Beit Midrash are the best-trained and intellectually most well-equipped human resource at the Interfaith Center's disposal, representing the Center on various local, national, and international stages.

In 2022, the Beit Midrash published its first book in Hebrew: *God Shall Be One: Healing Judaism's Relations with World Religions.* You are now holding the English-language version of this groundbreaking book. *And They Shall Live With You: A New Perspective on Minorities in a Jewish State,* in both Hebrew and English, is already in production. Additional planned publications include *Healing Jewish-Muslim Relations, Abrahamic Religions and the Prophetic Vision,* an interfaith guide for diplomats, and a review of *Muslim-Jewish Encounters.* The Beit Midrash also supports the Interfaith Center's secondary publications, social media activity, and joint study sessions with leaders of other faiths.

Thank you to our dear friends of the Beit Midrash for Judaism and Humanity:

> *Dr. Michelle Friedman and Benjamin Belfer*
> *Dr. Giti and Mr. Jack Bendheim*
> *Mr. David Harris*
> *Mrs. Gloria Harris*
> *Mrs. Jodi and Mr. Jeff Harris*
> *Mrs. Rachel and Mr. Alan Jacoby*
> *Dr. Monique and Dr. Mordecai (z"l) Katz*
> *Mrs. Danielle and Mr. Jeffrey Wild*

Maggid Books
The best of contemporary Jewish thought from
Koren Publishers Jerusalem Ltd.